ALASKA BY ⌕ W9-CRY-945

DOCUMENTATION

Passenger Name _____

Ship Name_____

Captain's Signature_____

Date of Voyage _____

Cabin Number_____

ALASKA
By Cruise Ship

THE COMPLETE GUIDE TO CRUISING ALASKA

Eighth Edition

ANNE VIPOND

YOUR PORTHOLE
COMPANION

OCEAN CRUISE GUIDES

Guidebooks to the world of cruising

Vancouver, Canada   Pt. Roberts, USA

Published by: Ocean Cruise Guides Ltd.
Canada
325 English Bluff Road
Delta, BC V4M 2M9
USA
PO Box 2041
Pt. Roberts, WA 98281-2041
Phone: (604) 948-0594 Email: info@oceancruiseguides.com
Editors: Mel-Lynda Andersen, Diane Luckow, Duart Snow
Contributing Editors: William Kelly, Michael DeFreitas, Katharine Dawe
Artwork by Alan H. Nakano.
Cartography: Reid Jopson, Doug Quiring, Cartesia, OCG.
Design: Ocean Cruise Guides Ltd
Publisher: William Kelly
Visit our web site: oceancruiseguides.com

Printed in China

Eighth Edition - 2015

Library and Archives Canada Cataloguing in Publication

Vipond, Anne, 1957-
    Alaska by cruise ship : the complete guide to cruising Alaska / Anne
Vipond. -- 8th ed.

Includes index.
"Your porthole companion".
ISBN 978-1-9277470-3-2

    1. Cruise ships--Alaska--Guidebooks. 2. Cruise ships--British
Columbia--Pacific Coast--Guidebooks. 3. Alaska--Guidebooks.
4. Pacific Coast (B.C.)--Guidebooks. I. Title.
F902.3.V56 2014   917.9804'52   C98301478-7

Kenai River

CONTENTS

PART TWO

THE VOYAGE & THE PORTS

SEATTLE 100

VICTORIA 112

VANCOUVER & CANADIAN ROCKIES 122

CANADA'S INSIDE PASSAGE 150

KETCHIKAN 180

PIONEER PORTS – WRANGELL & PETERSBURG 198

JUNEAU & TRACY ARM 208

SKAGWAY & THE YUKON 226

GLACIER BAY & ICY STRAIT POINT 248

SITKA 264

HUBBARD GLACIER & YAKUTAT BAY 280

PRINCE WILLIAM SOUND – WHITTIER & VALDEZ 292

ANCHORAGE / SEWARD / KENAI............................... 302

DENALI NATIONAL PARK / FAIRBANKS.................................... 320

EXPEDITION CRUISING... 334

CRUISE LINES GLOSSARY 343

INDEX 348

COLOR PULL-OUT MAP (Inside Passage & Gulf of Alaska) 353

A laska – the Great Land – is inextricably tied to the sea. With nearly 34,000 miles of shoreline, Alaska is very much a coastal state. Its waterways have been traveled over the centuries by dugout canoes, sailing vessels and steamships delivering people and materials to far-flung ports. I first traveled this vast coastline in a sailboat skippered by my husband. Together we voyaged up and down the intricate channels of Southeast Alaska, anchoring in magnificent fjords and visiting tiny boardwalk communities. Eventually we headed further north into the Gulf of Alaska to explore the waters of Prince William Sound and Kodiak Island. In the course of our seaborne travels we met many of the people who live and work along this coast. And somewhere along the way, Alaska changed us. We were challenged by the weather and sea conditions, awed by the grandeur of the landscapes, and touched by the warmth of strangers who welcomed us into their homes.

Modern cruise ships travel the same waterways as mariners past and present, and passengers are treated to the same ongoing panorama of mountains, forests and fjords. Much can be seen from the ship's rail: snowcapped summits, cascading waterfalls, glaciers dropping their ice straight into the sea. Whales feed in these waters, bears roam the land, eagles soar overhead and schools of salmon swim homeward to the rivers that gave them life.

The natural wonders are there for all to see, but there's more to Alaska than meets the eye. This book is designed to help you, the traveler, better appreciate the splendid scenery gliding past your porthole.

Perhaps no traveler loved Alaska more than John Muir. A naturalist, mountaineer and writer, Muir was a man of strong opinions who quickly lost patience with others who didn't show sufficient interest in the natural forces – glacial action in particular – that have shaped and are still shaping the landscapes of Alaska. "Most people who travel look only at what they are directed to look at," he wrote in *Travels in Alaska*. "Great is the power of the guidebook maker, however ignorant."

As the maker of this particular guidebook, I can only hope that Mr. Muir – were he alive today – would not call me ignorant and that he might agree with some of the sentiments expressed here about his beloved Alaska.

As for you the traveler, I hope this book will help you see things that might otherwise go unnoticed as you cruise one of the most spectacular coastlines in the world.

Sitka National Historical Park

Anne Vipond

PART I

GENERAL INFORMATION

Ketchikan in full bloom

When to go?

The Alaska cruise season stretches from May through September, with late June to mid-August being the high season for fares. June and July are the brightest months, with early dawns and daylight lasting well into the evening during the northern summer. Flowers are in full bloom, and Pacific humpback whales can be sighted in local waters, for coastal Alaska is their summer feeding grounds. In June salmon start swimming upstream along rivers and creeks, and passengers have numerous opportunities to witness the fascinating and heroic efforts of these sleek fish returning to their natal streams to spawn. Bears and bald eagles appear along shorelines and streams to feed on the salmon.

The shoulder seasons of spring and fall offer more than just reduced fares and fewer people. Springtime brings heavy run-off from mountain snowfields, producing a multitude of cascading waterfalls along the steep channels and inlets of the cruise route. The southern ports of Seattle, Vancouver and Victoria are pleasantly warm in spring (average mid-May temperature, 60° F) and their surrounding mountain peaks look their most stunning, still crowned with snow at higher elevations. Fall is the time of year to see Pacific white-sided dolphins rejoice in their annual rite – mating – and their acrobatics are a delight to watch when dozens of these swift swimmers make a beeline toward a large cruise ship to leap in its bow wave.

Weather in Alaska is unpredictable and localized, with rain always a possibility along the coast, even in the middle of summer. Fog can also occur in late summer and early fall, but is not prevalent in spring or early summer.

JUNEAU WEATHER

AVERAGE TEMP (F)	MAY	JUNE	JULY	AUG	SEPT
Daily max:	55.4	62.0	63.6	62.3	56.1
Extreme high:	82	86	90	83	72
Extreme low:	25	31	36	27	23
RAINFALL (in inches)					
Average	3.31	2.93	4.69	5.00	6.90
Greatest	6.33	5.34	7.88	12.31	11.51
CLOUD COVER					
Days with cloud	23	22	23	23	24

Which itinerary?

The selection has never been better for travelers pondering an Alaska cruise. The ships servicing this region range from some of the newest and largest, carrying 2,000-plus passengers and offering a myriad of on-board amenities, to small cruisers carrying less than 100 passengers and able to get close enough to a berg to plunk ice into your drink.

The majority of cruises depart from Vancouver or Seattle in the south, and from Seward or Whittier (both near Anchorage) in the north. Weekend departures are the most popular and seven-day itineraries are widely offered. Longer itineraries of 10 or more days are also available, notably on ships departing from San Francisco. At the beginning or end of the season, a few cruises are offered that leave from Vancouver and terminate in Seattle, or vice versa.

Organized shore excursions can be taken at each port of call, and for passengers who want to see more of interior Alaska and Canada, extended land tours are offered by most cruise lines. (These are described in the next section.)

The large ships trace two main routes: **Inside Passage** – a round-trip cruise from Vancouver or Seattle to the Alaska Panhandle; and **Gulf of Alaska** – a one-way cruise between Vancouver and Seward or Whittier. The small ships that service these routes call both at the major ports and at minor ones not normally visited by large ships, and they offer imaginative itineraries into less-traveled fjords of the coast. The Inside Passage can also be traveled by government-operated ferries, which follow the same channels as the cruise ships but don't make sightseeing detours into glacier-fed inlets and their schedules don't always provide ample time in port to fully enjoy the local attractions.

Alaska cruises include at least one visit to a tidewater glacier.

The Inside Passage to Alaska is so named because it lies 'inside' a long chain of coastal islands that act as a protective buffer from the open seas of the North Pacific Ocean. Rugged capes, cliffs and fjords define this coast, and each hour of cruising brings another spectacular scene into view. This route remains extremely popular with its dramatic scenery, friendly Alaskan ports and numerous port-of-call attractions.

The Inside Passage cruise is an excellent introduction to Alaska. Starting and ending in Vancouver or in Seattle, the turn-around point is Skagway (at the top of the Inside Passage) or Hubbard Glacier, near the top of the Alaska Panhandle. Usually seven days in duration, this round trip will take you past hundreds of miles of intricate coastline as the ship threads its way along narrow, winding channels, past forested islands and mountain-bound inlets. This cruise will stop at three or four ports of call and will include a close-up look at a tidewater glacier.

A full day is spent traveling to Alaska and the exact route a ship takes is often at the captain's discretion, depending on the weather and other factors. Time constraints are the main reason most ships departing from Seattle bypass British Columbia's Inside Passage, instead heading up the west side of Vancouver Island and Haida Gwaii (Queen Charlotte Islands) on their way to and from Alaska.

Ships departing from Vancouver travel inside waters, transiting Seymour Narrows and Johnstone Strait, where killer whales are often sighted. The route taken along British Columbia's north coast is at the captain's discretion and depends on various factors, including visibility (i.e. fog) and whether commercial fishboats are clogging any of the narrow channels.

Victoria is British Columbia's southernmost port and is included in most roundtrip cruises from Seattle. The main Alaskan ports of call are Ketchikan, Juneau, Skagway and Sitka (the latter vis-

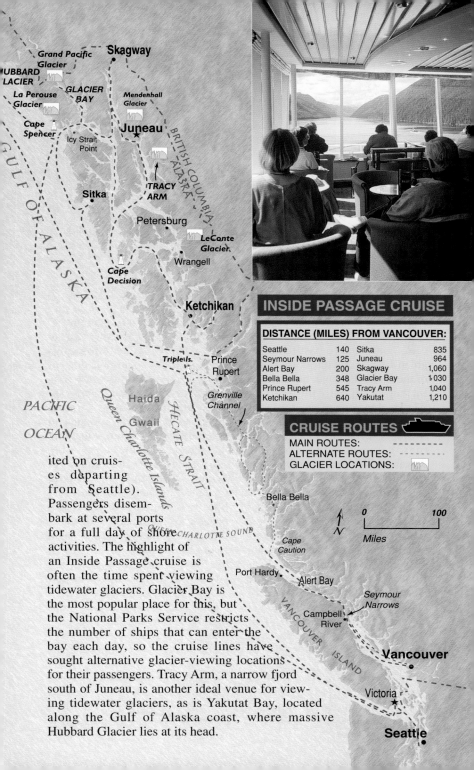

Skagway

Grand Pacific
Glacier

HUBBARD
GLACIER

La Perouse
Glacier

GLACIER
BAY

Mendenhall
Glacier

Cape
Spencer

Icy Strait
Point

Juneau ★

TRACY
ARM

Sitka

BRITISH COLUMBIA
ALASKA

Petersburg

LeConte
Glacier

Cape
Decision

Wrangell

GULF OF ALASKA

Ketchikan

Triple Is.

Prince
Rupert

PACIFIC

OCEAN

Haida

Gwaii

Queen Charlotte Islands

HECATE STRAIT

Grenville
Channel

QUEEN CHARLOTTE SOUND

Bella Bella

Cape
Caution

Port Hardy

Alert Bay

Campbell
River

Seymour
Narrows

VANCOUVER ISLAND

Vancouver

Victoria ★

Seattle

INSIDE PASSAGE CRUISE

DISTANCE (MILES) FROM VANCOUVER:

Seattle	140	Sitka	835
Seymour Narrows	125	Juneau	964
Alert Bay	200	Skagway	1,060
Bella Bella	348	Glacier Bay	1,030
Prince Rupert	545	Tracy Arm	1,040
Ketchikan	640	Yakutat	1,210

CRUISE ROUTES

MAIN ROUTES: - - - - - - -
ALTERNATE ROUTES: - - - - - - -
GLACIER LOCATIONS:

0   100

N   Miles

ited on cruis-
es departing
from Seattle).
Passengers disem-
bark at several ports
for a full day of shore
activities. The highlight of
an Inside Passage cruise is
often the time spent viewing
tidewater glaciers. Glacier Bay is
the most popular place for this, but
the National Parks Service restricts
the number of ships that can enter the
bay each day, so the cruise lines have
sought alternative glacier-viewing locations
for their passengers. Tracy Arm, a narrow fjord
south of Juneau, is another ideal venue for viewing tidewater glaciers, as is Yakutat Bay, located
along the Gulf of Alaska coast, where massive
Hubbard Glacier lies at its head.

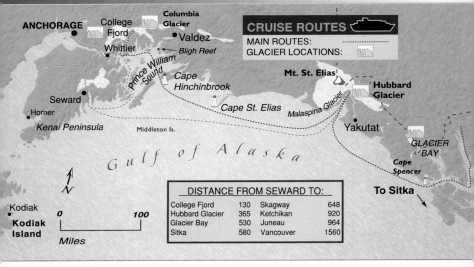

ANCHORAGE

College Fjord

Columbia Glacier

Whittier

Valdez

Bligh Reef

Prince William Sound

Cape Hinchinbrook

Mt. St. Elias

Hubbard Glacier

Seward

Homer

Cape St. Elias

Malaspina Glacier

Yakutat

GLACIER BAY

Kenai Peninsula

Middleton Is.

Cape Spencer

To Sitka

CRUISE ROUTES	
MAIN ROUTES:	--------
GLACIER LOCATIONS:	

Gulf of Alaska

N

Kodiak

Kodiak Island

0   100

Miles

DISTANCE FROM SEWARD TO:			
College Fjord	130	Skagway	648
Hubbard Glacier	365	Ketchikan	920
Glacier Bay	530	Juneau	964
Sitka	580	Vancouver	1560

These increasingly popular Gulf of Alaska cruises not only weave past the evergreen islands and turquoise fjords of the Inside Passage, but proceed further north into the Gulf of Alaska along one of the most rugged and remote coastlines in the world. A seven-day glacier cruise runs between Vancouver and Seward or Whittier, spending four days traveling the Inside Passage and visiting several popular ports, such as Ketchikan, Juneau and Skagway. The Inside Passage portion of this itinerary sometimes includes a day of glacier viewing in Glacier Bay. Ships bound for Hubbard Glacier at the top of the Alaska Panhandle will usually bypass Glacier Bay and proceed along Icy Strait into the Gulf of Alaska to visit Hubbard Glacier, a spectacular glacier at the head of Yakutat Bay.

Ships traversing the Gulf of Alaska take their passengers past one of the most spectacular stretches of coastline anywhere.

Here the snow-covered mountains of the Fairweather Range rise abruptly from the ocean's edge, their steep summits glistening with ice. Fishing boats look like toys as they pass beneath these magnificent peaks, where the sprawling La Perouse Glacier discharges its icebergs directly into the open Pacific.

More glaciers are found in Prince William Sound, where College Fjord is often the highlight of a Gulf of Alaska cruise because of the numerous glaciers lining this stunning inlet. Situated at the top of the Gulf of Alaska, the Sound's mainland shores are surrounded by snowcapped mountains and indented by dozens of glacier-carved fjords containing Alaska's greatest concentration of tidewater glaciers, 20 of them active. Columbia Glacier, near the port of Valdez, is the Sound's largest glacier and one of Alaska's most active.

Ships visiting Prince William Sound will pass within a few

miles of Bligh Reef where the *Exxon Valdez* ran aground in March 1989. Cruise companies were just starting to venture into this area when the oil spill occurred and several cruise lines donated substantial funds to assist with clean-up efforts. There is little visible evidence today of the spill, although ongoing studies continue in coves and bays where foreshores and salmon streams were adversely affected.

Cruise ships pick their way carefully through the ice-clogged waters in front of Columbia Glacier before proceeding to College Fjord, its slopes lined with glaciers named in 1899 after the various Ivy League Schools associated with a team of research scientists exploring the region by steamship. Nearby is the port of Whittier, beautifully situated in a fjord of Prince William Sound.

Whittier is an emerging cruise port with rail and road access to Anchorage. Seward is the other base port for cruises between

A ship visiting College Fjord nudges close to a glacier's snout where chunks of ice will often drop with a thunderous crash into the sea.

Vancouver and Anchorage, and is located west of Prince William Sound, at the head of Resurrection Bay. Lying at the foot of the Kenai Mountains, this scenic fishing and cargo port is the headquarters for Kenai Fjords National Park, with boat excursions departing daily for tours of the nearby glacier-carved fjords.

Choosing A Ship

Once you've decided which areas of coastal Alaska you want to see, the next step is deciding which cruise line to book with. If you are new to cruising, you are well advised to see a travel agent who specializes in cruises and can explain the individual style of each cruise line (a good starting

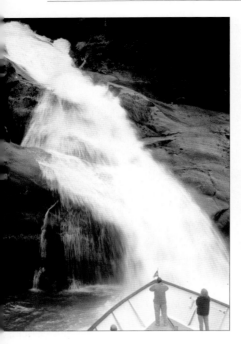

Small ships can cruise closer to the scenery (above); large ships have more facilities (below).

point is the Cruise Lines Glossary at the back of this book). Let your cruise agent know what you're looking for in terms of atmosphere and activities, i.e. a casual, family-oriented vacation versus a more elegant ambience.

The cost of an Alaska cruise can vary, depending on your choice of cruise line and month of travel. Stateroom selection (ranging from an inside cabin to an outside deluxe suite with balcony) is another factor in the cost of a cruise. While it is possible to incur few additional expenses once you board a cruise ship, most passengers buy optional shore excursions and these also vary widely in price, depending on the excursion's length and mode of transportation.

Cruise ships have been compared to floating resorts, with the large ships offering an astounding array of onboard facilities and entertainment. The small expedition ships offer more intimacy and closer proximity to the scenery. They also tend to be more casual than the large ships, the latter retaining traditions from the golden age of ocean liners, such as a Captain's Gala and dress codes for dinner, although optional casual dining is becoming a standard feature on the large ships. Luxury ships are small to medium in size, with spacious staterooms and exceptional service but not as many onboard amenities as the large premium and contemporary ships.

Although cruises can be booked online, this isn't necessarily where the best deals are or where good advice can be found. Cruise

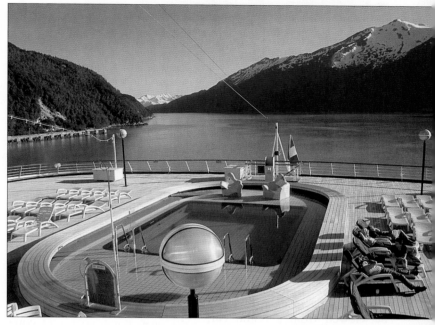

lines are very loyal to cruise agents and if a hot price or new itinerary is coming, agents know about it first.

When booking a cruise, use an agent who is affiliated with Cruise Lines International Association (CLIA) – an independent marketing and training organization for the cruise industry. CLIA offers courses for travel agents which earn them various levels of Cruise Counselor Certification and provide them with a high level of expertise in cruise travel. Veteran cruise agents have gained their expertise through years of experience and will be able to guide you through the maze of ship choices, cabin considerations and itineraries.

Cruise lines reward people who book early with generous discounts, shipboard credits and, if

Cruise ships are floating resorts, offering a daily change of locale.

the opportunity arises, upgrades. If you know when you want to take your cruise vacation, book early and purchase cancellation insurance. Another advantage of booking early is the opportunity to make specific requests regarding your stateroom. If you are booking an outside stateroom on a northbound Gulf of Alaska cruise, ask to be placed on the starboard side of the ship so you will have views of the coastline from your cabin. If yours is a southbound cruise, ask to be on the port side. The same applies to flights to or from Anchorage – the starboard seats provide the best views when flying north; the port seats are best for southbound flights.

Land Tours

There is more than one Alaska. The vast and varied landscape of this northern state encompasses several ecosystems, from temperate rainforests to arctic tundra. A relatively short distance inland from the glacier-carved fjords and coastal ports visited by cruise ships lies the land of legend, where gold prospectors once toiled by the light of summer's midnight sun and where sled dogs are still used to travel the snow-covered mountain valleys and frozen rivers of winter. While the rugged scenery of coastal Alaska is best enjoyed from the deck of a cruise ship, the inland regions can be viewed from a rental car, motorcoach, rail car or riverboat.

To experience Alaska's interior entails booking a **land tour** in combination with a cruise, or independently arranging a pre- or post-cruise land trip. The major cruise lines offer an assortment of land tours that must be confirmed when you book your cruise, the complete package referred to as a **cruisetour**. Ranging from three to 12 days in duration (in addition to the cruise), these land tours cover hundreds of scenic miles by road, rail, river and air. Organized land tours provide driver-guides who explain the sights and whose local knowledge includes entertaining anecdotes about the various places you are visiting.

If you prefer **traveling independently**, you can rent a vehicle or ride the Alaska Railroad, following the same routes as an organized land tour and staying at the same hotels and wilderness lodges used by the cruise lines. The train ride to Denali National Park is slightly more scenic than the parallel highway, for the train traces the shorelines of lakes and generally provides a more intimate look at the countryside. The advantage to traveling by car, however, is that you can set your own schedule and be spontaneous, stopping anywhere you like along the way to take advantage of the many viewpoints and hiking trails. Generally speaking, Alaska's highways are well maintained and free of heavy traffic. Major **rental car firms** are locat-

Mt. McKinley dominates the horizon north of Anchorage, where the scenic Parks Highway leads to Denali National Park.

(Above) Cruisetours to Denali include luxury rail travel on private railcars. (Right) You can make spontaneous stops when traveling Alaska's scenic highways (such as the Seward Highway) by rental car.

ed in Anchorage, Fairbanks and throughout Alaska at communities serviced by an airport.

If you're traveling independently, you should reserve your overnight **accommodations** well in advance during the peak summer season, when many of the lodges often become fully booked. The advantage of taking a cruisetour is that all arrangements are taken care of by the cruise line, leaving you free to focus entirely on enjoying the scenery.

The **Alaska Railroad** has provided a vital transportation link to Alaskans since 1923 and now caters to summertime visitors, providing regular rail service as well as an assortment of tour packages which include overnight accommodations and side trips. The Denali Star provides service between Anchorage and Fairbanks, with stops at Talkeetna and Denali National Park. The Coastal Classic runs south from Anchorage to Girdwood and Seward, and the Glacier Discovery runs between Anchorage and Whittier with stops at Girdwood and Portage. The cruise lines' private railcars also ride the Alaska Railroad and these offer luxury rail travel with their large domed windows providing panoramic views of the passing scenery. The cruise lines book their guests into their own lodges or those of comparable quality to ensure their passengers a consistent level of accommodation and service on the land portion of their cruisetour. Optional guided side trips are available at each destination, including river rafting, sportfishing and flightseeing. Or a person can just sit back and relax, enjoying the lodge's pristine setting and nearby nature trails.

Which Cruisetour?

One of the most popular land tours is the trip to **Denali National Park and Preserve**, home to the tallest mountain in North America – Mt. McKinley. Rising above the surrounding countryside and visible from

Mt. McKinley Princess Wilderness Lodge is a classic example of the lodges featured on Alaska land tours.

Anchorage on a clear day, this massive mountain's twin peaks stand in isolation, often shrouded in clouds that collect at the summit. Mt. McKinley is part of the 600-mile long Alaska Range, and the rail journey between Anchorage and **Fairbanks** provides breathtaking views of this range. Overnight accommodation is provided at lodges located just outside the entrance to Denali Park, which is 240 miles north of Anchorage and 120 miles south of Fairbanks. There are regular shuttles from these lodges to Denali Park, where park buses transport visitors to scenic landmarks, wildlife viewing spots and hiking trails. More lodges are located south of the park, near **Talkeetna**, where the views of Mt. McKinley (weather permitting) are stunning.

There are many variations of Alaska cruisetours, some including a visit to the **Copper River Valley**. Others focus on Canada's Yukon where the Klondike Gold Rush can be relived in **Whitehorse** and **Dawson City**. Some tours (specifically those offered by Holland America Westours) begin or end at the Alaskan port of Skagway, where disembarking cruise passengers are whisked by rail over the Chilkoot Mountains to retrace the Trail of '98 to Dawson City. The Yukon's rugged and remote landscape encompasses **Kluane National Park**, which contains the most extensive non-polar icefields in the world, and the subarctic terrain of **Tombstone Territorial Park**. Another way to see this beautiful Canadian wilderness is by rented vehicle from Anchorage or Fairbanks.

Gates of the Arctic National Park lies north of Fairbanks, nearly 100 miles north of the Arctic Circle, and it too can be visited on a cruisetour, as can **Prudhoe Bay**, on the shores of the Beaufort Sea. To cover these vast distances in a reasonable amount of time, air travel to or from Fairbanks is used in addition to highway driving. This trip can also be arranged independently in Anchorage through tour companies which are often stationed in the large hotels.

Another, more accessible region to explore by land tour is the **Kenai Peninsula**. Passengers embarking or disembarking in Seward will have an opportunity to see some of Kenai's magnificent mountain scenery while transferring to or from Anchorage by railcar or motor coach. However, those who opt to spend a few days in the area can visit **Kenai Fjords National Park** by tour boat from Seward, and visit **Exit Glacier** by road, where a trail leads from the parking lot to the face of the glacier.

Other attractions include the scenic fishing port and artists' enclave of **Homer**, situated on the shores of Kachemak Bay. Luxury lodges in the area include the **Kenai Princess Wilderness Lodge**, nestled on the banks of the Kenai River, and the **Seward Windsong Lodge**, located in a forest setting along the road to Exit Glacier.

Visitors hike the tundra-covered slopes of Canada's Kluane National Park.

Talkeetna Alaskan Lodge

At the head of Turnagain Arm is Mount Alyeska, where the luxury **Alyeska Prince Hotel & Resort** near Girdwood is the area's premier accommodation. The nearby **Portage Valley** is ideal for independent travel, with numerous hiking trails, including one that winds along the edge of a meltwater stream to **Byron Glacier** where you can climb onto its snow-covered snout and gaze down the green valley that was once filled with ice.

Whether you book a cruisetour, or travel independently, the lodges owned or utilized by the cruise companies are an integral part of the Alaska land experience. Princess is the leader in this category, owning an impressive network of luxury lodges in Alaska, including the **Denali Princess Wilderness Lodge** near the park entrance and the **Mt. McKinley Princess Wilderness Lodge** near Talkeetna. Also in the vicinity is the **Talkeetna Alaskan Lodge**, operated by Alaska Heritage Tours, which is an Alaskan-owned and operated company whose resort properties include

the Seward Windsong Lodge and whose services include day cruises of the Kenai Fjords and Prince William Sound. The **Westmark** chain of hotels (owned by Holland America Westours) has properties throughout much of Alaska and Canada's Yukon.

One of the most enduring land tours available to Alaska cruise passengers isn't even in Alaska. It's the ever-popular trip to Canada's Rocky Mountains where **Banff National Park** has drawn visitors for more than a century to its famous mountain lakes and river gorges. The Canadian Rockies can be reached by road or rail from Vancouver and Seattle. Passengers on a pre-cruise land tour usually fly to **Calgary**, situated an hour's drive east of Banff in the foothills of the Rockies. From Calgary you proceed by train or motorcoach to Banff National Park where famous sights include the turquoise blue waters of Lake Louise and the Banff Springs Hotel, which resembles a Scottish castle on the banks of the Bow River. From Banff, a tour might proceed

(Above and right) Relaxing at the Kenai Princess Lodge. (Below) Hiking onto Byron Glacier in the Portage Valley.

north along the scenic Icefields Parkway to **Jasper National Park** and an overnight stay at the Jasper Park Lodge before turning westward, past Mount Robson (highest peak in the Rockies) toward Vancouver, stopping overnight in Kamloops. Rocky Mountaineer Railtours is often used by the cruise companies for these classic land tours. **Whistler**, a ski resort to the north of Vancouver, is another popular pre- or post-cruise destination, as is the British-flavored city of **Victoria** and nearby **Butchart Gardens**. Victoria, the provincial capital of British Columbia, is also a popular port of call for cruises out of Seattle.

For more detailed information on specific places mentioned in this section, please refer to the Table of Contents or the Index.

Shore Excursions

A cruise to Alaska offers many highlights, and shore excursions often top the list. These port-of-call activities are purely optional but usually worth the additional expense, and the cruise lines offer a wide selection of high-quality excursions. It's possible, of course, to independently explore each port's local attractions, many of which are within easy walking distance of the cruise dock. **Information on bus and shuttle service to a town's local and outlying attractions is provided in the 'Getting Around' section of each port's respective chapter in Part II of this book.**

Captivating as the ports themselves are, their outlying wilderness areas are what many people envision when they think of Alaska. And there's no better way to see a large wilderness area in a short time than from a **floatplane**

A helicopter flight to a glacier is one of the most exciting shore excursions offered in Alaska.

or **helicopter**. The floatplanes usually take off right beside the ship or a short distance from where it's docked, and helicopters lift off at nearby airports.

Weather checks are made every hour and if your flight is cancelled, you will receive a full refund. However, aircraft still fly in cloudy weather – when the crystal blue ice of a glacier looks even bluer and the fjords are said to be their most beautiful, with mist rising from the water. A few of the day-long excursions depend on evening light for return flights and may not be offered late in the season, but most run throughout the entire cruise season in all types of weather. Headsets are provided with commentary to keep you informed while in flight, but such narration is secondary to the incredible landscapes passing beneath your aircraft.

Glaciers come in many forms and from the air you'll gain a different perspective of them. You'll see entire valleys filled with ice and thick sheets of snow blanketing mountainsides. You'll also see blue ice hanging from valley walls, and row upon row of icy pinnacles frozen in a downhill march. If you choose a helicopter tour, your pilot will land the plane right on a glacier and in the moon boots provided you will walk on the surface of a glacier and peer down its deep crevasses. Some heli-seeing flights include a visit to a **dog-sled camp** where you have the opportunity to meet dog teams that compete in the Iditarod Trail Sled Dog Race and mush with them across a glacier before reboarding your helicopter. In late summer, however, this ice can become too soft to continue the sled-dog excursions and these will be cancelled in such conditions. Also, the air temperature on these icefields is considerably colder than at sea level, so pack a warm jacket, wool hat and gloves if you plan to go dog-sledding.

Flightseeing trips are not the only adventures offered while in port. Water-borne excursions abound. **River rafting, lake canoeing** and **sea kayaking** are all offered. Beginners are welcome and although wet weather gear is sometimes provided, it's best to come prepared. Wear warm clothing in layers – the outer layer should be waterproof.

Whale-watching is offered in several ports, notably Juneau, Icy Strait Point and Sitka, which are located near summer feeding grounds for the Pacific humpback. While it's possible to see a whale from the ship, you're much more likely to see humpback whales on an excursion boat that takes you to specific spots where these mammals are known to feed.

Juneau shore excursions include dog mushing on a glacier (above) and whale watching in Lynn Canal (below).

(Above) Independent sportfishing and whalewatching excursions are offered in Juneau. (Below) Taxi drivers are a friendly source of local insight.

Sportfishing is offered in most ports, usually on boats that carry four to six fishermen per vessel. Tackle and bait are provided, and your catch can be prepared locally (smoked or frozen) and shipped to your home for an additional charge. Wear boating attire, including rubber-soled shoes and a rainproof jacket.

Land-oriented excursions include **zip-lining, mountain biking** and **off-road jeep and ATV safaris**. Even seemingly sedate tours by **motorcoach** are informative, entertaining and a good way to get an overview of a port before setting off by yourself on foot. These tours also give you an opportunity to meet the people who live and work in Alaska, and to ask them a few questions.

Children are welcome on most excursions (often at a reduced price), although some activities have age restrictions. Be prepared for **changeable weather** by dressing in layers to stay warm and dry.

Reserving: Shore excursions can be viewed at each cruise

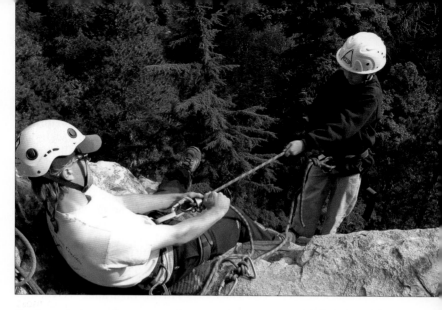

line's website and, once you've booked a cruise, you can reserve shore excursions online. These are grouped by port of call, with their activities described and their prices indicated. Those worth booking in advance are the ones that have limited capacity, such as flightseeing, and these are sold on a first come/ first served basis. In addition to advance booking, once you're on board the ship you can usually book (or cancel) excursions right up to the evening before you pull into that port – assuming a particular shore excursion isn't sold out.

The ship's Shore Excursion Desk is there to help with bookings and answer questions. The shore excursion staff can help you co-ordinate your excursions if you decide to take two while in a port and are concerned about a conflict in timing. If you book your shore excursions through the cruise line, there's no need to worry about getting back to the ship on time – the shore excursion

Rock climbing with trained mountaineers is a popular shore excursion in Skagway.

staff will make sure everyone's back on board before the ship departs.

It's also possible to book shore excursions with **independent tour operators** (which have kiosks at the docks of most ports), either on the spot at the port or in advance through their websites. Prices are about 10 per cent cheaper, although many tour operators will not undercut the cruise lines. Generally speaking, it makes sense to book a shore excursion through the cruise line if the activity involves helicopters, floatplanes or other specialized equipment. Should you book your excursion directly through a local operator, be aware that you're responsible for getting yourself back to the ship before its departure – if you're late, the ship will leave without you.

Documentation & Currency

A valid passport is the best proof of citizenship you can carry and is recommended for all American and Canadian citizens taking a cruise to Alaska. All air travelers, from any country, are required to present a passport and children must present their own.

Under the Western Hemisphere Travel Initiative, American and Canadian citizens entering the U.S. at land and sea ports of entry without a passport must carry a WHTI-compliant document. If you're a non-U.S. citizen residing in America, verify with your travel agent the existing identification requirements.

Before your departure, leave a detailed travel itinerary with a family member, friend or neighbor. Include the name of your ship, its phone number and the applicable ocean code, as well as your stateroom number – all of which will be provided with your cruise documentation. With this information, a person back home can place a satellite call to your ship in an emergency.

Another precaution is to photocopy, on a single sheet of paper, the identification page of your passport, your driver's license and all credit cards. Keep one copy with you, separate from your passport and wallet, and leave another one at home.

Travel insurance is recommended. A comprehensive policy will cover travel cancellation, delayed departure, medical expenses, personal accident and liability, lost baggage and money, and legal expenses. You may already have supplementary health insurance through a credit card, automobile club policy or employment health plan, but you should check these carefully. Carry details of your policy with you and documentation showing that you are covered by a plan.

American currency is used in Alaska of course, and is also accepted by most Canadian businesses, but you'll receive the best rate of exchange at a bank or currency exchange service when in Canada. Automatic tellers in Canada and Alaska are connected to major ATM networks, and the large ships have an ATM, usually located near the front desk (purs-

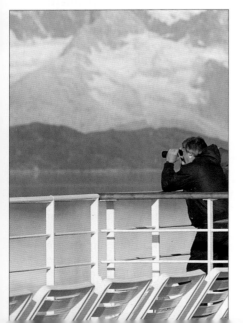

From the ship's rail, a pair of binoculars will give you a closer look at the scenery and wildlife.

er's office). Visa, MasterCard and American Express credit cards are widely accepted.

What to Pack

Bring casual attire for daytime wear – both on board the ship and in port. The weather in Alaska can change rapidly, so dress in layers. Start with slacks and a light shirt, then a sweater or sweatshirt, and end with a rainproof jacket (or jacket and rain poncho). Also take an umbrella or wide-brimmed hat, in case you get caught in a downpour. If the sun shines, you can peel off a couple of layers, and if the sky suddenly clouds over, you won't be cold. Also bring resort wear – on sunny summer days it will be warm enough to sunbathe by the swimming pool. The southern ports of Vancouver and Seattle can reach temperatures of 80 F in summer, as can the interiors of Alaska and Canada's Yukon. Nights can be cool.

Footwear is also important. Your shoes should be comfortable, with thick soles and good ankle support, and leather is preferable to canvas in wet conditions. Give your shoes a good spray of all-weather protector before packing them and bring along a second pair in case your first pair gets soaked and needs time to dry. A woolen hat is also recommended for brisk days at sea or when your ship is

Pack mostly casual attire, except for the one or two formal nights on your ship.

approaching a tidewater glacier, where the air is cool. Sunglasses are another must. There is always some glare off the water, even on overcast days. If you plan on taking a helicopter excursion to a glacier, be sure to pack a warm jacket, wool hat and gloves. Boots will be provided by the tour operator. If you're heading inland on a cruisetour, bring insect repellent.

Your evening wear should include something suitable for the one or two formal nights held on board the large ships. Women wear gowns or cocktail dresses on these occasions and men favor dark suits or tuxedos. For informal evenings, women wear dresses, skirts or slacks, and men wear a shirt and tie, or a sports jacket with an open-necked shirt.

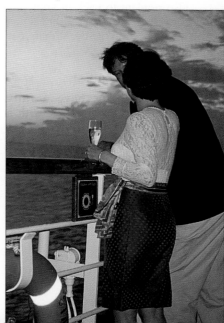

Check with your travel agent or the cruise line's website regarding your ship's on-board facilities, such as whether there will be a hair dryer in your cabin, and whether the ship has coin-operated launderettes with irons and ironing boards. Those that don't will provide a laundering service (the cost is approximately $15 for a bag of clothes, washed and pressed), and hand washing can be done in your cabin. Dry cleaning is another service offered on the large ships. Basic toiletries can be purchased aboard the ship.

Keep any valuables (jewelry, travelers checks, etc.) in your carry-on luggage as well as all documentation (tickets, passport, etc.), prescription medicines and eyeglasses. Keep prescribed medication in original, labeled containers and carry a doctor's prescription for any controlled drug. If you wear prescription eyeglasses, consider packing a spare pair. It's also prudent to pack in your carry-on bag any other essentials you would need in the event that your luggage is late arriving.

Health Precautions

All large ships have a fully equipped medical center with a doctor and nurses. Passengers needing medical attention are billed at private rates, which are added to your shipboard account. This invoice can be submitted to your insurance company upon your return home.

The overall standards of cleanliness on board cruise ships are extremely high, yet contagious viruses that are spread by person-to-person contact (such as the Norovirus, which is a brief but severe gastrointestinal illness) do occasionally plague a small percentage of passengers. To avoid contracting such a virus, practise frequent, thorough handwashing with warm, soapy water.

Sea sickness is not a widespread or prolonged problem on Alaska cruises, especially in the protected waters of the Inside Passage. Modern ships also use stabilizers to reduce any rolling motion when in open seas. However, if you're susceptible to motion sickness, there are a number of remedies. One is to wear special wrist bands, the balls of which rest on an acupressure point. Over-the-counter medications include Dramamine or Gravol pills, which should be taken ahead of time, before you start to feel nauseous. Another option is to chew Meclizine tablets (usually available at the ship's infirmary). Check first with your doctor before taking any medication. Natural remedies include taking ginger in capsule form or sipping on ginger ale and nibbling on dry crackers. Fresh air is another antidote.

Shopping

Luxury goods are sold (tax and duty-free) at the on-board shops, but if Alaskan handcrafted items are what you're looking for, the ports of call are where you'll be doing much of your shopping. The shopping districts at most Alaskan ports are located within walking distance of the ship pier or tender docks. The shops themselves are

(Left) Native artwork is widely available, including decorative wood carvings.
(Right) Logos of authenticity appear on Alaskan-made souvenirs.

often housed in or among the town's historic buildings and are part of a walking tour – so you can mix sightseeing with shopping.

If you're looking for 'authentic' Alaskan souvenirs, be sure the item carries one of two symbols: the Silver Hand on authentic native handicrafts from Alaska, or the Made in Alaska polar bear on items made by Alaskans. Handicrafts and fine art by native artists living in Washington State, British Columbia and Northern Canada are also sold in Alaska galleries and gift shops. (For more detail on regional styles, see the Native Art section on page 93.)

Northwest Coast native crafts include engraved silver jewelry, wood and soapstone carvings, silkscreen prints, ceremonial masks and beaded moccasins. Different native groups specialize in different art forms and use a variety of materials, including argillite (a compact, grayish-brown rock used primarily by the Haida) and soapstone (a soft rock with a soapy feel that ranges in color from gray to green). If a sculpture you are considering for purchase is warm to the touch, it is likely made not of soapstone but of resin. Stone is cool to the touch and is heavier than plastic.

The quality of native art can vary, and the price usually reflects the level of artistry or craftsmanship that created the piece. Shop at reputable venues, i.e. museum gift shops or galleries recommended by the cruise line, and ask for written proof of an expensive piece's authenticity. If you buy an ivory carving, the U.S. Fish & Wildlife Service requires that you buy an export/transit permit unless you choose to mail it home. In Canada, whalebone and walrus ivory are both banned imports, but not mammoth tusk ivory which has beautiful honeycomb patterns. Walrus ivory is a

Ivory carvings are popular items for purchase in Alaska shops.

popular medium in Alaska, and only Native Alaskans are allowed to carve a piece of new walrus ivory, its thin black lines occurring naturally when a walrus experiences abrupt changes in temperature as it leaves its rock haul-out and dives into icy cold Arctic water.

Gold nugget jewelry is another popular Alaskan souvenir. These nuggets are sold in their natural shape – unaltered and mounted with prongs onto pendants. Each nugget is unique and has a gold content of 70 to 95 percent (compared to 41 percent in 10 karat gold and 58.5 percent in 14 karat gold). The nuggets are weighed by troy ounce, which is slightly heavier than a standard ounce. Every gold nugget is unique and

gold experts can identify its source creek by examining the nugget's color and texture. Local gems include jade (in a variety of colors) and blue topaz – also called 'glacier ice.'

Smoked salmon comes vacuum-packed and is handsomely packaged for take-home gifts. Russian stacking dolls, lacquer boxes and hand-painted icons are other popular items.

Vacation Photos

Digital images have largely replaced photographs, but the goal of capturing your holiday's highlights remains the same. If you're using a digital camera, be sure to pack an extra battery pack, which can be recharged in your stateroom. For print-quality reproduction, shoot at a fine setting and large size. Most onboard photo departments can develop digital images into prints.

The ship's photo gallery is also a good place to purchase snapshots taken of yourself, friends and family members as you disembark at each port of call. These make nice mementos of your cruise.

On formal nights, when everyone is looking their best, the ship's photographers are set up at locations around the ship to take studio-quality portraits that are displayed the next day in the photo gallery. There is no sitting fee and no obligation to purchase these framable prints but people often do because it's a convenient way to obtain a professional portrait.

Connecting with Home

You can phone home from the ship by placing a satellite call on your stateroom telephone. This is expensive, however, and unless the call is urgent you may want to wait and place your call from a land-based phone when the ship is in a port or use your cell phone. Most of Southeast Alaska is serviced by the same cell zone, and your phone should get reception in roaming mode (which can also be very expensive). Long-distance calls can be made without dialing a country code. Washington State and British Columbia are part of the Pacific Time Zone; Alaska has its own time zone, which is one hour behind Pacific Time (the zone in which Vancouver, Seattle and Los Angeles are located).

(Above) Taking big pictures with small cameras is one of the joys of visiting Alaska. (Below) Internet cafes are found on the large cruise ships.

Perhaps the easiest and cheapest way to contact family and friends back home is either text messaging or email. Most large ships have an Internet cafe on board and offer flat-rate use. Passengers log onto the Internet through their shipboard card (issued on boarding) and within seconds are online. At the end of your session, the ship's system shows your time spent on the Internet and the total cost. No matter where you are, at sea or in port, you can send an e-mail instantly from most ships in the Alaska fleet. Some ships allow passengers to plug their own computers into the ship's connection, which is usually a 56k speed or better, so e-mailing images of your trip to friends and family is an easy, if slow, procedure.

Mariners have long dominated the evolution of the Inside Passage. First they plied its waters in dugout canoes, then in square-rigged sailing ships. Over time, they conducted arduous surveys and drew detailed marine charts for future mariners.

When the noted writer and naturalist **John Muir** first arrived in Alaska by steamship in 1879, his subsequent writings about Glacier Bay sparked tremendous interest in the area. Soon more ships, including those of Canadian Pacific, were bringing travelers to view this unique area. However, it wasn't until 1957 that Alaskan cruises came into their own.

In that year, Westours became the first dedicated Alaska cruise-ship operator when it purchased two 110-passenger steamships, *Coquitlam* and *Camosun*, from Union Steamships Ltd. of Vancouver.

Westours was founded by a Fairbanks tour operator named **Chuck West** who pioneered nearly every element of Alaska's travel industry and eventually sold his company to Holland America

P&O's **Arcadia** *was one of the first large liners to cruise Alaska's Inside Passage in the late 1960s. Built in 1954, the ship was 30,000 tons and carried 647 first-class and 735 tourist-class passengers.*

Line. Westours was joined in Alaska in 1969 by P&O's Princess Cruises and the cruise business became a thriving industry.

How Ships Move

Ships are pushed through the water by the turning of propellers, two of which are usually used on cruise ships. A propeller is like a screw threading its way through the sea, pushing water away from its pitched blades. Props are 15 to 20 feet in diameter on large cruise ships and normally turn at 100 to 150 revolutions per minute. It takes a lot of horsepower – about 50,000 on a large ship – to make these propellers push a ship along. The bridge crew can tap into any amount of engine power by moving small levers that adjust the angle (or pitch) of the propeller blades to determine the speed of the ship. Cruise ships normally travel at 15 to 20 knots, depending on the ship's schedule and distances to be covered between ports. Distances at sea are measured in nautical miles (1 nautical mile = 1.15 statute miles = 1.85 kilometers).

Ships use diesel engines to transmit power by supplying electricity either to motors that smoothly turn the prop shafts or to motors mounted on pods hung from the stern of the ship, like huge outboard motors, which can swivel 360 degrees. The amount of soot smoke from today's ships is a fraction of that produced by earlier ships, but stricter emission regulations have prompted the cruise lines to retrofit their ships with exhaust-cleaning systems (called scrubbers). A growing number of ships have also been configured to plug into shoreside electrical power (cold ironing) when docked. Ports equipped with this technology include Juneau, Vancouver and Seattle.

The modern cruise ships currently sailing Alaskan waters have been dubbed 'floating resorts' for their extensive onboard facilities, from swimming pools and health spas to show lounges and casinos. Cabins, formerly equipped with portholes, now are fitted with picture windows or sliding glass doors that open onto private verandas.

Modern cruise ships are quite different from those of the Golden Age of ocean liners, when ships were designed for the rigors of regular year-round ocean crossings and some of the worst weather imaginable. Constructed with heavy riveted plating, their design features included a deep draft (more stability in rough seas) and a low profile (less windage, more maneuverability in storms).

Ships built today are generally taller, shallower, lighter and powered by smaller, more compact engines. Although their steel hulls are thinner and welded together in numerous sections, modern ships are as strong as the older ocean liners because of advances in construction technology and metallurgy.

An Alaskan cruise is mainly along protected coastal waters and rough conditions are uncommon. Two areas where some ocean swell will be felt are in Queen Charlotte Sound and the Gulf of Alaska. Challenges for the crew when navigating Alaska include making tight turns around the numerous islands of the Inside Passage. Officers begin the turn well ahead of time and the stern – because of the ship's flat bottom – seems to slide across the water for some distance before it gains way (or speed) in the new direction.

The Engine Room

Located many decks below the passenger cabins is the engine room – a labyrinth of tunnels, catwalks and bulkheads connecting and supporting the machinery that generates the vast amount of power needed to operate a ship. A large crew keeps everything running smoothly, but its size is a far

A ship's bow bulb, the protruding red shape at the front of the ship, reduces fuel consumption.

cry from the hundreds once needed to operate coal-burning steam engines that were used before the advent of diesel fuel.

Technical advancements below the ship's waterline include the bow bulb, stabilizers and thrusters. The **bow bulb** is located just below the waterline and displaces the same amount of water that would be pushed out of the way by the ship's bow. This virtually eliminates a bow wave, resulting in some fuel saving because less energy is needed to push the ship forward. **Stabilizers** are small, wing-like appendages that protrude amidships below the waterline and act to dampen the ship's roll in beam seas. These are normally not needed during an Alaskan cruise. **Thrusters** are port-like openings with small propellers at the bow and sometimes at the stern, located just below the waterline. They push the front or rear of the ship as it is approaching or leaving a dock and they greatly reduce the need for tugboat assistance.

The Bridge

The bridge (located at the bow or front of the ship) is an elevated, enclosed platform bridging (or crossing) the width of the ship with an unobstructed view ahead and to either side. It is from the ship's bridge that the highest-ranking officer, the **captain**, oversees the operation of the ship. The bridge is manned 24 hours a day by two officers working four hours on, eight hours off, in a three-watch system. They all report to the captain, and their various duties include recording all course changes, keeping lookout and making sure the junior officer has a fresh pot of coffee going. The captain does not usually have a set watch but will be on the bridge whenever the ship is entering or leaving port, transiting a pass or approaching a tidewater glacier. Other conditions that would bring the captain to the bridge would be poor weather or when there are numerous vessels in the area, such as commercial fishboats.

An array of instrumentation provides the ship's officers with pertinent information. The electronic **Global Positioning System** (GPS) uses a system of satellite signals to provide a fix of where the ship is, accurate to within a few feet. This position is displayed in a series of numbers indicating the latitude and longitude, which is compared with a chart (usually an electronic chart) to determine the ship's location.

Radar is used most intensely in foggy conditions or at night. Radar's electronic signals can survey the ocean for many miles, and anything solid – such as land or other boats – appears on its screen. Radar is also used for plotting the course of other ships and for alerting the crew of a potential collision situation. **Depth sounders** track the bottom of the seabed to ensure the ship's course agrees with the depth of water shown on the official chart.

A young passenger sizes up the ship's bridge.

The **helm** on modern ships is a surprisingly small wheel. An automatic telemotor transmission connects the wheel to the steering mechanism at the stern of the ship. Ships also use an 'autopilot' which works through an electronic compass to steer a set course, and is used when cruising in open water.

Other instruments monitor engine speed, power, angle of list, speed through water, speed over ground (which is affected by the numerous currents encountered in the Inside Passage) and time arrival estimations. Along intricate sections of coastline, large ships must have a **pilot** on board to provide navigational advice to the ship's officers. These pilots have local knowledge of every back eddy, stray current and dangerous reef in their territory, and help thread the big ships through the narrow passes and channels that make Alaska cruises so thrilling. Canadian pilots are on board

The bridge on a cruise ship contains banks of navigational aids.

when a ship is traveling the inner channels of British Columbia's Inside Passage, and American pilots are on board when the ship is inside Alaskan coastal waters. These pilots embark and disembark the ship at various pilot stations along the cruise route. When a ship is in open waters, a pilot isn't required.

There are many navigational challenges encountered on an Alaska cruise. Here are a few cited by cruise ship officers: Seymour Narrows (fast currents), Cape Caution (reefs and choppy seas), Snow Passage (fast currents, shallow and twisting passage), Cape Decision (choppy seas and poor visibility combined with a blind corner), Cape Spencer (steep seas and contrary currents) and Cape St. Elias (choppy seas, poor visibility). Icebergs are generally not a safety factor because they usually melt before they drift into the shipping lanes, with the exception of the icebergs calving off Columbia Glacier near the Port of Valdez.

Ship Safety

The cruise lines treat passenger safety as a top priority. The International Maritime Organization maintains high standards for safety at sea, including regular fire and lifeboat drills, as well as frequent ship inspections for cleanliness and seaworthiness.

Cruise ships must adhere to a law requiring that a **lifeboat drill** take place within 24 hours of embarkation, and many ships schedule this drill just before leaving port. You will be asked to proceed to your lifeboat station or designated gathering place (directions will be displayed somewhere in your cabin). Ship's staff will be on hand to guide you through the safety drill so you know what to do in the unlikely event of an emergency.

On the ship's bridge, a large area of instrumentation is devoted to the monitoring of numerous fire alarms placed throughout the ship. If an alarm sounds, it rings on the bridge and is illuminated on a ship's diagram so that its location is immediately known and the officers can promptly secure the area to prevent the blaze from spreading. Next to ship navigation, the threat of a fire is the most serious concern for the ship's officers, and deck crews regularly practise fire safety drills.

At some ports, the ship will anchor rather than dock. In such an instance, passengers are tendered ashore in the ship's launches. Passengers on organized shore excursions will be taken ashore first. If you're heading ashore independently, wait an hour or so

A tender pulls alongside a ship that's lying at anchor.

to board a tender, when the line-ups are much shorter or even non-existent.

Hotel Staff

The Purser's Office/Front Desk is the pleasure center of the ship. And since a cruise is meant to be an extremely enjoyable experience, it is fitting the Hotel Manager's rank is second only to that of the Captain. In terms of staff, the **Hotel Manager** (or Passenger Services Director) has by far the largest. It is his responsibility to make sure beds are made, meals are served, wines are poured, entertainment is provided and tour buses arrive on time – all while keeping a smile on his face. Hotel managers generally have many years' experience on ships working in various departments before rising to this position, and usually have graduated from a university or college program in management. Often they train in the hotel or food industries, where they learn the logistics of feeding hundreds of people at a sitting.

A Hotel Manager's management staff includes a Purser, Food

Services Manager, Beverage Manager, Chief Housekeeper, Cruise Director and Shore Excursion Manager. All ship's staff wear a uniform and even if a hotel officer doesn't recognize a staff member, he will know at a glance that person's duties by their uniform's color and the distinguishing bars on the sleeves. The hotel staff on cruise ships come from countries around the world.

Life Aboard

Cruise ship cabins – also called staterooms – vary in size, from standard inside cabins to outside suites complete with a verandah. Whatever the size of your accommodation, it will be clean and comfortable. A telephone and television are standard features, and storage space includes closets and drawers ample enough to hold your clothes and miscellaneous items. Valuables can be left in your stateroom safe or a safety deposit box at the front office, also called the purser's office.

If your budget permits, an outside cabin – especially one with a verandah – is preferable for enjoying the coastal scenery and orienting yourself at a new port. When selecting a cabin, keep in mind its location in relation to facilities on the decks above and below. If you're a light sleeper, you may want to avoid a stateroom that's situated below the disco or dining room, or is next to a stairwell or elevator. For passengers prone to seasickness, cabins located on lower decks near the middle of the ship will have less motion than a top outside cabin near the stern. If you have preferences for cabin location, be sure to discuss these with your cruise agent at the time of booking.

Both casual and formal dining are offered on the large ships, with breakfast and lunch served in the buffet-style lido restaurant or at an open seating in the main dining room. Traditionally, dinner was served at two sittings in the main dining room and passengers were asked, when booking their cruise, to indicate their preference for first or second sitting. While this option is still offered on most large ships, they also offer open seating for passengers who want more flexibility. Luxury cruise lines usually have one open seating for dinner. Many ships also offer alternative dining – small

(Above) In addition to the main dining room, alternative dining in a variety of specialty restaurants is also offered on most ships. (Below) An outside suite with verandah.

specialty restaurants that require a reservation and for which there is usually a charge (about $20-$30 per person). Room service is also available, free of charge, for light meals and in-between snacks.

Extra Expenses

There are few additional expenses once you board a cruise ship. Your cabin and meals are paid for, as are any stage shows, lectures, movies, lounge acts and other activities held in the ship's public areas. If you make use of the personal services offered on board – such as dry cleaning or a spa treatment – these are not covered in the basic price of a cruise. Nor are any drinks you might order in a lounge (although you can certainly sit there and enjoy the ambience without ordering a drink). You will also be charged for any wine or alcoholic beverages you order with your meals. Optional shore excursions are another additional cost.

Gratuities are extra, with each cruise line providing its own guidelines on how much various crewmembers should be tipped – provided you are happy with the service. Gratuities for your cabin steward, dining room steward, assistant waiter and head waiter were traditionally handed out individually in cash-filled envelopes on the last night of the cruise. However, most ships now offer a service that automatically bills to your shipboard account an aggregate amount for gratuities (about $12 per passenger per day). Should you prefer to personally hand out your tips or adjust the amounts charged to your account, you simply notify the purser's office. These gratuities do not cover bar bills, to which a 15% tip is automatically added. (On luxury cruise ships, gratuities are included in the all-inclusive fare).

Most ships are cashless societies in which passengers sign for incidental expenses. These are itemized on a final statement which is slipped under your cabin door during the last night of your cruise and settled at the front office by pre-approved credit card. It's best to check your account balance (which can usually be accessed on your stateroom television) before the last full day of your cruise and thus avoid long line-ups at the front desk should you need to clear up any discrepancies.

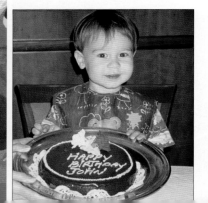

(Above) A lone jogger on the sports deck. (Left) Birthdays and anniversaries are celebrated with a complimentary cake.

Alaska's Bumpy Beginnings

Alaska, were it rated by Hollywood censors, would receive an 'R' for violence. A battle scene on a planetary scale is occurring along the west coast of North America where sections of the earth's crust – called tectonic plates – are colliding.

As the Pacific plate rams into the North American plate, dramatic action is taking place along the Gulf of Alaska coastline. Here, some of the world's tallest coastal mountains, caught between these two plates, are being shoved upwards. Others are slipping into the sea as they are dragged under along the collision zone. Something's got to give with this constant pushing and pulling going on, and that something is the occasional earthquake or volcanic eruption. Mountains twist, shake and heave tons of snow and rock from their slopes, or spew from their cores a fiery ash that turns day into night.

The tectonic tug of war that eventually formed Alaska started when the earth's crust began dividing into plates – a process which seems to have started shortly after the crust was formed. As these large plates rubbed against each other, pieces chipped off and became terranes. These fragments could move more freely than the large plates and the earth's crust became a sort of jigsaw puzzle as pieces slowly moved from one location to another. An island, perhaps where the Philippines are today, gradually made its way across the Pacific Ocean to lie off Canada's West Coast and become part of Vancouver Island.

Over the last few hundred million years, terranes off the Pacific Plate have been pushed, as if on a conveyor belt, up the west side of the North American Plate where they docked against ancestral Alaska, and against one another, at the top of the Gulf of Alaska.

Alaska's dramatic Gulf of Alaska coastline was formed by terranes – pieces of the earth's crust – being jammed between two major plates.

These terranes are still moving today, with the Yakutat terrane riding on the Pacific plate but also docking against the earlier arrivals. If the terrane upon which Los Angeles sits continues moving north at its rate of two inches per year, it will reach the northern Gulf of Alaska in 76 million years.

The current era – the Cenozoic – began 65 million years ago. It began with volcanism and huge slices of crustal rocks stacking one upon the other to form the Rockies and other mountain ranges. Early whales appeared, as did the hardwoods and redwoods of North America.

Then the warm, humid climate cooled and fur-bearing animals such as the bear, seal and raccoon came into being. As the climate continued to cool about five million years ago, the widespread giant ape evolved into a manlike ape, and the earliest human artifacts date from this period, which ended about two million years ago.

The Pleistocene epoch – the age of glaciers – came next and it contained a series of major glacial advances and retreats. These rumbling fields of ice eroded rock and transported huge deposits of clay, sand and gravel across large sections of North America.

The First Arrivals

Ice covered much of Alaska during the age of glaciers, extending across the northern Gulf of Alaska. Sea levels were also lower, and an ice-free corridor of land connected Alaska with Siberia via the Bering Land bridge – now referred to as

The Aleuts wore ceremonial cloaks made from the skins of hundreds of tufted puffins.

Beringia. About 30,000 years ago, humans began to migrate from Asia to North America, where they established hunting camps in Alaska's interior and Canada's Yukon. Others may have come not by land, but by water, working their way around the Pacific rim and using as stepping stones the ice-free coastal refuges that were exposed by retreating glaciers when the last great ice age drew to a close some 15,000 years ago.

When the glaciers began staging their retreat, these giant bulldozers of ice left behind valleys that would eventually become channels and fjords of the Inside Passage. Initially, however, the land uplifted when relieved of the massive weight of ice fields. It was during this time of retreating ice and dropping sea levels, before the growing torrents of glacial meltwater further inland swelled the oceans and turned valleys into waterways, that a migration of ancient seafarers likely took place along the edge of today's Inside Passage.

Sea levels finally stabilized about 5,000 years ago, and the Inside Passage as we now know it became permanently inhabited by people. The maritime climate was mild, the rivers were filled with salmon, and the lush forests of cedar, spruce and hemlock provided an endless supply of building material.

Prime waterfront locations were snapped up as groups established summer and winter villages within their fishing and hunting territories. These highly organized societies thrived along the entire Inside Passage, from Puget Sound in northern Washington State to the top of the Alaskan Panhandle. The rest of Alaska's coastline was inhabited by Eskimos and Aleuts, while Athabaskans – possibly the region's first inhabitants – lived in the interior.

Each of these native groups was affected in different ways when European explorers arrived at their shores and engaged them in the fur trade. The Aleuts were traumatized by the Russian *promyshlenniki* (frontier men) who enslaved them as hunters, but the coastal Indians initially profited from the fur trade – exchanging their furs for metal and tools. Eventually, rum and firearms became popular items of exchange, and native social structures began to unravel. The deadliest European import was disease, and whole villages were wiped out by smallpox and other epidemics.

European Explorers

The 18th century was an era of great naval exploration. Russian explorers – led by the Danish sea captain Vitus Bering – set off from the shores of Siberia to discover what lay to the east. Spanish, French and British ships also ventured into the Pacific's northern waters in search of the elusive Northwest Passage.

During this Age of Enlightenment, naval commanders such as Britain's Cook, France's La Perouse and Spain's

A wooden cross at Three Saints Bay on Kodiak Island marks the location of Alaska's first permanent European settlement established there by the Russians in 1784.

British naval survey expeditions charted the Inside Passage throughout the 19th century.

Malaspina all led scientific expeditions to the New World.

The logbooks of these and other commanders provide a wealth of information on the native cultures that thrived at this time of First Contact. Some natives, upon initially seeing these strangely clad, pale-skinned men, fled into the forest. Others, overcome with curiosity, ran their hands across their visitors' faces to see if darker skin lay beneath a layer of white paint.

Captain Cook speculated that cannibalism was practiced by North Coast natives, but this rumor was dispelled by Captain Vancouver when he wrote that his men, while camped on shore, offered venison to some natives who mistook it for human flesh and made their aversion quite clear, refusing to eat any of it until the British sailors produced a deer carcass to prove that they were not cannibals.

The natives were duly impressed with the sailing ships that magically appeared on the horizon. Captains were honored guests in the homes of village chiefs and, in a show of reciprocal hospitality, ship's tours were often held for high-ranking village members. The ships and their nautical instruments fascinated the natives. One chief, when shown how a telescope worked, asked a naval officer if he could see around a bend in a channel with it and watch for approaching enemy canoes.

The Spanish explored much of the Pacific Northwest in the mid-to-late 1700s but were secretive about their discoveries. When the journals of Captain Cook's final voyage were published in America and Europe in 1783, merchant ships began flocking to these northern waters in pursuit of sea otter pelts. Dubbed 'soft gold,' these luxuriant pelts fetched a phenomenal price in China.

As more merchant ships (from Europe and America) frequented

the coast, inevitable misunder-
standings erupted in bloodshed.
The natives became increasingly
wary of white fur traders and, at
times, openly hostile. Captain
Vancouver's men reported incidents in which they were
approached in their open survey
boats by canoes filled with weap-
on-bearing natives. A few shots
fired over their heads, however,
would prompt the natives to
unstring their bow-and-arrows
and offer them in trade.

Settlers eventually followed the
fur traders, and their arrival
changed the coastal landscape.
The natives' territorial boundaries
became obsolete as homesteaders
farmed, logged and mined the
land, while Spain, Britain, Russia
and America disputed borders and
trade monopolies.

Spain withdrew from the North
Pacific in the late 1700s after a
political showdown with Britain
over territorial rights. The dispute
centered around control of
Nootka Sound – a strategic harbor
on the west coast of Vancouver
Island.

In 1867, Russia withdrew from
the North Pacific by selling
Alaska to the United States for
what now seems like a fire sale
price of $7.2 million – about two
cents an acre. However, the lucrative fur trade had dwindled and
the American people showed little
enthusiasm for this large tract of
distant land their government had
just acquired.

America's New Frontier

The man who masterminded the
purchase of Alaska, Secretary of
State William H. Seward, was ridi-
culed for his efforts and Alaska –
dubbed 'Seward's icebox' – was
largely neglected by its new
owner. The U.S. army and navy
were sent to police this vast territory but no civil government was
established until 1884 – at the urg-
ing of Reverend Sheldon Jackson,
a Presbyterian missionary who
traveled throughout Alaska establishing missions to educate the
natives and assimilate them into
the American way of life. Jackson
also supported prohibition in
Alaska, to protect the natives from
the influence of rum, but the Klondike gold rush proved too much of
a match for the prohibitionists.

Gold changed many Americans'
perception of Alaska. The first
strikes saw prospectors hurry to
Wrangell and Sitka in 1872.
Juneau was founded almost overnight when gold was discovered
in the area in 1880. More strikes
followed at Forty Mile River,
Yakutat Bay, Lituya Bay,
Mastodon Creek and the Kenai
Peninsula. Then came the really
big one – the Klondike strike on
Bonanza Creek in Canada's
Yukon. Men and women flocked
by the thousands to Skagway for
a chance to get rich in the
Klondike, where the gold fever
ended as quickly as it began, with
many rushing to Nome to try and
cash in on yet another strike.

The 20th century brought con-

Nome's tent city sprang into being when gold was discovered on the beach in 1898, attracting 20,000 prospectors.

tinuing social changes to Alaska. Bush planes opened up the rugged interior – formerly the domain of riverboats, pack animals and dogsleds. The first flight up the Inside Passage, from Seattle to Ketchikan, was made in 1922, and 10 years later the first plane to land on an Alaskan glacier touched down on Mt. McKinley's Muldrow Glacier.

In 1942, during World War II, the U.S. Army Corps of Engineers built the Alaska Highway – a supply route safe from the hazards of wartime shipping. In just eight months they constructed a 1,500-mile road from Dawson Creek, in northern British Columbia, through Canada's Yukon to Fairbanks. Alaska was now joined to 'the Outside' and the next step was statehood – achieved in 1959,

making Alaska the 49th State of the Union.

The discovery of North Slope oil and natural gas deposits in 1968 transformed Alaska's economy. A pipeline was built from Prudhoe Bay on the Beaufort Sea to Valdez on Prince William Sound. Completed in 1977, this 800-mile-long pipeline is half underground and half above ground where it's supported in a flexible, zigzag pattern to withstand earthquakes.

The city of Anchorage, economic center of the state, now has a population exceeding a quarter of a million and is home to two-fifths of the state's total population of 670,000. The majority of Alaskans live in an urban setting, yet the region continues to attract people of pioneer spirit whose jobs pit them against the elements.

America's two largest fishing fleets are stationed in Alaska – at Kodiak Harbor and at Dutch Harbor in the Aleutians. In the early 1980s, a sudden population boom of king crab in the Bering

Sea, coupled with a strong demand for this product in Japan and the U.S., turned fishermen not yet out of their twenties into instant millionaires. The money madness made for some interesting stories. One year, during a protracted strike, hundreds of boats sat moored in Dutch Harbor waiting for a settlement. When word came, fishermen dashed to their vessels and, during this chaotic mass departure, boats were rammed and skippers accidentally left behind. One frenzied crew forgot to untie the docking lines and had to cut themselves loose. The end came as quickly and mysteriously as it arrived. Old myths die hard though, and each summer college kids flock to Alaska's legendary fishing ports, drawn by tales of lucrative deckhand jobs. The greenhorns often have trouble getting hired as crew and have to settle for work in the canneries.

When the Exxon oil spill of March 1989 threatened the fisheries of Prince William Sound and Kodiak Island, entire fishing fleets stayed home that year to help with clean-up operations. Ironically, this environmental disaster focused world attention on the natural beauty of Prince William Sound. Oil tankers now share these waters each summer with increasing numbers of cruise ships and tour boats bringing people to view the area's beautiful fjords and tidewater glaciers.

Although petroleum taxes and royalties produce about 85 percent of Alaska's general revenue, the state's greatest resource may prove to be its spectacular scenery. America's 49th state is enjoying a tourism boom right now and, unlike the rush for furs, gold and other natural resources, this one looks like it will last. Although climate change can affect the size of icefields and cause sea levels to fluctuate,

Kodiak is a major port for Alaska's commercial fishing fleet for both crab and salmon.

humankind cannot deplete the mountains and fjords that took millions of years to create. All we can do is gaze at them in wonder.

A Few Words About Place Names

Thousands of place names have, over the centuries, been bestowed on the islands, channels and mountains of the Inside Passage and Gulf of Alaska coastline. The natives who first inhabited the coast had their own names in place when European naval ships began appearing on the horizon in the mid-1700s.

These survey expeditions continued in the 1800s. In Canadian waters these were conducted by the British Royal Navy, while the United States surveyed Alaskan waters after purchasing the territory from Russia in 1867. The Bostonian William Dall was a member of various American survey expeditions from 1865 to 1899, and his name now graces an island in Southeast Alaska, not far from Annette Island which he named for his wife. Dall's romantic streak is further evidenced by his naming Marmiom Island to commemorate a poem by Sir Walter Scott.

Then there was Captain Pender

of the British Royal Navy who, while surveying the Canadian Inside Passage in 1864, named a point of land Connis after his Skye Terrier. Alma maters, winning racehorses and wives, mothers and sisters have all been honored with place names along this coastline.

The rules for naming landmarks were never cut and dried. The natives often had more than one name for certain places and when explorers from various countries were busy surveying this coast, it was anyone's guess which name would endure. Some names are misnomers, such as British Columbia's Gulf Islands – named when the Strait of Georgia was incorrectly called the Gulf of Georgia. Others, such as the city of Seattle and the country of Canada, are derivatives of native names. Alaska's name comes from the Aleut word Alyeska, meaning The Great Land.

The last word on place names goes to John Muir, an explorer who harbored a healthy skepticism about the relevance of place names. "People look at what they are told to look at or what has been named," he wrote in *Travels in Alaska*. "Nameless things, however fine, go unnoticed."

Glaciers

These rivers of ice are always in movement. Fed by layers of compacted snow at higher elevations, they flow at varying speeds, depending on a variety of factors such as the height and slope of the mountain collecting the snow. The causes of glacier movement are complex and unique to each glacier, with the center and surface of a glacier moving more rapidly than the sides and bottom, which encounter friction. Decreased snow accumulation or increased ablation (losing ice through melting or calving) will result in a retreating (or shrinking) glacier. Those still advancing (or expanding) have a positive mass balance (accumulation exceeds ablation). A stable glacier is one in which its rate of accumulation and rate of ablation are in balance.

The retreating Norris Glacier flows into Taku Inlet and is part of the massive Juneau Icefield.

Most glaciers stopped expanding in the mid-1700s, at the end of the Little Ice Age, which began about 4,000 years ago. Prior to that numerous advances and retreats of the glaciers took place as the climate fluctuated between cooling and warming. At the height of the Great Ice Age, which began more than 12 million years ago in parts of Alaska, a massive ice sheet extended across half of Alaska's land mass and right across the northernmost Gulf of Alaska. Some of these mountains have never emerged from the Ice Age, supporting almost continuous glaciation for as far back as scientists can determine.

The future is uncertain for the 100,000 glaciers covering nearly 30,000 square miles of Alaska. Currently, 95% of Alaska's glaciers are thinning, stagnating or retreating.

The few that are increasing in volume and advancing are all tidewater glaciers lying at the head of long fjords. Each is characterized by a large accumulation area and a constricted area in which to shed ice at its terminus. A tidewater glacier's calving cycle of slow advances and relatively rapid retreats is not greatly affected by climate until late in the advancing phase. This is why the glaciers currently advancing in Alaska are doing so in spite of global warming.

The movement of glaciers is a complex process. No two glaciers are exactly alike and their unique anatomies – determined by local topography and localized weather conditions – can cause them to often behave differently within the same general area. Regardless of whether a glacier is retreating, advancing or stationary, its ice always flows in a downhill direction (due to gravity).

Glaciers carve deep valleys, and when valley glaciers flow together at the base of a moun-

GLACIER GLOSSARY

BERGY SELTZER – Also called 'ice sizzle', in reference to the crackling or sizzling sound emitted when a melting iceberg is relieved of the intense pressures that formed it and trapped air bubbles are released.

CALVING – The breaking away of ice from the terminus (or snout) of a tidewater glacier.

CIRQUE – A valley head shaped like an amphitheater, its vertical walls eroded by a mountain glacier's source.

CREVASSE – Deep, elongated cracks that form in a glacier's brittle surface due to tensions caused by the glacier's movements. A snowbridge is a layer of snow concealing a crevasse.

DRIFT – The sedimentary deposits of a glacier, including till, which is unsorted drift deposited directly by a glacier.

FIRN – The intermediate stage in the transformation of snow to glacier ice. The compression of snow into dense firn takes about one summer.

MORAINE – Unsorted glacier deposit of rock and gravel that collects, through erosion, along the sides and snout of a glacier.

NEVE – The upper end, or source, of a glacier covered with perennial snow.

ROCK FLOUR – Pulverized rock ground by a glacier to a fine powder.

SERACS - Spires of ice pointing skyward.

SURGING – A sudden rapid movement (up to 300 feet per day) of a glacier, that may or may not involve an advance of the glacier's terminus. Factors causing a surge include the build-up of water pressure beneath the ice. Famous surges include those of Hubbard, a tidewater glacier that advanced hundreds of feet within a few weeks in the summer of 1986 (see page 286).

TERMINUS – Also called the snout or toe, this lower extremity of a glacier can be rounded in shape or form a sheer wall of ice. In the case of tidewater glaciers, the terminus is often several hundred feet in height with much of it submerged in water.

(Above) Icebergs are slippery and can suddenly roll, but some people can't resist climbing aboard for a quick ride.

tain, they become a fan-shaped piedmont glacier. An icefield forms when numerous alpine glaciers join together and cover a large land mass with solid ice and snow. A tidewater glacier is a valley glacier that flows right down to the sea and lies at the head of a fjord or inlet.

When chunks of ice fall from the snout of a tidewater glacier and crash into the sea, the glacier is said to be calving. The causes of glacial calving are still being studied and debated, but one known factor involves ice melting faster when in contact with water versus air. This results in an erosive undercutting of a glacier's snout below the high water mark. Each time the tide drops, an eroded section of the snout loses the water's support and this weakening of the ice may hasten its col-

An upthrust rock formation at Taku Harbor in Stephens Passage is evidence of a now-inactive fault of the earth's crust.

lapse. Blue ice at the face of a glacier means it's actively calving. The water near a glacier often appears milky turquoise because of fine sediments carried by glacier meltwater.

Although Alaska's glaciers are millions of years old, they flush their ice fairly rapidly, and the chunks we see dropping off the face of a tidewater glacier are usually a few hundred years old. These bergs are much smaller than those discharged from the polar ice caps and they melt quickly as they drift seaward toward the open waters of the Gulf of Alaska.

One of the largest bergs recorded in Alaska was about 300 square feet and 100 feet above the water. It was discovered in May 1977 floating in Icy Bay, which is located on the Gulf of Alaska at the base of the massive Bering Glacier complex.

An iceberg's blue color is the result of compressed ice absorbing light's short wave colors (reds) and reflecting the long

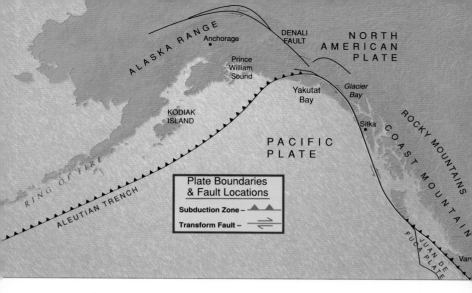

wave colors (blues). If a piece of ice is relieved of pressure, air bubbles form and create a porous surface which is rough (like snow) and doesn't allow any light to penetrate, with light coming back as white. When afloat, about five-sixths of a berg is usually submerged. This ratio can vary, depending on the iceberg's shape and the amount of rock debris it might be carrying.

Earthquakes

The coastal belt of the Pacific Ocean is one of the world's most active earthquake zones. This is due to the earth's surface being divided into crustal plates, some of which meet along the edges of the Pacific Ocean. Blocks of rock move along these plate boundaries, passing one another along fault lines (fractures in the earth's crust). Their relative movements can be vertical, horizontal or oblique and are usually measured in inches per year, except when a sudden release of stress along a fault triggers an earthquake.

An earthquake begins with tremors, followed by more violent shocks which gradually diminish. The origin (focus) of a quake is underground or underwater, and the epicenter is a point on the surface directly above the focus. The magnitude and intensity of an earthquake is determined by the Richter scale, which measures the ground motion to determine the amount of energy released at the quake's origin.

A reading of 4.5 on the Richter scale indicates an earthquake causing slight damage; a reading of 8.5 indicates an earthquake of devastating force. The energy of a quake measuring 8 on the Richter scale is equal to that of a 250-megaton thermo-nuclear bomb. (The atom bomb dropped on Hiroshima in 1945 was .02 megatons.)

The Good Friday earthquake that hit Alaska in 1964 measured between 8.4 and 8.6 on the Richter scale then in use and has since been upgraded to 9.2, the strongest recorded earthquake ever to hit North America. Its epi-

Downtown Anchorage, built on glacial silt deposits, was devastated by the 1964 earthquake when streets collapsed.

center was 15 miles north of Prince William Sound and about 80 miles east of Anchorage causing the death of 131 people. Damage was widespread with sections of Anchorage's downtown collapsing. A block of the earth's crust tilted, causing parts of the Gulf of Alaska to rise 30 feet and coastal land to sink as much as 10 feet.

Tsunamis (Tidal Waves)

A tsunami – meaning 'harbor wave' in Japanese – is often referred to as a tidal wave. However, tsunamis are not caused by tidal action (although a high tide can increase their onshore damage) but by sea floor earthquakes or underwater landslides. Such seismic disturbances rarely trigger tsunamis, but when they do – watch out.

Up to several hundred miles in length but with heights of only a few feet, a tsunami can travel thousands of miles across the open ocean at speeds reaching 450 miles per hour. Its movement is undetected by ships at sea, but when it approaches a shelving coastline, it builds into a series of waves of catastrophic proportion. Anywhere from 10 to 40 minutes can pass between crests and the highest wave may occur several hours after the first wave (generally the third to eighth wave crests are the largest). The sudden withdrawal of water from a shoreline could be the trough of an approaching tsunami, so people who venture onto these newly exposed beaches risk being engulfed by a wave's huge crest.

A tsunami warning system is in place for the Pacific Ocean (where almost two-thirds of all tsunamis occur). Countries with gauge stations include the United States, Canada, Japan, Chile, New Zealand and the Philippines. Should any of the stations record a drastic change in water elevation, direct telephone contact is made with the warning center located in Honolulu, Hawaii.

The 1964 Alaska earthquake was of such intensity that it sent a series of waves to the far reaches of the Pacific. Waves over 20 feet high swept ashore in Oregon and California, killing 15 people. The Gulf of Alaska ports were hardest hit, with 107 people losing their lives. In 1946, an earthquake in the Aleutians sent 100-foot waves sweeping onto Unimak Island where the lighthouse was destroyed and five people perished. Tsunamis of such magnitude are extremely rare. However, the Alaska Tsunami Warning Center – established at Palmer in 1967 – now provides timely

Star marks 1964 earthquake's epicenter in Prince William Sound. Shaded area shows crustal uplift (+) and subsidence (-). Curved lines show leading edge of resultant tsunami, generated at 7:36 p.m.

warnings to prevent loss of life from an approaching tsunami. The 2004 Boxing Day tsunami that struck Indonesia and other countries bordering the Indian Ocean was caused by an earthquake off Sumatra that registered 9.0 on the Richter scale. More than 200,000 people perished, many standing on beaches watching the approaching tsunami waves, as no warning system was in place for the Indian Ocean at the time of this calamitous event.

Volcanoes

There are about 500 active volcanoes on our planet, more than 70 of these located in Alaska. They are part of the Ring of Fire that encircles the Pacific Ocean basin and marks the collision zone of various tectonic plates that comprise the earth's crust. Volcanoes also exist beneath the ocean's surface and are called seamounts. About 100 of these extend from the Gulf of Alaska to the Oregon Coast.

Volcanoes form around an aperture in the earth's crust,

through which gases, lava (molten rock) and solid fragments are ejected. A dormant volcano quickly loses its conical shape to erosion, so any mountain that is cone-shaped can be considered a potentially active volcano.

A volcano's crater is formed when the cone collapses during an eruption. Steam vents often cover a crater floor or the collapsed summit may fill with glacial meltwater. The crater lake atop Mount Katmai on the Alaska Peninsula is a unique robin's-egg blue, due to glacial silt and sulphur in the water which remains ice-free for most of the year because of volcanic heat.

The Alaska Peninsula contains 15 active volcanoes, its most famous being Mount Katmai which erupted in June 1912 through a vent in its base. One of

Volcanic ash from Mount Katmai's 1912 eruption still lies on the nearby mountains of Geographic Harbor.

the greatest volcanic eruptions in recorded history, it was twice the size of Krakatoa, which killed 35,000 Indonesians in 1883, and ten times the force of Washington State's Mount Saint Helens which erupted twice in 1980 and killed 60 people. Because of Katmai's remote location, no humans were killed, but the residents of Kodiak (90 miles away) were rained with ash so thick that for two days a person couldn't see a lit lantern held at arm's length. Acid rain fell 2,000 miles away in Vancouver, Canada, where laundry hanging on clotheslines disintegrated. An entire valley was filled with burning ash that spewed from Mount Katmai. In total, the volcanic eruption blanketed 40 square miles with ash that was 700 feet deep in places.

The 1992 eruption of Mount Spurr, near Anchorage, was merely a hiccup in comparison, sending a giant cloud of ash into the upper atmosphere that disrupted air traffic in Canada and the northern United States for three days.

When a jet plane flies into volcanic ash, the finely ground rock is sandblasted onto the aircraft, clogging its engines and degrading its wing surfaces. One of the most graphic examples of this occurred in December 1989 when a jumbo jet flew into a mass of ash the day after Mount Redoubt, near Anchorage, began erupting. All four engines quit. The pilot tried to restart the engines, unsuccessfully, seven or eight times before two of them finally kicked in, followed by the other two. The plane landed safely at Anchorage, but this and other similar incidents prompted the Civil Aviation Organization to establish a worldwide network of Volcanic Ash Advisory Centers. The one in Anchorage is responsible for Alaska, analyzing information it receives from satellites, volcano observatories and weather agencies to forecast movements of ash clouds and alert airlines and air-traffic control centers of potential danger.

Alaska's chain of volcanoes extends westward along the Alaska Peninsula and Aleutian Islands. Pavlof Volcano, near the tip of the Peninsula, erupted in 1996, and Mount Cleveland Volcano, on the uninhabited Aleutian island of Chuginadak, erupted in 2001. The Aleutians are a string of volcanic islands standing on the edge of the Aleutian Trench. This ocean trench is a subduction zone in which the Pacific plate is descending beneath the North American plate, and the waters along this trench are thousands of feet deeper than the nearby ocean bottom.

Aurora Borealis (Northern Lights)

A poet would describe the Northern Lights as curtains of shimmering light that flutter across the sky. A scientist would say they are high-speed particles from the sun colliding with the earth's air molecules. Both descriptions are correct.

When charged electrons and protons – released during sunspot activity – drift toward the earth, they are magnetically pulled to the planet's northern and southern latitudes. These charged particles strike gases in the earth's upper atmosphere and turn luminous – ranging from silvery white through the colors of the rainbow. The

The aurora borealis lights up a northern sky.

Bathers relax in the hot mineral waters of Warm Spring Bay on Baranof Island

shimmering effect is caused by the differing intensities of light.

The aurora borealis is most prevalent over the Arctic Circle but can occur throughout the northern latitudes. (Those which occur over the Antarctic Circle and southern latitudes are called the aurora australis.) The Northern Lights appear most often during the spring and fall equinoxes, when the sun crosses the equator and night and day are of equal length. Northern Lights can also occur on dark winter nights and during increased sunspot activity. The last phase of intense sunspot activity was during the late 1950s.

Hotsprings

The hot water flowing from a natural spring is the result of ground water seeping to great depths through faults in the earth's crust, where it is heated and recirculated back up to the surface. A soak in a steaming mineral bath is consid-

ered by many to be a most therapeutic pastime. Alaskans are fortunate to have about 80 such thermal springs scattered throughout their state. Half of these are located along the volcanic Alaska Peninsula and Aleutian chain, with another concentration of hotsprings in southeast Alaska.

Some of these natural springs are developed, with bath houses built over tubs that collect the flow of spring water. The village of Tenakee Springs on Chichagof Island grew up around its hotsprings. Enclosed by a cement bathhouse with bathing hours for men and women posted on the door, the springs at Tenakee attract plenty of visitors seeking relaxation, including state legislators from Juneau. The Alaska ferry calls at Tenakee Springs, as do fishermen and pleasure boaters looking for a good soak in a hot bath – compliments of Mother Earth's ingenious plumbing system.

Marine Weather

Alaska encompasses a number of climatic zones: maritime along its southern coastlines; continental in its vast interior; arctic along its northern shores. The cruise ship routes remain within the moderate maritime zone, which is dominated by the Pacific Ocean.

Weather systems flow in an easterly direction in the northern hemisphere, so the west coast of North America enjoys the moderating effects of the Pacific Ocean throughout the year. Wet and windy weather prevails along the Pacific coast in winter as storms originating offshore flow into the Gulf of Alaska where its mountain-rimmed coastline acts as a catch basin and precipitation falls as snow at higher elevations. Summer weather in the North Pacific is dominated by a subtropical high which brings reduced precipitation and increased sunshine. Autumn is a transition season as the North Pacific High gradually shrinks and the relatively light breezes of summer are replaced with winter storms generated by the Aleutian Low.

Ocean currents also flow eastward across the Pacific from Asian waters, but the warm Japan Current never reaches the shores of Alaska.

This slow-moving current joins the North Pacific Current (a broad, slow, easterly drift), which eventually veers south somewhere off the Oregon or California coast. The Subarctic Current runs parallel with the North Pacific Current and it gradually splits as it approaches the Washington/British Columbia coast, with one branch veering south to become the California Current, and the other veering north to become the Alaska Current. This current flows in a counter-clockwise direction along the Gulf of Alaska coastline and keeps it free of winter ice, except in protected waters.

It can take two to five years for a parcel of water carried by the Subarctic Current to cross the North Pacific. Along the way its temperature is determined not by the current's origin but by the surface water's constant heat exchange with the atmosphere.

This archival shot of Kodiak's harbor shows the smoking waters of a winter storm as it sweeps ashore.

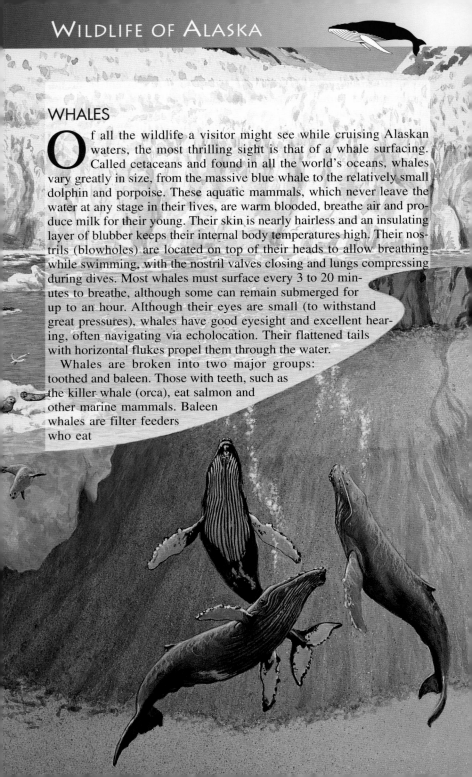

WHALES

O f all the wildlife a visitor might see while cruising Alaskan waters, the most thrilling sight is that of a whale surfacing. Called cetaceans and found in all the world's oceans, whales vary greatly in size, from the massive blue whale to the relatively small dolphin and porpoise. These aquatic mammals, which never leave the water at any stage in their lives, are warm blooded, breathe air and produce milk for their young. Their skin is nearly hairless and an insulating layer of blubber keeps their internal body temperatures high. Their nostrils (blowholes) are located on top of their heads to allow breathing while swimming, with the nostril valves closing and lungs compressing during dives. Most whales must surface every 3 to 20 minutes to breathe, although some can remain submerged for up to an hour. Although their eyes are small (to withstand great pressures), whales have good eyesight and excellent hearing, often navigating via echolocation. Their flattened tails with horizontal flukes propel them through the water.

Whales are broken into two major groups: toothed and baleen. Those with teeth, such as the killer whale (orca), eat salmon and other marine mammals. Baleen whales are filter feeders who eat schooling fish, plankton and other small organisms, which they catch by swimming with their mouths wide open. When the whale closes its mouth, it raises its tongue to force the scooped water out the sides where the bristles of its baleen plates trap the food.

Humpback Whale

The humpback whale, a filter feeder, is frequently sighted in Alaskan waters during the months of June, July and August. An estimated 6,000 to 8,000 humpback whales spend their summers in the North Pacific, with several thousand of these feeding in Alaskan waters each summer. In winter, most of them migrate south to breed and calve in the tropical waters off Hawaii. December and January are the birthing months, following a 12-month gestation period. Cows give birth to a single calf weighing about a ton and measuring 12 to 15 feet in length. Calves are born without a blubber layer and nurse on their mother's milk which contains 50 percent butter fat.

Adult humpbacks are, on average, 45 feet long and weigh up to 40 tons. Their large flippers provide maneuverability and the pleats on the sides of their mouths can create a pouch large enough to hold six adult humans. When feeding, they blow columns of bubbles that create a ring around a school of fish which they then lunge at with their mouths wide open. Sea birds, attracted by the water disturbance, feed on shrimp-like krill and herring which swim to the surface. A humpback whale consumes up to 3,000 pounds of seafood per day.

Humpbacks travel in threesomes – a female, her calf and a male escort. The male earns his position as escort. He serenades the female by performing a repeated pattern of sounds (called a song) at depths of 60 feet or more. If this doesn't win her, the male will confront her current escort by smacking him with his

(Facing page) Humpbacks blow air bubbles in a column to collect krill. (Below) Humpback whales are observed bubble-net feeding near Juneau.

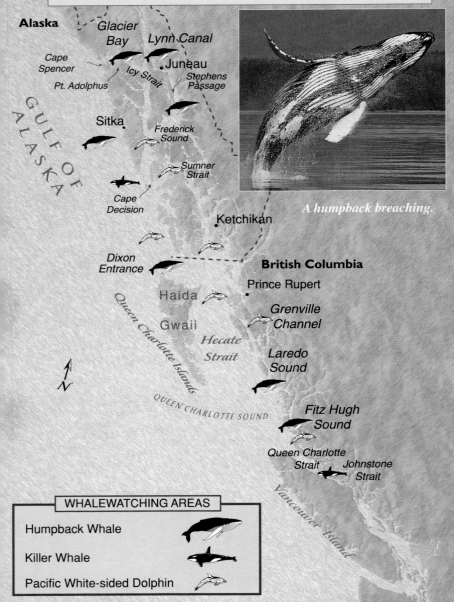

WHALE WATCHING:

Good areas to sight humpback whales include Frederick Sound and Stephens Passage (south of Juneau), Lynn Canal (north of Juneau) and the waters off Point Adolphus (opposite the entrance to Glacier Bay). One telltale sign to watch for is the appearance of a plume of mist in the distance, which could indicate a pod of whales surfacing. While it's always possible to sight whales (including dolphins and porpoises) from the ship's rail, the surest way to see a humpback whale is by taking a whalewatching boat excursion out of Juneau.

Alaska

Glacier Bay

Lynn Canal

Cape Spencer

Juneau

Icy Strait

Pt. Adolphus

Stephens Passage

GULF OF ALASKA

Sitka

Frederick Sound

Sumner Strait

Cape Decision

Ketchikan

A humpback breaching.

Dixon Entrance

British Columbia

Prince Rupert

Haida

Grenville Channel

Gwaii

Hecate Strait

Laredo Sound

Queen Charlotte Islands

QUEEN CHARLOTTE SOUND

N

Fitz Hugh Sound

Queen Charlotte Strait

Johnstone Strait

Vancouver Island

WHALEWATCHING AREAS

Humpback Whale

Killer Whale

Pacific White-sided Dolphin

A humpback doing a deep dive.

fluked tail which packs 8,000 pounds of muscle and, studded with barnacles, is a humpback's most powerful weapon. No two humpback tails are alike and scientists identify each whale by the pattern on its flukes which are visible when the whale raises its tail high out of the water before making a deep dive.

Only the males sing and they seldom do this while feeding in Alaska. They do, however, perform their usual acrobatics such as breaching (heaving themselves out of the water), lobtailing and flippering (smacking the water's surface with their tail or flippers). This surface activity and close-to-shore feeding by the humpback made it an easy target for commercial whalers in the 19th century. By the time humpbacks in the Pacific were protected in 1966, their number had dwindled to a few thousand from an estimated high of 125,000. Their numbers are now rebounding.

Killer Whale (Orca)

Killer whales belong to the dolphin family of toothed whales and for decades they were much feared by humans because of their swift, ferocious attacks on seals and other prey, their mouths holding more than four dozen sharp teeth. Today the social habits of this handsome species are a source of fascination for both scientists and enthusiastic whale watchers.

Males, which can reach 30 feet in length, live for about 30 years while females, which average 23 feet in length, can live 50 years, sometimes longer. The male is distinguished from the female by his taller, straighter dorsal fin (up to six feet high on mature males). Each sub-group within a pod consists of a mature cow and her progeny of all ages. Females give

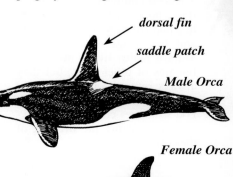

dorsal fin

saddle patch

Male Orca

Female Orca

A killer whale's most distinguishing features are its prominent dorsal fin and the white marking just behind it, called a saddle patch.

birth to single calves following a gestation period of 15 months.

A killer whale's most distinguishing features are its prominent dorsal fin and the white marking just behind it, called a saddle patch. Scientists who observe killer whales in the waters of the Pacific Northwest have developed a database in which regularly sighted pods and their members – identified by individual markings – are given reference names. Every killer whale belongs to a pod – the extended family group into which it was born. Each sub-group within a pod consists of a mature cow and her progeny of all ages. Mature males likely mate with females of other pods, but they always return to their own pod and remain with it until death. Pod structures change very slowly, many lasting the lifetime of the cow.

Resident pods, with up to 50 members, form the largest groups, remaining near established salmon runs along inshore waters. Transient pods form smaller groups and travel a wider area in search for food, preying primarily on marine mammals such as seals and sea lions. Offshore pods are found farther out to sea, well away from coastal waters, and apparently feed on fish.

Killer whales can swim for long distances at a cruising speed of about seven knots, but can accelerate dramatically when attacking prey or leaping from the water (breaching). Resident pods communicate with high-pitched sounds that can be heard on hydrophones. These vocalizations include sonarlike clicks, squeaks and whistles. Transient pods remain silent, so as not to alert potential prey of their presence.

Killer whales are frequently sighted in Johnstone Strait (feeding on salmon) and in the waters off Victoria, but can appear anywhere along the Inside Passage, Prince William Sound and Gulf of Alaska. Their distribution is worldwide.

OTHER WHALES

The smallest baleen whale to frequent Alaskan waters is the minke which reaches lengths of 33 feet. The blue whale, the largest known animal ever to have lived (reaching 100 feet in length), is sometimes sighted in the Gulf of Alaska. The gray whale is another large baleen whale, about 40 to 45 feet in length and weighing up to 40 tons. Strongly migratory but a relatively slow swimmer, the gray whale travels near shore on its twice-yearly migration between Mexico's Baja coast and the Beaufort Sea.

The beluga (or white whale) is a small toothed whale. Reaching lengths of 19 feet, the beluga is sometimes called a 'sea canary' for the variety of noises it makes. Traveling in large groups, belugas winter in the Arctic Ocean and in summer enter northern rivers and inlets, such as Turnagain Arm, south of Anchorage in Cook Inlet.

The legendary sperm whale, largest of the toothed whales, is usually blue-black in color and has a blunt snout containing up to a ton of sperm oil (a liquid wax). Males can grow to over 70 feet and their range extends from the Bering Sea to Antarctica. Females, which grow to 30 feet, remain closer to the tropics.

(Above) The beluga, a northern whale, can often be sighted close to shore in Turnagain Arm south of Anchorage. (Below) Dall porpoises skim the water's surface at speeds reaching 30 miles per hour.

Dall Porpoise

These small but speedy toothed whales are sometimes confused with killer whales because their black-and-white coloring is similar. However, Dall porpoises are much shorter (about seven feet long) and stockier in shape, and their dorsal fin is topped with white. They are the world's fastest marine mammals, reaching speeds of 30 miles per hour. Travelling in groups of a half dozen or more, they swim just beneath the surface of the water, kicking up splashes called rooster tails when they leap partially out of the water.

These sociable creatures love to ride the bow wave of a moving vessel and will perform dazzling, crisscross patterns as two pairs race toward the front of the bow, one from either side, only to veer off at the last moment to prevent a collision. Their split-second reflexes and swift speed allow them to dart through the water and turn quickly. They range from the Bering Sea to Baja California.

Pacific White-sided Dolphin

Playful and sociable, these high-spirited dolphins travel in large groups (115 members on average) and are, like the Dall porpoise, attracted to the bow waves of moving vessels. The larger and faster the vessel, the better the surfing as far as a Pacific white-sided dolphin is concerned.

Slightly longer than the Dall porpoise, these dolphins are black with a white belly and a hooked

dorsal fin. During the fall mating season, they go crazy with acrobatics – leaping with total abandon in front of large fishboats and cruise ships. Passengers watching from a forward lounge are often treated to the sight of hundreds of dolphins leaping and somersaulting in front of the ship.

Fall sightings can occur in Sumner Strait, Dixon Entrance, Grenville Channel and Queen Charlotte Sound.

SEAL & SEA LION

These fin-footed marine mammals have a thick layer of fat beneath their outer, hair-covered skin and spend much of their time in the water. They do, however, leave the water to rest, breed and give birth, but they always remain close to the water's edge. They haul out onto rocky islets, sandbars and ice floes where land predators cannot reach their pups. Sea lions gather in colonies to breed, with mature males assembling harems. Seals and sea lions live for about 30 years and feed on fish.

Harbor seals are commonly seen throughout the Inside Passage and Prince William Sound, often poking their large-eyed faces above the water to take a look around. They fear the transient killer whale and will quickly climb onto the closest rock or shoreline if such a pod is in the area. In one instance, a seal that

Pacific white-sided dolphins are playful and sociable, often seen leaping in the bow wave of a moving vessel.

was being circled by killer whales leaped into a whalewatching vessel to escape its predators.

Steller sea lions are larger than seals, with the males reaching 13 feet in length and weighing up to 2,000 pounds. Seals and sea lions will steal fish from fishermen's nets, and sea lions have been known to pull fishermen into the water from docks and skiffs, but it's illegal to shoot them under the 1972 Marine Mammal Protection Act. The Steller sea lion has, in recent years, suffered a dramatic decline in population – due possi-

(Above) Sea lions haul out on rocky outcroppings to breed and tend their young. (Below) A female harbor seal and her pup rest on a piece of glacier ice giving some security from predators.

bly to an unexplained shortage of forage fish.

Two popular haul-out and pupping sites for seals and sea lions are Benjamin Island in Lynn Canal and Seal Rocks at the entrance to Prince William Sound.

Sea otters spend much of their time floating on their backs – grooming, eating and nursing their young.

Sea Otter

The largest member of the weasel family, a sea otter can reach five feet in length and weigh close to 100 pounds. Although an aquatic mammal, the sea otter is kept warm not by blubber, like other marine mammals, but by its extremely thick fur coat – the most dense of any mammal at 675,000 hairs per square inch (a German shepherd has about 40,000 hairs per square inch). The outer guard hairs are long and course while the under fur is shorter and finer and must be kept fluffed to trap tiny air bubbles at the base of the fur which insulate the otter and block out the cold water. Sea otters regularly groom themselves because if their fur becomes matted, it cannot hold air bubbles.

Sea otters have huge lungs for diving and floating. They congregate in large groups in kelp beds, with females and their pups usually floating in rafts apart from the males. Kelp, a type of seaweed with fronds that float on the water's surface, is rooted to the sea bottom by a long rubber stem, and sea otters anchor themselves with kelp when they need to nap. A mother will wrap her pup in kelp fronds to stop if from drifting away on an ocean current while she dives for sea urchins.

Sea otters spend much of their time floating on their backs, eating sea urchins and other shellfish on their chests, breaking apart their food with a rock. A young otter will ride on its mother's stomach as she floats on her back. Sea otters also like to play together in pairs, hugging each other while they roll and perform somersaults in the water. They're real crowd-pleasers with their playful personalities and their round, whiskered faces.

Sea otters once ranged from the Aleutians to Baja California, their population about 150,000. Russian fur traders, realizing how quickly these animals were being decimated for their valuable pelts, eventually set quotas to limit harvests, and by the mid-1800s the species was recovering. However, when the U.S. purchased Alaska in 1867, unlimited hunting was again allowed and the total sea otter population was reduced to about 2,000. In 1911 sea otters were given complete protection and they have now returned to numbers approaching their original population.

Sea otters are often sighted along the northern and western shores of Chichagof Island and on sightseeing expeditions out of Sitka. They are also a common sight in Prince William Sound, near Seward in Resurrection Bay, and around Kodiak Island.

River otters, like sea otters, belong to the weasel family. With webbed feet, they are agile both on land and in the water. They run humpbacked because of their long bodies and relatively short legs. Males reach four feet in length and weigh up to 25 pounds. River otters are very sociable and playful. They like to slide head-first on their bellies down mud banks into the water.

FISH

Salmon

Salmon are at the top of the fish evolutionary ladder and, with a very streamlined body and a powerful tail fin, they are fast, agile swimmers. The meat on all species of salmon is rich in protein, providing an important food source for humans and animals.

Many coastal towns and cities owe their existence to this fish, which every year returns in large schools to natal spawning streams along the Pacific coast. There are five species of Pacific salmon caught in Alaskan waters: king (chinook) is the largest; silver (coho) is prized by sportsfishermen; red (sockeye) with its rich red meat, is the highly valued commercial salmon; pink (humpy) is the most common and an important commercial fish for the canneries; and chum (dog) salmon, when smoked, is a tasty delicacy.

Salmon spawn in fresh water, usually streams, where they spend varying lengths of time depending on the species, before heading out to sea. Some juveniles migrate directly to saltwater while others linger in river estuaries where they grow and adapt to the mix of fresh- and saltwater habitats. Depending on the species, salmon will spend one to seven years in the open ocean before returning to their natal streams to spawn.

Coho (silver) salmon, is a favorite catch of sportfishermen.

Salmon struggle against incredible odds to return to the stream of their birth. If a fish makes it past the sport and commercial fisheries, there will be other predators – such as bears and eagles – waiting along stream banks to make a meal of the weary fish. Salmon often have to leap up waterfalls and swim against rushing currents to return to their spawning grounds. Once there, the females dig nests in the gravel and lay their eggs while their male partners release milt which fertilizes the eggs. All Pacific salmon spawn only once – in summer or fall – then die.

Salmon stocks are suffering serious depletions in some areas of the Pacific Northwest. A complex combination of factors is likely to blame, including overfishing and destruction of stream habitat. Salmon are also extremely sensitive to temperature fluctuations, and a recent increase in ocean temperatures, possibly due to global warming, is another likely culprit.

Each salmon stock, which is grouped according to its stream of origin, has a specific genetic make-up which has evolved over tens of thousands of years. Sudden environmental changes, whether natural or man-made, threaten a specific stock's ability to adapt and survive.

Halibut

While salmon are generally found within 100 feet of the ocean's surface, halibut are always found near the bottom. Salmon is a pink or red meat; halibut is white. This fish is highly valued in Alaska, and around the world, for its delicate taste and texture. Pacific halibut can grow to over eight feet and weigh over 800 pounds. Halibut fishing is generally good near Sitka and Seward where numerous charter operations are available for fishing.

King Crab

In 1976, a sudden and inexplicable explosion in the number of harvestable king crab occurred in the Bering Sea. Within months hundreds of young men rushed to cash in on a boom which lasted almost eight years. Some came away millionaires, but many ended up with only memories of exciting years in the tough waters off Kodiak and in the Bering Sea. King crab can weigh up to 15 pounds and measure six feet across from claw to claw. Although the king crab population has declined since the mid-1980s, a large number of crab boats still operate out of Dutch Harbor and Kodiak.

BIRDS

The Inside Passage is part of the Pacific Flyway, a migratory route for millions of birds, and this coastal region's river estuaries and tidal passes provide habitat for a variety of species, with over 400 documented in Alaska and British Columbia. If you're interested in birds, it's well worth bringing a pair of binoculars and a field pocketbook to identify birds along your cruise.

Birds differ dramatically in size, shape and plumage but wing shape is an indication of a bird's survival strategies. Some, like gulls and shearwaters, have long-tapered wings suitable for gliding long distances over water with little effort. Others, like auklets and murres, have short and less efficient wings more suitable for propelling themselves underwater.

Eagles, whose flight muscles account for half of the bird's total weight, have long wide wings with a powerful downstroke (the muscles pulling the wings down are larger than those pulling the wings up). An eagle can glide with ease on thermal convection currents with its large but lightweight wings.

The flight of any bird is a marvel to behold. It derives both forward power and upward lift from its wings. As a bird propels itself forward by flapping its wings, a slight vacuum (low pressure area) is created above the wing, lifting the bird's body. As the bird picks up speed, the wing and tail feathers fold in to streamline the bird's shape and provide greater flying efficiency. A bird can turn very quickly using movements of its body, such as tilting the head, fanning the wings' secondary feathers, or subtly angling the tail feathers.

While cruising the Inside Passage you'll see gulls, herons, sea ducks, bald eagles and cormorants, which often perch on pilings or buoys with their wings outstretched to dry. In the Gulf of Alaska, shearwaters and albatross can be identified by the keen birder, and near Seward you're likely to see large colonies of horned and tufted puffins which thrive by the thousands near the western end of Prince William Sound, along the Kenai Peninsula and around Kodiak Island. The Mendenhall Valley marshlands near Juneau is another prime location to spot many species of birds.

Bald Eagle

Without a doubt, the bald eagle is one of the most magnificent sights of an Alaskan cruise. With a wingspan of between six and eight feet and weighing up to 15 pounds, the bald eagle is the largest member of the hawk family. The bald eagle gets its name from its distinctive snow-white head. Its bill is yellow and it has a thin, chittering call.

A high-soaring eagle can spot a fish from over a mile away and can dive from the sky at 100 miles per hour. Eagles, which glide effortlessly on thermal convection currents, don't always swoop down on their prey but will sometimes spread their wings wide and silently float toward their target.

Eagles perch on high points.

Although they are birds of prey, using their keen eyesight, swift speed and sharp talons to pluck salmon from the water, eagles are also scavengers and will gather by the hundreds along riverbanks to feed on spawning salmon.

Eagles mate while somersaulting through the air with their talons locked. The female lays one to three eggs in late April and the young birds leave the nest in early fall. Their mortality rate is high, with over 90 per cent failing to survive the first few years of life. Juvenile eagles retain their ragged plumage until the age of five, when they attain the distinctive markings of a mature bald eagle.

Eagles usually build their nests in the tallest tree of their nesting territory (a range of one to five miles) and close to the water. Since eagles mate for life, the couple will return to their nest each year and do minor upgrading, renovations, and the occasional expansion. One excellent opportunity to see a nest is the Eagle Tree on the ground floor of the Alaska State Museum in Juneau. This exhibit includes the nest, eggs and mounted specimens of juvenile and adult eagles.

(Above) The rough bumps on a bald eagle's talons enable the bird to hold onto slippery salmon. (Left) The bald eagle's nest is the largest of any bird in North America, built five to eight feet in diameter and two to 10 feet in depth.

Once the target of bounty hunters, the bald eagle became a protected species but its population has stabilized. About 35,000 to 45,000 bald eagles live in Alaska, and the bird was delisted in June 2007.

Raven

Ravens and crows use their sense of curiosity as a survival technique. Anything dropped or odd in shape or color will be quickly spotted by these black birds, which promptly swoop down to investigate. Ravens are larger than crows and have thicker bills. They are very intelligent, capable of making diverse sounds, and are highly respected in Northwest native cultures, the raven an integral creature of Haida mythology.

Seabirds

Unlike eagles, who don't like to get their feathers wet, are the many species of duck. Sea ducks eat intertidal invertebrates (mussels, hermit crabs, snails) and dominate the bird populations in many coastal areas of Alaska. They are robust, noisy and have colorful summer plumage, most notably the Harlequin duck. Sea ducks can be observed near shore while in port, often parading past in single file.

Sub-species include dabbling ducks, who feed on the surface or by dipping their heads and bodies until only their tail protrudes from the water. Dabblers include the well-known mallard, the drake (male) sporting an emerald green head and chestnut chest. Other dabbler species are the teal, northern pintail, wigeon and wood duck.

Diving ducks, as the name implies, completely submerge when feeding. Scoters, goldeneye and bufflehead are diving ducks, as are scaup and harlequin. Mergansers are nicknamed 'sawbills' due to their long, tapering bills lined with sharp 'teeth' for grabbing fish. A mother merganser will carry her brood of newborn chicks on her back as she swims near shore.

Puffins, like murres and auklets, are alcids (a type of seabird) and are able to swim underwater to great depths using their wings. These birds are not great flyers, however, and are often seen bouncing off wave tops trying to take off. Puffins come ashore only to breed and nest. A boat tour from Seward will take you to

Horned puffins, when gathering food for their young, hold several small fish in their large bills.

Seabirds, gulls and eagles hover above a feeding minke whale in Queen Charlotte Strait.

some of the largest nesting colonies in Alaska at the entrance to Resurrection Bay.

Shorebirds include sandpipers and the Black Oystercatcher, which has a long orange beak with which it pries open shellfish. The feet of the Pigeon Guillemot are also bright orange and quite a sight when this seabird runs across the surface of the water, gaining speed for take off. Ducks look like water skiers when landing as they dig the heels of their webbed feet into the water. In contrast are the balletic landings of gulls, which flutter their wings like backwinded sails to delicately set themselves down on the water.

Cormorants, which enter the water only to feed, are often seen perched on rocks or buoys, their wings outspread to dry. Loons, on the other hand, remain mostly in the water and come ashore only to nest, for they cannot walk on land and they cannot fly during moult. Swimming is their specialty and their heavily built bodies are designed for diving.

Albatross

Glacier cruise passengers, while traversing the Gulf of Alaska between Yakutat Bay and Prince William Sound, may be fortunate to spot the black-footed albatross. These beautiful gliders spend most of their lives at sea and, for survival, have special adaptations. To meet their freshwater needs, they drink seawater which is filtered and secreted through enlarged nasal glands to remove the salt. These birds, along with shearwaters and petrels, are called "tube-nosed swimmers" because their nostrils are situated in raised tubes on their bill. This gives them a sense of smell so acute they are believed to track fish and squid underwater.

Gull / Jaeger

Gulls are buoyant swimmers and strong fliers with well-developed scavenging abilities. Most common are white and light grey glaucous-winged gulls, herring gulls (with black-tipped wings) and mew gulls – smaller birds with cries similar to a child's. Another member of the gull family is the kittiwake, flocks of which feed on tiny krill near tidewater glaciers. The predatory jaeger may be sighted in the northern Yukon and Alaska. Jaegers are known to migrate many thousands of miles.

The long-tailed jaeger is a small gull-like bird renowned for its annual migration between northern Alaska and Southern Hemisphere oceans.

LAND MAMMALS

Bear

Of all the land mammals in Alaska, none excite the imagination quite like bears – most particularly the brown bear (Ursus arctos) and the grizzly, a sub-species of the brown bear. The brown bears that inhabit the Alaska coast are especially large because they have an advantage over interior (grizzly) bears – namely large numbers of available salmon spawning in shallow streams. This protein-rich diet combined with a mild climate produces bears that are between eight and nine feet tall (when standing upright) and weigh well over 1,000 pounds. In 1969 a brown bear measuring over ten feet was recorded on Kodiak Island.

Black bears can be viewed at Neets Bay near Ketchikan.

The black bear (Ursus americanus) is the most widespread and numerous of North American bears. Although smaller and seemingly more docile than the brown bear, it can still pose a serious threat when hungry, startled or injured. Black bears forage mainly on berries and occasionally on salmon along the coast. Adult male black bears weigh an average

A brown bear feeds on spawning salmon at the McNeil River.

of 500 pounds, are 6 feet long and vary in color from blonde to black, including the rare blue (or glacier) bear, which is found in the Yakutat Bay area along the Gulf of Alaska. Black bears have been known to spend their entire lives within five miles of their birthplace, and a transplanted black bear will travel many miles to return to its home range.

Brown bears are solitary animals, usually avoiding one another, but will exhibit a site-specific tolerance for one another at particularly abundant salmon feeding streams, such as Pack Creek on Admiralty Island (28 air miles south of Juneau) and the McNeil River on Cook Inlet (200 air miles southwest of Anchorage), a site that draws photographers from around the world. Brown bears may also be spotted on the foreshore from ships or ferries traveling through Peril Strait or along Lynn Canal. Brown bears can occasionally be seen along the north shoreline of Chichagof Island and in Glacier Bay.

The polar bear is rarely sighted by the casual traveler to Alaska, for this large white bear (an adult male can reach nine feet in length and weigh up to 1600 pounds) lives mainly on the drifting pack ice. Its hair is extremely dense and its paws have hairy soles for gripping the ice. A fearless and wily hunter, the polar bear will stalk any prey, including humans. Well aware that its black nose gives it away, a polar bear stalking seals will often hold a paw in front of its nose to conceal it.

Bears have an excellent sense of smell and hearing, and can run with bursts of speed reaching 35 mph. Black bears are also good tree climbers and polar bears are exceptional swimmers, crossing 30 miles of water at a time. Bears sleep through most of the winter in dens made in caves or holes in the ground but they do not truly hibernate, for their metabolism remains normal and they may even awake and emerge during warm spells. Polar bears wander all winter, except for pregnant females who dig dens in the snow. Cubs are born in pairs during the winter and remain with their mothers for about a year.

Sled Dogs

Dogs in the north have always been highly valued, both as working animals and as man's best friend. The early gold prospectors relied on dogs for winter transportation, and stealing someone's dog was a serious crime leading to arrest. The Alaskan malamute is one of the oldest arctic sled dogs and is often referred to as a 'husky', although this term actually applies to the purebred Siberian husky. The snowmobile threatened to replace the working dog-sled team, but dog mushing has made a comeback and was named Alaska's official state sport in 1972, with races held in various locales throughout the winter. Each March, the state's famous Iditarod Trail Sled Dog Race is run between Anchorage and Nome. The race, first held in 1973, follows an old dog-team

(Above) A brown bear family forages along the shoreline. (Below) Sled dogs are working animals as well as beloved pets.

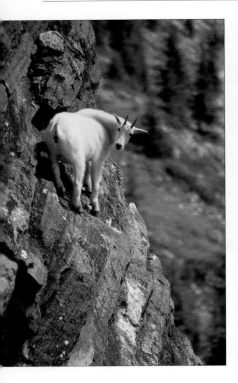

(Above) Mountain goats can scramble up steep mountainsides on spreadable hooves cushioned with skid-proof pads. (Below) A Dall sheep.

mail route blazed in 1910. Strictly a winter trail of frozen muskeg and river ice, over 1,000 miles in length, it was made famous in 1925 when teams of mushers relayed a life-saving diphtheria serum from Seward to epidemic-threatened Nome.

Wolf

Close to extinction in the Lower 48, the gray wolf (also called timber wolf) is thriving in Alaska where it enjoys a high reproductive rate and is protected by strict trapping and hunting regulations (aerial sporthunting of wolves has been banned since 1972). Resembling a German Shepherd dog, the gray wolf stands three feet at the shoulder and weighs about 100 pounds. Wolves usually travel in a pack (family group) which averages five to eight members and they hunt just about everything from moose to mice, wearing down even the swiftest of prey with their ability to run at about 20 mph for many hours. The wolf is of the genus Canis and can be bred with dogs to produce hardy animals for pulling sleds. The coyote is a small, swift wolf and resembles a medium-sized dog. Its cry – mournful high-pitched yelps – is heard early in the evening.

Mountain Goat

This agile animal inhabits mainland mountains, alongside Dall sheep, and is often spotted on windswept ridges and the steep slopes of fjords and inlets. With a body designed for balance (short legs and heavy shoulders), the mountain goat climbs steep rocky terrain on spreadable, padded hooves. Its double coat of long coarse outer hair over a thick layer of cashmere-quality wool insulates the mountain goat from winter winds as it battles sub-zero temperatures and snow-covered slopes in search of exposed forage. The mountain goat's ability to survive in steep terrain is its main protection from predators.

Dall Sheep

A white, wild sheep, this animal inhabits Alaska's mountain ranges and alpine meadows. Its current population is about 50,000. Dall sheep graze on grasses and other plants, and climb above the timberline in summer in pursuit of succulent new growth. The ram's horns are heavy and curled, and their growth rings determine the sheep's age.

Deer Family

Sitka blacktail deer, caribou and moose all belong to the deer family. Males are called bucks, females are does and babies are fawns, except for moose and caribou, which are called bulls, cows and calves. All deer are strictly plant eaters, with vegetation hard to find in winter. (A moose can eat up to 20,000 leaves or weeds a day, often foraging underwater in the bottom of shallow lakes and ponds.) Deer have a stomach divided into four chambers for digesting the tough leaves and grasses, allowing the deer to dine and dash. After retreating to a safe spot, the deer digests its food by returning it to the mouth in small bits, called cud, and chewing this slowly before swallowing it again.

Sitka blacktail deer are superb athletes, able to run up to 45 miles per hour, and to dodge boulders and trees without slowing down. By taking long leaps, especially over streams, the agile deer leaves little scent for predators, such as wolves and cougar, which a deer can outrun. With eyes located on the side of its head, a deer can see

Caribou range across Alaska's tundra regions and can be seen at Denali National Park.

movement in every direction except right behind, so it usually has a head start.

The **moose** is the largest member of the deer family, with mature males standing as high as eight feet at the shoulder and weighing nearly 2,000 pounds. The moose inhabits mixed woods and wetlands. The spread of a bull moose's antlers can measure six feet, and males become very aggressive during the fall mating season. In winter, to avoid deep snow, moose often travel at night along highways and train tracks where they present a serious traffic hazard.

Made of solid bone, **antlers** are shed every winter and a new set is grown, which is soft and tender and covered with a thin skin called 'velvet' while growing. This velvet is covered with fine short hairs and consists of thousands of blood vessels that carry calcium and other minerals for building strong bones. A young male's first set of antlers are just spikes; the second set branches into points (called tines). Over time, a full set develops which forks into many points and weighs about 80 pounds. Antlers protect males when fighting one another. A large set attracts females and acts as a deterrent to other males who might challenge his position as leader of the herd.

Both the male and female **caribou** grow antlers. On a mature bull, the antlers extend four feet from base to tips. Caribou number more than 300,000 statewide. They often travel in large herds and have been called 'nomads of the north' because they are always on the move in search of food – and thus hard to track. Alaska's interior and the Alaska Peninsula are where these elusive animals roam.

Moose often wander into Alaska towns when they are unable to forage beneath a deep snowpack. One November, a male moose wandered into a yard on the Kenai Peninsula where the owners watched him take off with their children's swing set after his antlers got entangled in the metal structure. After following the animal's trail of shredded blue plastic, state biologists concluded some of the ropes and chains were still tangled in the moose's antlers but the animal would be free of these once it lost its rack for the winter.

Moose are plentiful in Denali National Park and the Kenai Peninsula. In winter, when snow cover restricts their grazing range, they often show up in Anchorage in search of food.

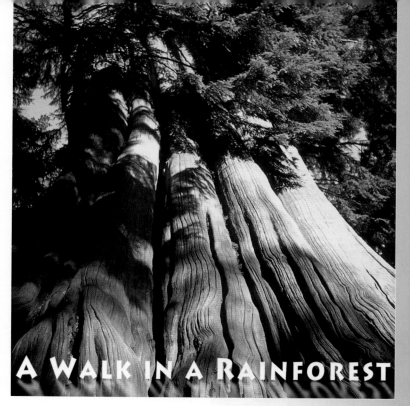

A WALK IN A RAINFOREST

Alaska's coastal rainforests flourish during the long, warm days of summer. Fronted by shoreline meadows of tall grass and leafy alders, these forests contain towering evergreens that can grow over 200 feet tall and live for hundreds of years.

The two common species of conifer found in Southeast Alaska are the Sitka spruce (Alaska's official tree) and the Western hemlock. The **Sitka spruce** grows quickly (up to three feet per year), reaches an average height of 160 feet and is three to five feet in diameter. Its branches project at an upward angle from its straight trunk, giving the tree a conical crown, and its spiky green needles are a deep green. The tree's strong, lightweight timber is used for boat building, piano sounding boards and, in the early days of aviation, aircraft construction.

The Sitka spruce grows in pure stands or alongside the **Western hemlock** – a tall, slender tree with branches that droop slightly and with twigs containing two rows of needles that are flat and soft. At an average height of 100 to 150 feet and a diameter of two to four feet, the Western hemlock covers 75 percent of Southeast Alaska's forested area. This tree is tolerant of shade and often sprouts up among the faster-growing Sitka Spruce. Western Hemlock is a major source of pulpwood and lumber.

Another member of the pine family that thrives along the

Pacific Northwest coast is the **Western red cedar** – the giant of the forest with a massive trunk (two to eight feet in diameter) and an average height of 100 to 175 feet. Its shiny needles grow in splayed clusters from the cedar's drooping branches and its aromatic wood is straight grained, durable and resistant to decay – the perfect material for dugout canoes and totem poles, as well as for

panels, posts and other outdoor objects. The Western red cedar grows throughout the southern half of the Panhandle and along the Inside Passage.

Carpeting the forest floor are ferns, mosses and flowering plants. In an old-growth forest, toppled trees are reclaimed by mosses and become 'nurse' logs to evergreen seedlings. Skunk cabbage is found in wet areas of the forest, near streams and bogs, and is easy to spot with its yellow, tulip-shaped inner leaf and large outer leaves. These leaves are eaten by deer and geese, and were traditionally used by natives to wrap salmon for baking.

Blueberry and salmonberry bushes are plentiful and are a major food source for bears. Blue lupine, its tall spires thick with pod-like flowers, is a common sight, and brilliant fireweed grows in dense stands on recently cleared land, its bright rosy-pink petals blooming on stalks that grow four feet high.

Other plants to look for include the poisonous toadstool (*amanita muscaria*) which thrives in the forests above Skagway, and devil's club – a big, prickly, maple-leafed plant that belongs to the ginseng family, its medicinal properties long ago applied by the natives who would make a tea brewed from the root to cure colds and other ailments. Found in rainforests throughout Alaska, this plant's

(Top) Skunk cabbage, as its name implies, has a pungent odor. (Middle) A poisonous toadstool. (Bottom) Devil's club.

tough, prickly spines can inflict bad scratches on bare-legged hikers. However, if you stay on park trails, you will have to watch out for nothing more than the odd slug lying on the path

Slugs feed at night on roots and plants and they grow to grand proportions in Alaska, earning such labels as Banana Slug, so named for its yellow-green color with brown or black spots.

HIKING TIPS

The wilderness is always close at hand in the Alaskan ports of call, and hiking a maintained trail is a good way to enjoy the great outdoors. The cruise lines often offer a few organized hikes at each port of call, with guides/ naturalists escorting the group. However, it's also possible to go for an independent hike along trails near town that are easily accessed from the cruise docks. Check with the local visitor center or parks office for information on trails and wildlife safety.

Be sure to wear sturdy shoes and a waterproof jacket with a hood because the weather can change quickly. Pack drinking water and a high-energy snack, and always hike with at least one other person. Also, let someone other than your fellow hiker(s) know where you are going.

Never approach or feed a wild animal. Make noise when hiking so you don't surprise an animal, especially a bear. If you encounter a bear, do not run but instead back away very slowly without making eye contact (which is perceived as aggression by the bear). If a moose charges at you, run behind the nearest tree.

Slime mold is a fungus that grows under the damp leaves and rotting logs found lying on the ground. Coral slime looks much like frost covering a log, and scrambled-egg slime resembles an unappetizing helping of powdered eggs fried sunny side up.

A conk is a type of bracket fungus that grows on dead tree trunks. When conks become hard and dry, Alaskans like to snap them off and turn them into decorative ornaments.

A variety of birds and animals live in the forest, including black bears who feed on wildberries in late summer, and Sitka blacktail deer who forage here for food throughout the winter.

Trails near ports of call offer excellent hiking for day visitors.

Thousands of years ago, when the inhabitants of our planet lived in isolated pockets, few locations were more remote than the Aleutian Islands. A string of barren, volcanic islands, the Aleutians dot the open waters west of Alaska where the North Pacific meets the Bering Sea. The **Aleuts** who lived here were highly skilled at open-ocean hunting. They set out to sea in *baidarkas* (kayaks made of animal skin) and they used harpoons with poisoned tips to kill whales many times the size of their tiny vessels. Their waterproof clothing was made from strips of sea lion intestine stitched together and their boots were made from sea otter flippers.

When winter came and the hunting season ended, the **Aleuts** spent much of their time feasting and dancing. They lived in pit dwellings with sod roofs, and their villages extended throughout the Aleutians and along the Alaska Peninsula to the Shumagin Islands.

Sharing many of the Aleut customs, such as matrilineal descent and a similar language, were the **Southern Eskimos** whose territory bordered the Bering Sea and Gulf of Alaska coastlines, including Kodiak Island and Prince William Sound. They too hunted from kayaks and wore wooden visors to protect their eyes from rain and ocean glare.

Kodiak Island is covered not with forests but tall grasses, and the **Alutiiq** who first lived here resided in semi-subterranean sod houses. The **Chugach Eskimos**, living on the forested shores of Prince William Sound, built planked wooden houses.

Alaska's **Northern Eskimos**, living along the Arctic coastline, built homes to withstand the freezing temperatures of winter. An underground entrance tunnel, which trapped any cold air coming in from outside, led into a semi-subterranean dwelling where seal-oil lamps were used for light and warmth. For clothing, they wore two layers of fur-lined garments.

The **Northern Eskimos** hunted for whale and walrus from *umiaks* (large, open skin boats) but also used kayaks and, on land, sleds. They often saved Yankee whalers when their ships became trapped in Arctic ice.

Aleuts and **Eskimos** believed in reincarnation and in maintaining a positive relationship with animal spirits through special rites performed at the beginning of each hunting season. The blanket toss, in which a person is bounced high in the air off a trampoline made of seal skins and held taut by a circle of onlookers, was traditionally held after a successful whale hunt. **Shamans** – who could cure illness and foretell the future – were important members of all native groups.

The **Athabascans**, who lived in the interior of Alaska and Northern Canada, were nomadic tribes who lived by hunting and fishing. Their clothing was often made of moose and caribou hides, and their homes were of various forms – from semi-subterranean log dwellings to dome-shaped tents made of animal skins. In the 18th century, the Athabascans increased their hunting and trapping of fur-bearing animals to supply the flourishing fur trade.

The natives who inhabited the Inside Passage enjoyed a mild climate in a region where rivers

NATIVE GROUPS OF ALASKA
AND BRITISH COLUMBIA

INUPIAT
ESKIMO

YUP'IK
ESKIMO

ATHABASCAN

Anchorage

Prince
William
Sound

ALUTIIQ

Kodiak
Island

ALEUT

BERING SEA

GULF OF ALASKA

TLINGIT

Sitka

TSIMSHIAN

HAIDA

KWAKIUTL

COAST SALISH

NOOTKA

Ocean going canoes were carved from huge cedar logs, then steamed to soften the wood and allow the sides to be spread. Separate prow and stern pieces were added and the hull torched to harden the wood before sanding it smooth with dogfish skin.

Today's visitors to the Inside Passage can view numerous shell beaches, which are prehistoric kitchen middens from native societies.

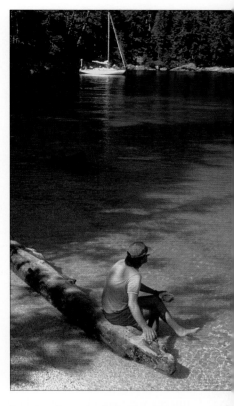

teemed with salmon and fore-shores were covered with shell-fish. These reliable food sources supported a thriving population which had free time to develop sophisticated art forms. Their ancient civilizations are today recognized as complex social structures that produced monu-mental works of art.

The pyramids of Egypt were being constructed when perma-nent settlement of the Inside Passage began about 5,000 years ago. People had already been inhabiting this region for four or five thousand years, following the last retreat of the glaciers, but wild fluctuations in sea levels kept forc-ing them to relocate. When sea levels finally stabilized, the area's inhabitants began establishing per-manent coastal villages. But their building materials, unlike those of the Egyptians, were not of stone but of wood.

Thick stands of cedar, spruce and hemlock provided an abun-dance of building materials but, just as uncut conifers eventually topple to the ground and slowly rot, so too did the natives' wood-en dwellings and monuments. What did survive, however, were their kitchen middens.

A **midden** is a prehistoric refuse dump of shells and bones. At first glimpse it appears to be a natural beach of crushed shell, when in fact it is an archaeological site containing clues to a lost civiliza-tion. The shell, neutralizing the acid in the soil, has preserved ancient tools and artifacts such as antler carvings and stone bowls engraved with human and animal figures. Weapons for hunting and warfare have also been found in middens, as well as skeletal remains and the caches of chiefs.

Middens were formed from empty clam and mussel shells tossed into heaps which, over time, were crushed and com-pressed into beaches several yards deep. These white beaches were easily spotted by villagers returning after dark in their canoes. Another feature marking ancient village sites is a **fish trap** – stone barriers designed to trap salmon near shore at low tide. The fish could swim across the trap at high water, but as the tide dropped they could not get past the row of stones blocking their way seaward.

While the Athenians of Ancient Greece were erecting the Parthenon on the Acropolis some 2,500 years ago, a complex and artistically productive civilization was also thriving in the Pacific Northwest. Archaeological digs reveal a society that produced masters at weaving, woodworking and sculpturing. Personal adornments were miniature works of art depicting human, animal and supernatural figures carved from stone, bone, antler and tooth. **Petroglyphs** were cut into foreshore stones, and pictographs were drawn on rock walls. These images were possibly inspired by shamanism – a belief in supernatural powers – or some may have had a more pragmatic purpose,

such as marking a good fishing hole or a territorial boundary.

As the knights of medieval Europe rode off to battle, chiefs and warriors of the Northwest Coast also engaged in warfare, paddling their canoes hundreds of miles into enemy territories. The northern tribes often headed south to raid villages and capture slaves, who were the lowest rank of a social hierarchy consisting of nobility, commoners and slaves. During this period, mortuary practices shifted from burying the dead in middens to placing their remains in boxes hung from trees or inside small mortuary houses near the village.

When European explorers first landed on the Northwest Coast, they encountered various native groups who shared some general traits but spoke different languages and displayed regional differences in their architecture, art and social customs. Their territories ranged from the top of the Alaska Panhandle to the lower reaches of the Inside Passage.

The three northern groups – the Tlingit, Tsimshian and Haida – were highly respected as warriors and artisans. The **Haida**'s cedar dugout canoes were considered top-of-the-line and the Haida would often tow a newly carved canoe across Hecate Strait to the mainland where they would trade it to the Tsimshians for candlefish oil. The Haida, skilled mariners, traveled as far away as present-

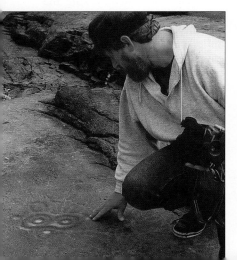

Ancient petroglyphs, such as this one at Port Neville, are found along the Inside Passage.

day San Francisco in these sea-worthy craft.

Although their languages were unrelated, the northern groups' social structures were similar. The **Tlingit** (klink-it) and Haida were divided into two sub-groups (called moieties by anthropologists) which were symbolized by the Eagle and the Raven. (The **Tsimshian** were divided into four sub-groups, termed phratries.) Sub-groups were further divided into kinship clans represented by **totems** (crests) depicting the Frog, Beaver, Wolf, Grizzly Bear and Killer Whale. Each clan was further subdivided into family households.

Descent was through the female line and a person was not allowed to marry someone from the same moiety or phratry. This intermarriage among sub-groups forged alliances between village chiefs and their heirs. Etiquette and ceremony were fundamental to these structured societies in which power and wealth were manifested in **potlatch** celebrations of feasting, dancing and gift-giving. Custom

dictated that invited guests would repay the host chief's hospitality with a reciprocal potlatch, preparations for which could take years. Totem poles were often raised at a potlatch.

The **post-and-beam houses** of the northern groups were solidly built. Massive corner posts and cross beams – which sometimes took 300 men to raise – supported the roof and sides made of cedar planking. The main frontal pole and interior poles, elaborately carved, displayed the clan and moiety crests. Sometimes a portal was carved in the lowest figure of a frontal pole to serve as the entrance. **Freestanding poles** were raised in front of the houses to commemorate an important event, such as a birth, marriage or, most importantly, a death. When a high-ranking chief died, his cremated remains were even-

The Beaver Clan House at Saxman Village near Ketchikan is an example of Tlingit art and architecture.

tually placed in a niche at the back of a mortuary pole that was raised – with much ceremony – in his honor.

The architecture of the Wakashan groups to the south was slightly different from that of the northern groups. House planks were not permanently attached to the post-and-beam framework, allowing them to be dismantled and towed by canoe to a summer village during the salmon season. The earthen floors were also simpler than the recessed levels of northern homes, but common activities included burning indoor fires and hanging salmon to dry.

Wakashan is a linguistic term and the people of this language group consist of the **Kwakwaka'wakw** (Kwakiutl), who inhabit much of British Columbia's central coast, and the

Massive posts and beams supported this big house's removeable cedar planks.

Nuu-Chah-Nulth (Nootka), who live on the west coast of Vancouver Island. Because the natives' traditional languages were oral and not written, there is often a variation in the spelling of their words and names. Early explorers, attempting to phonetically record what they were hearing, gave certain groups erroneous names. For instance, the Nuu-chah-nulth were called Nootka by Captain Cook, and for decades the name Kwakiutl was applied to the Kwakwaka'wakw – "those who speak Kwakwala".

Kwakwaka'wakw potlatch festivities were the most flamboyant of all the groups, their theatrical dances performed with elaborate props and costumes, especially masks. They often painted themselves and even altered the shape of their heads by binding them in infancy to make them elongated and thus more beautiful. The Nuu-chah-nulth natives were skilled mariners who hunted whales and other sea mammals in the open waters of the Pacific.

The southernmost group is the **Coast Salish**, their territory encompassing the modern cities of Vancouver and Seattle. The Coast Salish inhabited flat-roofed houses that were often built in long rows under a common roof and divided by plank partitions, which could be removed for social and ceremonial occasions. At the time of European contact, their social structure was less rigid than the Wakashans or the northern groups, and class distinctions were less evident. Their winter festivities were more contemplative, less devoted to feasting and dancing than to personal acquisition of spirit power. To acquire a guardian spirit meant success at hunting and fishing. Those with the ability to foretell events and cure sickness became shamans and their supernatural powers were highly respected.

Also respected were the souls of other living creatures. In mythic times, it was believed that animals had the ability to transform themselves into humans. Elaborate rituals were conducted at the beginning of each fishing and hunting season to pay homage to the various species which were sought for food and clothing.

Native legends were passed orally from generation to generation. These traditional stories, set in a timeless past, are an expression of the universe's creation and the evolution of humanity. In native mythology, the **Raven** plays a major role as a supernatural trickster and transformer. Raven represents curiosity and he continually alters the world provided by the Creator. While steal-

ing, he accidentally released the sun and stars, and when he opened a clamshell he released the first humans.

Understanding Native Art

At the time of first contact by European explorers, Northwest native communities were filled with skilled artisans. The explorers engaged in a healthy trade with the natives, acquiring artifacts that were sometimes handcrafted on the spot. In exchange, the natives received European tools which enhanced their woodworking and carving. Glass beads were also a coveted trade item, especially with the Athabascans who used them to decorate their leather garments.

Basket weaving was a skill shared by all the native groups. The women of the coastal Indian

Haida dancers re-enact native myths, which were passed orally from generation to generation at potlatch celebrations.

tribes wove watertight hats and baskets out of spruce roots and cedar bark. The Athabascans used willow root, and the Southern Eskimos and Aleuts used beach ryegrass.

Another product of native craftsmanship was the **bentwood box** – made from a single cedar plank that was steamed until soft enough to bend at ninety-degree angles. Three of the corners were, as a result, perfectly smooth while the fourth corner was skillfully joined with pegs or spruce root stitches. These boxes held all sorts of items and were often decorated with ornate carvings.

Totem poles, made from the trunks of massive red cedars, were the most monumental of all native art. As the chosen cedar was felled, the cutters looked away while its spirit departed. Master carvers were commissioned to sculpture the pole and, upon its completion, they performed a dance around the base of the pole while it was being raised. A freestanding totem pole survived for about 60 years before the elements took their toll and the weathered pole toppled to the ground. Then, its spirit would depart and the fallen pole was left to return to nature.

Throughout the early years of the fur trade, native groups flourished and their art continued to evolve. But when white missionaries and schoolteachers moved into these regions, native customs were discouraged and a unique art form was all but abandoned. Its rebirth came in the late 1960s and gained momentum in the '70s when native artists discovered a new medium – the silkscreen print. The ensuing mass production of native art prompted the general public to take an interest.

Each group has its own artistic style but they share basic components. The **form line** defines the shape of the figure being portrayed. Its flowing outline varies in thickness and is usually painted black, with the figure's secondary features in red.

The sculptured figures of Tlingit totem poles can be viewed at Saxman Village, including works in progress in the carving shed.

Black and red are the traditional colors of native art. Red was made from ochre (a clay-like mineral) ground to a powder and turned into a paste with the addition of a binding agent such as oil from salmon eggs. Black came from charcoal, graphite or lignite. With the introduction of commercial paints, artists began experimenting with non-traditional colors; however, much of their work is still done in the original colors. The Kwakwaka'wakw traditionally used more colors than the northern artists, adding green, white and yellow to their palettes.

Another basic component is the **ovoid** – an oval that is pushed out of shape to fit inside the form lines. An ovoid can represent a face, eyes, major joints or simply fill in empty spaces. The **U form** is used to help contour the figure, fill in spaces or represent features such as feathers. The **S form** is also used in a variety of ways, such as joining elements, filling in space or representing part of a leg or arm. The four basic design elements – form lines, ovoids, U forms and S forms – are closely assembled to create other shapes in the spaces between them.

Split figures (mirror images) are also widely used, as are **transformation figures** (i.e. half human/half animal). The basic elements of a figure are sometimes dismantled and rearranged to fit inside a given shape, such as a blanket, hat or spoon. The key to recognizing the figures portrayed in native art is to learn a few of their dominant features.

For example, a **raven** has a long, straight beak whereas an **eagle** has a shorter, hooked beak. The legendary **Thunderbird** – a crest used only by the most pow-

(Far right)
Silkscreen
scarf. (Right)
Bentwood box.

erful and prestigious chiefs – is always portrayed with outstretched wings and a sharply recurved upper beak. A **bear** will have flared nostrils, clawed paws and sharp teeth, sometimes with its tongue hanging out. The **beaver** has two large front teeth and a cross-hatched tail. The **wolf** is often shown standing on all four legs whereas the bear and beaver are usually sitting upright.

One of the easiest motifs to recognize is the **killer whale**, frequently portrayed in an arched position with a tall dorsal fin protruding from its back and two saw-like rows of teeth in its mouth. The **moon**, an exclusive crest of high-ranking Haida chiefs, is round with a face in the center. The **sun** is similar to the moon but with long rays projecting from the outer circle. Human figures are also part of native art and those wearing

high-crowned hats atop a totem pole are **watchmen** who can see outsider approaching. In Kwakwaka'wakw art, the eyes of supernatural beings are hollow and those of animals and people protrude.

Haida drawings and sculptures embody Northwest native art's classical purity. The trademarks of **Haida art** are a fluid, stylized use of well-defined form lines and a complex intertwining of figures. Poles and other objects are minimally altered by shallow carvings that blend with the basic shape. Heads are often large (especially those portrayed on totem poles) and in print works the blank spaces are seldom left unadorned.

Tlingit art is similar to Haida, although the figures on a Tlingit totem pole are more isolated and sculptured. The Tlingit are well known for their **Chilkat blankets** – woven of goat hair and decorated with clan crests – and for their **button blankets** on which intricate crests are outlined with thousands of buttons.

This 19th-century Haida drawing represents Raven in the belly of a killer whale.

U form

Form line

Ovoids

Split U form

S form

Tsimshian artists implement many of the traditional northern elements but with slight variations, such as detaching certain components from the main figure. Kwakwaka'wakw art is recognized by its variety of colors, abundance of small elements and protruding beaks, fins and wings that are added to totem poles.

Nuu-chah-nulth (Nootka) art is more flexible than classic northern art, with frequent breaks in the form lines or even the complete absence of form lines. Shapes are often geometrical and fewer design elements, such as ovoids, are used.

Coast Salish natives used no crest system, so their art traditionally depicted animal and human figures rather than clan emblems. They are noted for their excellent weaving and basketry as well as their carved spindle whorls. The **Cowichans** on Vancouver Island still employ traditional methods when making their famous **sweaters**.

With a renewed interest in preserving the traditions of native art, another concern has arisen – that of authenticity. By definition, anything created by a native Indian is authentic. However, some of the best native artists are not content to replicate the work of their ancestors but are experimenting with their art's classical components. As the acclaimed Haida artist **Robert Davidson** has said, if an art isn't changing, it's dead. Davidson's career as a Haida artist began with his carving miniature totem poles for customers at a Vancouver department store. His work is now displayed in art galleries, and his original prints and sculptures are collectors items.

The late **Bill Reid**, of Haida and Scots-American ancestry, is credited with reviving West Coast native art and reintroducing it to the world. His major works include *The Black Canoe*, which is the centerpiece of the Canadian embassy in Washington, DC. A second casting, *The Jade Canoe*, stands in the departure hall of the Vancouver Airport. His *Killer Whale* bronze is displayed outside the entrance to the Vancouver Aquarium, and his massive yellow cedar carving *The Raven and The First Men* is housed at the University of British Columbia's Museum of Anthropology.

When a Haida embarks on an artistic career, the first step is to become an apprentice – one who copies the art of predecessors. The next stage is that of journeyman – learning the symmetrical and classical forms of Haida art. The next stage is to become a master, which entails experimenting with what has been learned. Finally, those with exceptional talent become artists, their work reflecting both mastery and emotion.

A recent development in native art is the use of computer graphics. Tsimshian artist Roy Henry Vickers has recreated traditional forms on a computer screen. He says that his computer-generated ovoids and U-shapes look no different than those created by his ancestors a thousand years ago. The use of computer technology also provides for long-term storage of totem pole designs on disks.

Misty Fjords

PART II

THE VOYAGE AND THE PORTS

STRAIT of GEORGIA

Nanaimo

Vancouver
Int'l Airport

Vancouver

BRITISH COLUMBIA

Richmond
Sand Heads
Tsawwassen Ferry

99

1

White Rock

GULF ISLANDS

Pt. Roberts

Blaine

CANADA
U.S.A.

WASHINGTON

MT. BAKER
10185'

Active Pass

East Point

VANCOUVER ISLAND

1

Swartz
Bay

Haro Strait

Waldron I.

Bellingham

Orca I.   Lummi I.

San Juan
Islands

Victoria ★

Fisgard

San Juan I.

Lopez I.

Anacortes

LaConner

Whidbey I.

STRAIT OF JUAN de FUCA

Dungeness

Admiralty
Inlet

5

Port Angeles

Port Townsend

Everett

OLYMPIC

Port Ludlow

PUGET SOUND

PENINSULA

SEATTLE	
POPULATION:	610,000
POPULATION METRO AREA:	3.7 million
ANNUAL RAINFALL:	37 inches
DISTANCE TO KETCHIKAN:	760 miles
DISTANCE TO JUNEAU:	1,084 miles

Port Gamble

Poulsbo

Bainbridge I.

Seattle

Bellevue

CRUISE ROUTES 🚢	
MAIN ROUTES:	– – –
ALTERNATE ROUTES:	·········
FERRY ROUTES:	————

0   20

Miles

Bremerton

Mercer Is.

Renton

Sea-Tac
Airport

N

5

Tacoma

★ Olympia

GRAYS
HARBOR   •Aberdeen

MT. RAINIER
13367'

SEATTLE

Seattle is a city to be reckoned with. Ranked in various surveys as the number one place in America to live, do business and raise children, Seattle is also known for its music scene. The city's rock-and-roll legacy includes native son Jimi Hendrix and such home-grown bands as Nirvana and Pearl Jam. Microsoft was founded by hometown school pals Bill Gates and Paul Allen, and Starbucks originated in Seattle when three entrepreneurs opened the company's first coffee bean outlet at Pike Place Market in 1971. Holland America Line's head office is also located in Seattle, which is a burgeoning base port for Alaska-bound cruise ships. The city enjoys a superb setting at the head of beautiful Puget Sound, on the shores of Elliott Bay. To the west, across the water, lies the Olympic Peninsula, and stretching along the eastern horizon are the snow-capped Cascade Mountains.

Elliott Bay, Port of Seattle

Seattle became a bustling port during the Klondike Gold Rush.

Seattle's History

The lands around Puget Sound were still part of Oregon Territory in 1851 when settlers arrived from Portland and built a sawmill at Alki Point. When this venture failed, a group of them relocated four miles away on the east side of Elliott Bay in what is now Seattle's downtown core. Land claims were quickly made and the new town named Sealth (later altered to Seattle), after a local chief. Their settlement slowly grew into a supply center for nearby mining and logging camps, but the town's fate remained uncertain. Its future hinged on the Northern Pacific Railroad, and land speculators eagerly anticipated that Seattle would be chosen as a western terminus. When Tacoma got the nod over Seattle, her disappointed citizens joined together to build their own railroad. This civic pride and energy became known as the Seattle Spirit.

In 1889 a fire wiped out 60 city blocks but the Seattle Spirit, fueled by immigrants from other parts of the country and Europe, propelled the city forward with dogged determination. Then, on July 17, 1897, the steamer *Portland* arrived from Alaska with gold prospectors on board. They had struck it rich in the Klondike and the great Gold Rush began. Seattle, already shipping freight to Alaskan ports, quickly established itself as the outfitting center and port of departure for prospectors heading north.

The city's economy diversified further with the establishment of Boeing Airplane Company in 1917, marking the start of Seattle's aerospace industry. Then, in the 1990s, the phenomenal wealth generated by Seattle's high-tech industries, such as Microsoft, triggered an unprecedented building boom in Seattle's downtown area as local billionaires redirected millions into civic projects. These include The Experience Music Project – an interactive rock-n-roll museum funded by Paul Allen – and Seattle's opera house, its construction funded by the McCaw brothers, after selling their cellular communications company to AT&T.

As for Bill Gates, his foundation pledges billions of dollars to various causes, charities and scientific research programs worldwide. One of the world's wealthiest individuals, he lives with his wife and children in a 50,000-square-foot, earth-sheltered home on the shores of Lake Washington. The five-acre property is set in the side of a wooded hill overlooking a man-made beach. One of their neighbors is Jeff Bezos, founder of Amazon, whose waterfront estate is mostly hidden from view by trees.

Seattle's new library – a space-age design of glass, unusual angles and a soaring atrium – is fully computerized with its nearly one million books sorted automatically on a conveyer belt.

The city's iconic landmark remains the Space Needle, built as the centerpiece of the 1962 Seattle World's Fair. America's space race with the Soviet Union was underway at that time and the fair's themes were science and the space age. Seattle has lived up to those themes, its high-tech wealth clearly visible, but its soul remains rooted in its pioneer past.

The Frank Gehry-designed Experience Music Project building also houses a sci-fi museum.

Getting Around

The cruise ships dock at Pier 66 (at the foot of Bell Street) and at the Smith Cove Cruise Terminal at Pier 91, which is located at the north end of the Seattle waterfront, about a 10-minute drive from downtown. Norwegian Cruise Line and Oceania Cruises use Pier 66; Carnival, Celebrity Cruises, Holland America Line, Princess Cruises and Royal Caribbean use Pier 91.

Long-term parking is available at both terminals – approximately $20 a day at Pier 66; $25 a day at Pier 91 (visit www.rpnw.com).

Seattle's Sea-Tac Airport is about a 30-minute drive to downtown. The metered taxi fare from the airport to Pier 66 is about $50 and to Pier 91 is about $60. Town cars can be reserved in advance and charge about $50 to downtown Seattle. The cheapest way to travel from the airport to downtown is by light rail to Westlake Station.

Seattle's waterfront is undergoing major reconstruction to replace the Alaskan Way Viaduct with a bored road tunnel. Much of the Elliott Bay seawall is also being rebuilt. Until this massive project is completed, pedestrians can still make their way from the waterfront piers to other downtown attractions, such as Pike Place Market and Seattle Center, by following marked pedestrian detours. The Bell Street Pedestrian Bridge is a good shortcut, and the stairs of Pike Place Hillclimb connect the market with the waterfront below.

(Above) Pier 91 is a 10-minute drive from downtown Seattle. (Right) On board the monorail as it leaves Seattle Center.

Trolley cars no longer run along the waterfront but their old route is serviced by a Route 99 metro bus. A high-speed monorail whisks riders between Westlake Center and the Seattle Center.

A Visitor Information Center is located in Pike Place Market.

Seattle Shopping

During the Klondike Gold Rush, prospectors shopped in Seattle for tents, picks and shovels, beans and bacon. Today, Seattle is a good place to do some pre-Alaska shopping for items such as a wide-brimmed felt hat, rain slicker and binoculars. If high fashion is more your taste, head for Fifth Avenue's shops and malls, such as Nordstrom, **Westlake Center** and Rainier Square.

Local art and crafts are sold at booths in **Pike Place Market**, and several **art galleries** are located in

Shore Excursions
SEATTLE

Ship-organized excursions include narrated driving tours of the city with walking stops at the Space Needle, Experience Music Project and/or Pike Place Market. A boat cruise from Lake Union along the Ship Canal and through the Chittenden Locks is sometimes included. Also offered are driving tours to out-of-town attractions such as the Future of Flight & Boeing Factory Tour at Paine Field Airport in Everett (north of Seattle) and a culinary tour of Woodinville's wineries.

Pike Place Market sells fresh seafood and farm produce – ingredients featured in Seattle's local restaurants.

the **Pioneer Square** area, such as Flury & Company (focusing on vintage photos of Edward S. Curtis) and Stonington Gallery, which features carvings and prints by contemporary masters of Pacific Northwest Coast and Alaska art, including Robert Davidson and Susan Point. The Legacy has moved to a new location across Lake Washington in Bellevue and visitors are welcome by appointment only (425-454-2363).

Where to Stay

In addition to the reliable chain hotels – Westin, Sheraton, Hyatt and Hilton – Seattle's distinctive establishments include the five-diamond **Fairmont Olympic Hotel**, built in 1924 in the Italian Renaissance style and noted for its stunning lobby. The **Inn at the Market** is a boutique hotel located near the waterfront on the edge of the historic Pike Place Market. **The Edgewater** at Pier 67 offers a mountain lodge decor and looks over Elliott Bay. When the Beatles stayed at the Edgewater in 1964 at the height of Beatlemania, a cyclone fence had to be erected around the hotel to keep the fans at bay but this didn't deter those who tried climbing in from the water.

The historic **Mayflower Park Hotel**, at Olive Way and 4th Avenue, features 1920s European elegance in its decor, and offers a cruise package that includes a full American breakfast for two and shuttle vouchers to the cruise terminals. The **Seattle Marriott Waterfront Hotel** is conveniently located opposite Pier 66 on Alaskan Way.

Seattle Dining

In the mid-1980s, a new culinary trend began in the Pacific Northwest. With its moderate climate, rich soil and access to both salt water and fresh water, the region enjoys a year-round bounty of fresh fruit, vegetables and seafood from nearby farms and fishboats. These locally harvested products are highlighted in Northwest cuisine. And to help wash down an oyster in the shell or a steaming bowl of clams, Seattle diners can choose from an extensive list of local wines and beers. Award-winning restaurants serving Northwest cuisine include

Dahlia Lounge (at 4th and Virginia), which is run by Tom Douglas – an Iron Chef famous for his crabcakes and whose other Seattle restaurants include **Etta's Seafood**, near Pike Place Market.

Pike Place Market contains a wide variety of brewpubs and restaurants, such as the highly touted **Cafe Campagne** (1600 Post Alley at Pine) and its sister restaurant, **Campagne**, which is located in The Inn at the Market. The original **Starbucks Cafe** is at 1912 Pike Place.

Excellent Italian food can be enjoyed at **Assaggio Ristorante** (on 4th Avenue between Virginia and Lenora Streets). For a succulent steak dinner served in a richly appointed dark wood interior, visit Morton's Steakhouse on 6th Avenue (between Pine and Pike). **Andaluca**, in the Mayflower Park Hotel, serves good Mediterranean cuisine, and the hotel's popular bar – Oliver's Lounge – is known for its martinis and classic cocktails.

Seafood lovers should head to **Chandler's Crabhouse** overlooking Lake Union, or to **Ray's Boathouse** on Shilshole Bay, just north of Pier 91.

(Top to bottom) The lobby of the Fairmont Olympic. The Edgewater Hotel at Pier 67. Waterfront dining at Ray's Boathouse.

Restaurants and attractions line the waterfront's boardwalk. (Below) Historic Pike Place Market overlooks Elliott Bay.

Local Attractions

Seattle's waterfront was formerly called The Gold Rush Strip when freighters and passenger liners from Alaska and other American ports docked here. It stretches the length of Alaskan Way, from Pier 70 – a restored wharf now filled with shops and restaurants – down to Pier 52.

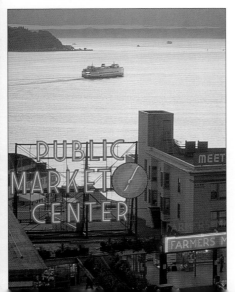

The **Olympic Sculpture Park** opened beside Pier 70 in early 2007. This former nine-acre industrial site was bought by the Seattle Art Museum and then transformed into an open green space for displaying public art.

Other attractions along the waterfront include the **Seattle Aquarium** (on Pier 59) where sea otters and other marine mammals can be observed.

At the end of Pier 57 is a giant ferris wheel, called **The Seattle Great Wheel**, its fully enclosed gondolas offering unmatched views of the city's waterfront.

The **King County Water Taxi** operates from Pier 50, offering 10-minute crossings to Seacrest Park at Alki Point in West Seattle.

Perched on a bluff overlooking the waterfront is the century-old **Pike Place Market** **1**. Its cobblestone streets are lined with stalls of fruit, vegetables, seafood, meats, cheeses, coffees, teas and spices. When you tire of strolling the busy aisles, there are three levels of shops and restaurants below the main arcade.

Four blocks up from the Pike Street Market, at Pine and 5th Avenue, is the **Westlake Center**

monorail terminal where you can embark on a two-minute monorail ride to **Seattle Center** and the famous Space Needle.

The perfect place to enjoy Seattle's beautiful mountains-and-sea setting is from atop the 600-foot **Space Needle 2**, built for the 1962 World's Fair. The observation deck's 360-degree view lets you gaze down at the city built on the hills between Puget Sound and Lake Washington. To the west lie the Olympic Mountains and eastward is the Cascade Range of snow-capped peaks, which includes Mount Rainier and Mount Baker.

The Space Needle is part of the 74-acre Seattle Center which encompasses a theater, opera house (McCaw Hall), children's museum and Pacific Science Center.

Near the base of the Space Needle is the **Experience Music Project**, an interactive rock'n'roll museum funded by Microsoft co-founder Paul Allen and housed in a modernist red, blue and purple steel-skinned building designed by Frank Gehry. In a corner of this unusual structure is the **Science Fiction Museum and Hall of Fame**, brainchild of sci-fi fan Paul Allen and packed with rare artifacts and memorabilia from sci-fi films, books and television shows.

The **Seattle Art Museum 3**, located on 1st Avenue and Union, is internationally known for its Native American and modern art of the Pacific Northwest.

Two blocks uphill from the Museum, on 3rd Avenue between Union and University Streets, is

(Above) The entrance to Olympic Sculpture Park.
(Below) Pioneer Square.

the Seattle Symphony's concert hall – **Benaroya Hall**.

On 5th Avenue, between Columbia and Cherry, the **Sky View Observatory** provides a 360-degree panoramic view of the city from the Columbia Center's 73rd floor ($12.50 per adult).

The restored brick buildings of **Pioneer Square 4** stand where settlers' shacks stood before the Great Fire of 1889. Yesler Way, which runs through the middle of Pioneer Square to the waterfront, was originally a skid road for logs. A guided underground tour follows sidewalks (one storey down) that were abandoned after the Great Fire. Located within Pioneer Square Historical District is the Seattle Unit of the **Klondike Gold Rush National Historical Park**. Consisting of a Visitor Center housed in the former Cadillac Hotel, this historic brick building is located at 319 2nd Avenue South and its exhibits commemorate Seattle's boomtown days as 'Gateway to the Gold'.

Next to Pioneer Square is **Century Link Field** (the Seattle

A retired Concorde supersonic jetliner is on permanent display at the Museum of Flight.

Seahawks' football stadium) and adjacent **Safeco Field 5**, home to the Seattle Mariners baseball club. Walking tours of both the stadium and the ballpark are available.

Due east is the **International District 6** where Asian restaurants, bazaars and exotic shops are bordered by the Kobe Terrace Park. Guided tours are available of this colorful area rich in Oriental culture.

To the north of downtown Seattle, and separated from it by the **Lake Washington Ship Canal**, is the Ballard area – settled by Scandinavian fishermen and loggers. The canal connects Lake Washington with Puget Sound and near its western entrance are the **Chittenden Locks**. Here sightseers can watch fishboats and other vessels being raised or lowered as they travel between fresh water and salt water. Seattle's huge fishing fleet moors at nearby Fisherman's Terminal and each spring hundreds of seiners and gillnetters head north to fish the waters of Alaska.

The **Woodland Park Zoo**, on Phinney Avenue North, is one of the best zoos in the U.S. with its re-creation of natural habitats.

On the southern outskirts of the city, off Airport Way, is the **Museum of Flight**, a national historic landmark. Built around the Boeing Company's original factory on the edge of Boeing Field (King County Airport) the museum's Great Gallery contains vintage aircraft suspended in simulated flight from the ceiling, which is six storeys high.

More vintage aircraft can be viewed at **The Flying Heritage Collection** in Everett (a 30-minute drive north of downtown Seattle). The World War II fighter planes on display here were donated by co-founder Paul Allen and are housed in a 51,000-square-foot exhibition facility.

Ninety miles south of Seattle is **Mount St. Helen's National Volcanic Monument**, where a new lava dome began forming in 2004. Whenever steam is billowing from the main crater, officials temporarily close the immediate area to visitors who come to hike the trails and view the destruction caused by the volcano's cataclysmic eruption in May 1980.

To the west of the city lies beautiful **Puget Sound**. The Washington State ferry system (the nation's largest) provides access from downtown Seattle to Bainbridge Island and to Bremerton on the Olympic Peninsula. A loop drive of the Peninsula can include stops at Poulsbo (settled by Norwegians), and the ports of Gamble, Ludlow and Townsend (all 19th-century towns where schooners loaded lumber for shipment to California). Port Angeles, with its mile-long spit called Ediz Hook,

is the gateway to **Olympic National Park**, where attractions include the Sol Duc Hot Springs. Ocean beaches beckon on the Peninsula's west coast, and the state capital of **Olympia** is on Puget Sound's southern shore.

North of Seattle, the Interstate 5 is the quickest land route to Vancouver, Canada – a 3.5 hour drive of 140 miles. Time permitting, you can turn off at Conway for a visit to **LaConner** – a century-old port town with interesting shops and restaurants. Another recommended detour is to turn at Burlington onto the scenic **Chuckanut Drive**, which hugs the coastline. Chuckanut Drive reconnects with the I-5 at Bellingham – southern terminus of the Alaska State Ferry. From here Mount Baker is a 60-mile detour east.

Powell River

Whistler

Saltery Bay

Egmont

Texada Island

MALASPINA STRAIT

Pender Harbour

Sisters I

Smuggler Cove

Sechelt

Hornby Is.

Lasqueti I

Ballenas Is.

STRAIT of GEORGIA

BRITISH COLUMBIA

Gambier Island

Howe Sound

Bowen Is.
Pt. Atkinson

Horseshoe Bay

North Vancouver

Vancouver

Harris
Hot Spr

Entrance Is.

Nanaimo

Gabriola I

English Bay

Vancouver Int'l Airport

Richmond

1

Sand Heads

Steveston

GULF ISLANDS

99

White Rock

CANAL

U.S.A

Tsawwassen Ferry

Blaine

1

Active Pass

East Point

Haro Strait

Bellingha

Swartz Bay

Waldron I

Orca I

Butchart Gardens

Sidney

San Juan

Islands

Anacortes

San Juan I

LaConner

VANCOUVER ISLAND

Victoria

Lopez I

Port Renfrew

Pacific Rim Nat'l Park

Fisgard

Cape Flattery

Sooke

STRAIT of JUAN de FUCA

Port Townsend

WASHINGTON

Port Ludlow

PUGET SOUND

Ev

VICTORIA

METRO POPULATION:	355,000
ANNUAL RAINFALL:	24 inches
DISTANCE TO KETCHIKAN	680 miles

OLYMPIC

PENINSULA

Seatt

Bremerton

*Sea-Ta
Airport*

CRUISE ROUTES

MAIN ROUTES: – – – – –
ALTERNATE ROUTES: ·············
FERRY ROUTES: – · – · – · –

0   20

Miles

N

Tacoma

VICTORIA

More than any other Canadian city, Victoria has retained its British colonial heritage. The provincial capital of British Columbia, it's a city of tea rooms, English pubs, double-decker buses and flower gardens that bloom year-round in the temperate climate. Victoria began as a fur trading post when the Hudson's Bay Company built a fort here in 1843. British immigrants soon arrived in sailing ships, having rounded Cape Horn with their fine English china and Victorian ideals, ready to carve a piece of the old country out of this new land of rugged wilderness. The city was named in honour of Queen Victoria, Empress of India, whose statue graces the lawns leading to the Legislative Buildings – designed by British architect Francis Rattenbury and completed in 1898. By the end of Queen Victoria's reign in 1901, the city that bears her name was coming into its own. Rattenbury's architectural achievements would soon define the city's Inner Harbour, the sight of which prompted Rudyard Kipling to say that a visit to Victoria was "worth a very long journey" – a sentiment still expressed to this day.

VICTORIA AT A GLANCE

Victoria's Inner Harbour with Empress Hotel in background.

Getting Around

The cruise ships dock at Ogden Point, which is about a 10-minute taxi ride or a 30-minute walk to downtown Victoria, where most of the major attractions are clustered around the Inner Harbour. Passengers disembarking at Ogden Point can take a boat or bus shuttle ($11 round-trip) to downtown. The boat docks at Steamship Terminal and the bus

Locals and visitors enjoy the waterfront path to Ogden Point.

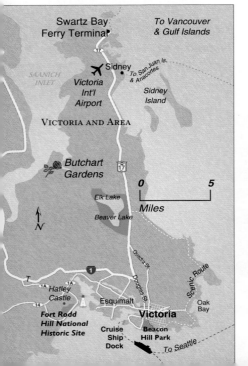

shuttle stop is on Government Street. Small cruise ships dock in the Inner Harbour at Ship Point. Victoria's area attractions – such as the Butchart Gardens – can be visited by ship-organized shore excursion, by taxi (about $50 each way) or by taking a tour that departs in front of The Empress and costs about $60 per adult (www.cvscruisevictoria.com).

The city's main **Visitor Info Centre** overlooks the docks in front of The Empress. Here you'll find helpful staff and a selection of maps and brochures. **City tours** are available by motor coach, double-decker bus and horsedrawn carriage. Local whalewatching tours are also available, with three resident pods of killer whales regularly sighted in the waters off Victoria.

Harbor tours ($22 per adult) can be taken on the small ferry boats operated by Victoria Harbour Ferry. These hop-on/hop-off boats make regular stops at various points around the waterfront (see city map) including Fisherman's Wharf and the docks in front of The Empress. The fare is $5 one way; pay the driver upon boarding. If you're looking for a scenic walk, a pedestrian seawall called the Oceanside Walk leads from Ogden Point to Beacon Hill Park.

Passengers planning to visit Victoria on a **pre- or post-cruise tour** from Vancouver can usually book this side-trip through their cruise line. Should you prefer to visit Victoria independently, your best options are to book a float-plane ride from Vancouver's Coal Harbour to Victoria's Inner

Harbour, or book a seat on a motorcoach that departs from downtown Vancouver and drops off behind The Empress hotel in downtown Victoria. Your other option is to rent a car and travel from Vancouver to Victoria by road and ferry but there can be line-ups and sailing waits at the ferry terminals in summer.

If you plan to stay overnight in Victoria, reserve ahead for a hotel. The **Fairmont Empress** – a city landmark and luxury heritage hotel – offers a central location for exploring the city on foot. The contemporary **Laurel Point Inn** is situated away from the hustle and bustle with a location overlooking the Inner Harbour. The waterfront **Delta Victoria Ocean Pointe Resort** is located on the opposite side of the Inner Harbour; guests here can take the hotel's free shuttle to downtown or hop on the passenger ferry that docks in front of the hotel.

(Above) A ferry boat pulls up to the Empress Docks. (Below) Delta Ocean Pointe Resort.

Shopping & Dining

For shoppers, some of the best browsing can be done on Government Street where the late Victorian era is preserved in chocolate shops, bookstores, tobacconists and tea merchants. Here you can buy Scottish

Shore Excursions
VICTORIA

Ship-organized excursions include coach tours to the Butchart Gardens, often combined with another attraction, such as the Butterfly Gardens. City tours are by motorcoach and horse-drawn trolley. Sightseeing tours of the city's highlights often include a visit to Craigdarroch Castle or The Empress for afternoon tea. Victoria's British-style pubs are featured in ale tours. Wine and cuisine tours are also offered. Whalewatching tours depart from the Inner Harbour.

tweeds and tartans, English bone china, Waterford crystal and Irish linen. Munro's Bookstore, Old Morris Tobacconist (which sells Cuban cigars) and Rogers' Chocolates are worth popping into just for a look at their splendid interiors. On Fort Street is 'Antique Row' and at **Market Square** (the Olde Town's former hotel and saloon district) the shops front an open-air square. Narrow **Fan Tan Alley** leads to the shops of Chinatown.

Restaurant choices range from **Barb's Fish & Chips** floating seafood restaurant at Fisherman's Wharf, to fine dining at The

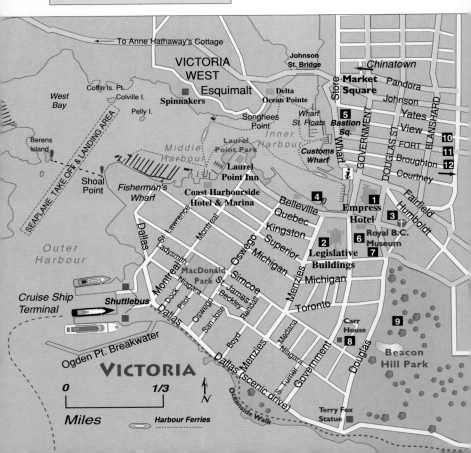

Fairmont Empress. A popular curry buffet is served in The Empress's famous **Bengal Lounge** where the British colonial decor includes a Bengal tiger skin over the marble fireplace. Afternoon tea is served with sandwiches, pastries and scones in the hotel's elegant **Tea Lobby** (reservations suggested).

For northern Italian cuisine, try **Il Terrazzo** on Johnson Street. Casual, west coast food can be enjoyed on the outdoor patio of the **Local Kitchen** on Wharf Street. Victoria's inviting pubs include **Swans Brewpub** near Market Square (corner of Pandora and Store) where draft ales and lagers are served on its flower-filled patio. **Garrick's Head Pub,** in Bastion Square, opened for business in 1867 and is one of the oldest English pubs in Canada. The **Irish Times Pub** occupies an historic bank building at the corner of Government and View, and the Scottish-themed **Bard & Banker**, one block south, is housed in an old bank where the Yukon-bound poet Robert Service once worked.

City Sights

There's no better place to start a tour of downtown Victoria than strolling the Inner Harbour. Replica historic vessels tug at their moorings while small passenger ferries whisk visitors around the harbour. In summer a festive atmosphere ensues when flowers spill from hanging baskets and spectators throng the seawall during various regattas, festivals and outdoor concerts. The harbour's dockside attractions are part of an imperial setting of lawns and lamp posts,

A horse-drawn carriage awaits customers outside The Empress.

overseen by the regal **Empress Hotel** **1**. This grand hotel, designed by Francis Rattenbury and built by the Canadian Pacific Railway, first opened its doors in 1908. The hotel has been restored to its original Edwardian opulence and afternoon tea at The Empress remains a Victoria tradition.

Equally imperial in style and scale are the **Legislative Buildings** **2**, designed by Rattenbury (who was in his early twenties when he won this commission) and completed in 1898. Built of granite and other indigenous materials, this Beaux-Arts structure is a mix of Victorian, Roman and Italian Renaissance styles. At night its neo-classical domes and arches are outlined by thousands of lights.

Rattenbury trained with his uncle in England before moving to Canada where the wide-open spaces of the west suited his grand schemes. His life ended in scandal back in England in 1935

(Above) The Rattenbury-designed Legislative Buildings. (Below) The waterfront entrance to Bastion Square.

when his young, second wife and her paramour (the chauffeur) were charged with bludgeoning Rattenbury to death. Alma Rattenbury was acquitted, only to commit suicide, while George Stoner was sentenced to life imprisonment and later released.

Right behind The Empress, near the bus depot, is the glass-roofed **Crystal Garden 3**. Based on Victorian England's Crystal Palace, it too was designed by Rattenbury and once housed an indoor pool in which Johnny Weismuller broke a world swimming record.

On the south harbourfront is yet another Rattenbury design – the former **CPR Steamship Terminal 4**. Modeled on a Greek temple with massive Ionic columns, this historic building once housed the Royal London Wax Museum. The Robert Bateman Centre currently occupies the top floor, and a gift shop is on the ground floor along with the Steamship Grill and Taphouse.

Wharf Street leads north from the Inner Harbour, past the original Customs House (1876), to historic **Bastion Square 5**, its restored brick buildings now housing restaurants, shops and art galleries. The original courthouse, at 28 Bastion Square, is now the **Maritime Museum**. Inside this turreted building, visitors can ride an ornate elevator built in 1900 for an elderly judge. Exhibits include a dugout canoe named *Tilikum* which was sailed by Captain Voss from Victoria to England.

Other downtown sights include the **Royal British Columbia Museum 6** which houses an outstanding exhibit on the area's natural and native history. Beside it is Thunderbird Park with an impressive display of totem poles, and behind it is **Helmcken House 7**, one of Victoria's oldest houses, built in 1852 by a pioneer doctor.

A 10-minute stroll away, heading south on Government Street, will take you to **Carr House 8**. Now a museum, this Italianate-style house, built in the 1860s, was the birthplace of Emily Carr (1871-1945) – one of Canada's most acclaimed artists.

Two blocks east of Carr House is Victoria's oldest and cherished municipal park – **Beacon Hill Park 9**, named for the navigational range markers which sat atop its hill in the 1840s. Today, visitors enjoy the classic English landscape garden while below in the strait a modern beacon guides mariners. The park's southwest corner marks Mile Zero of the

Craigdarroch Castle

Trans-Canada Highway (4,860 miles long from Victoria to St. John's, Newfoundland) and is where a bronze statue of Terry Fox was unveiled in 2005.

The colourful Butchart Gardens are stunning in every season.

A mile east of Victoria's downtown core, in the upscale Rockland neighborhood, is **Craigdarroch Castle** 🔟 – built in the late 1800s by the coal baron Robert Dunsmuir, a Scottish immigrant who became British Columbia's wealthiest and most influential businessman, and whose son James became premier of the province in 1900. The four-storey mansion, complete with a tower, turrets and French Gothic roof line, is now a museum with the family's original furnishings and artwork on display. Nearby, housed in an 1889 mansion, is the **Art Gallery of Greater Victoria** 🔢 where works of Emily Carr are exhibited.

City of Gardens

Victoria's rocky bluffs and sweeping sea views are tempered by gardens which bloom in early spring when other parts of the country are still in the grip of winter. Daffodils, rhododendron, honeysuckle and hyacinth are just a few of the flowers that thrive in Victoria's temperate climate. A British fondness for gardening is reflected everywhere – streets lined with blossoming cherry trees, lawns bordered by rockeries and rose bushes, and enough public gardens to satisfy any flower aficionado. The gated grounds of **Government House** 🔢 (official residence of the Lieutenant-Governor, who is the Queen's representative in British Columbia) are beautifully maintained and open to the public, as is **Hatley Park National Historic Site**, located eight miles west of downtown Victoria. The centerpiece of this 565-acre site is Hatley Castle, designed by Samuel Maclure for coal heir James Dunsmuir, which is today the main building of Royal Roads University campus. To see traces of an Elizabethan country garden, visit Anne Hathaway's replica cottage on the grounds of the **English Inn & Resort** (a Samuel Maclure-designed Tudor Revival building) in Esquimalt, across the harbour from downtown Victoria.

The gardens everyone wants to see, however, are the world-famous **Butchart Gardens**. A 20-minute drive north of Victoria, this 50-acre garden site took root in 1904 when Jennie Butchart decided to clean up the mess her husband left behind when his cement plant excavated a limestone quarry on their estate. Employing workers from the cement company, she transformed an eyesore into the Sunken Garden. She spent hours tucking ivy into the rock wall's crevices while hanging over the sides of the quarry in a bosun's chair.

For years the Butcharts welcomed all visitors to their gardens, serving afternoon tea in summer houses scattered about the property, until the sheer number of visitors made this impossible. Today more than a million visitors arrive annually to view the grounds which include a Japanese Garden, Rose Garden, Italian Garden, Concert Lawn and Fireworks Viewing Area. At night the gardens are transformed when hundreds of hidden lights illuminate the flowers and fountains.

Sidney by the Sea

The seaside town of Sidney is a pleasant detour for Victoria visitors heading to or from the B.C. Ferries terminal at Swartz Bay. Shop-lined Beacon Avenue runs through the center of Sidney to the waterfront, where a small passenger ferry departs regularly from the town pier to nearby **Sidney Spit Marine Park.** Summertime visitors to this Gulf Islands park can enjoy the sandy beaches and hiking trails.

A ferry transits Active Pass on its way to Swartz Bay, near Sidney.

Powell River

Saltery Bay

Egmont

Texada Island

Sisters I

Pender Harbour

Smuggler Cove

Sechelt

ornby I

Lasqueti I

Ballenas Is.

MALASPINA STRAIT

STRAIT of GEORGIA

Entrance I

Nanaimo

Gabriola I

GULF ISLANDS

Active Pass

BRITISH COLUMBIA

Gambier Island

Howe Sound

Horseshoe Bay

Bowen Is.
Pt. Atkinson

North Vancouver

English Bay

Vancouver Iht'l Airport

Vancouver

Harriso
Hot Spri

Fraser River

Richmond
Steveston

Sand Heads

Tsawwassen Ferry

99

White Rock

Blaine

**CANADA
U.S.A.**

1

Bellingham

VANCOUVER

1

ISLAND

Swartz Bay

Sidney

East Point

Haro Strait

Waldron I

Orca I

San Juan Islands

San Juan I

Lopez I

Anacortes

LaConner

5

Port Renfrew

Victoria ★

Fisgard

Sooke

STRAIT of JUAN de FUCA

Port Townsend

WASHINGTON

Port Ludlow

OLYMPIC

PENINSULA

PUGET SOUND

Ever

5

Bainbridge I

Seattle

Bremerton

Sea-Tac Airport

Tacoma

★Olympia

VANCOUVER

POPULATION METRO AREA:	2.4 million
ANNUAL RAINFALL:	48 inches
DISTANCE TO KETCHIKAN:	640 miles
DISTANCE TO JUNEAU:	964 miles

CRUISE ROUTES

MAIN ROUTES: – – – – – –
ALTERNATE ROUTES: ·············
FERRY ROUTES: –·–·–·–·–·

A cruise ship glides past the Tsawwassen ferry terminal.

0 — 20
Miles

N

VANCOUVER
& THE CANADIAN ROCKIES

Set against a magnificent backdrop of coastal mountains and inland sea, Vancouver is Canada's most beautiful city. It is also one of the fastest growing, with a steady influx of foreign investors creating a vibrant cosmopolitan centre.

Although vehicles clog its busiest streets, the city has retained a people-oriented core that is the envy of many a North American city planner trying to contain urban sprawl and car dependence. Situated on a peninsula, the downtown's compact neighborhoods are all within walking distance of each other, and most of the city's waterfront has been preserved as a green belt of parks,

public beaches and pedestrian seawalls.

Vancouver is a centre of film and television production, digital media and global finance, and its port is the largest in the Pacific Northwest, handling shipments to and from Asia and the rest of the world. The city celebrated its 100th birthday in 1986 by hosting Expo 86 – a world transportation fair. More recently, Vancouver was host city of the 2010 Winter Olympic Games.

Ships departing Vancouver pass beneath the Lions Gate Bridge.

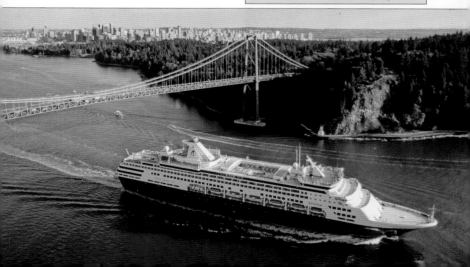

A History of Vancouver

Founded by British settlers in the late 1800s, Vancouver began as a small lumbering village on the shores of Burrard Inlet and gradually grew into a major shipping port.

The first people to appreciate Vancouver's natural harbor were the Squamish tribe of Coast Salish natives. Their local villages were well established when, in the summer of 1792, Captain George Vancouver of the British Royal Navy sailed his ship's boats into the harbor to survey the surrounding shores. He was looking for the Northwest Passage, not a good restaurant, so his visit was cursory to say the least.

In seamanlike fashion, he ordered that the boats proceed "under an easy sail" as a welcoming party of natives paddled out to

The City of Vancouver is named for the British sea captain George Vancouver.

greet these strange-looking visitors. An exchange of goods (salmon for iron) took place on the run as the British survey boats sailed toward the head of mountain-enclosed Burrard Inlet in search of an inland waterway. It was not to be found, so after a night spent camped on shore the British sailors left at dawn.

Spain had also dispatched ships to these waters, much to the surprise of Captain Vancouver who thought he was the first European to venture into what we now call the Inside Passage. The British and Spanish vessels crossed paths off Point Grey and the names English Bay and Spanish Banks commemorate this friendly encounter.

Apart from brief visits by naval ships, the waters off present-day Vancouver remained the domain of the Coast Salish natives who fished here for salmon and harvested shellfish. Merchant ships rarely ventured into the twisting channels of the Inside Passage, choosing to trade for furs with natives whose coastal villages bordered the open Pacific.

Eventually, however, the Hudson's Bay Company forged an overland route to the west coast where it established Fort Langley on the Fraser River in 1827. But it wasn't until gold was discovered in the Fraser Canyon, 30 years later, that settlers began moving into the area.

Gastown, Vancouver's original townsite, was founded in 1867 by a riverboat captain from Yorkshire named John Deighton who arrived at the local sawmill with a barrel of whiskey and told the thirsty mill workers they could have all the whiskey they could drink if they helped him build a saloon, which was up and open for business within 24 hours. His nickname of Gassy Jack, in reference to his smooth-talking personality, prompted locals to name the new settlement Gastown, although its official name was Granville.

In the 1880s, the Canadian Pacific Railway pushed its tracks through the Rocky Mountains to the west coast. Its termination point was Burrard Inlet, and with the arrival of CPR's first locomotive in 1886, the newly incorporated city of Vancouver was born, its name chosen by Cornelius Van Horne, chairman of the CPR.

Vancouver Harbour soon became a busy place. Merchant cargo ships – both the tall-masted and steam-driven variety – brought goods from overseas and loaded shipments of lumber, while CPR's Empress passenger ships offered luxury cruises to the Orient. In the 1950s, the Union

VANCOUVER'S ROYAL CONNECTION

Among Vancouver's early royal visitors were England's King George VI and Queen Elizabeth (the Queen Mother), who arrived by train in May of 1939. When Queen Elizabeth II arrived in the spring of 1982 on board the Royal Yacht *Britannia*, hundreds of Vancouverites sailed into English Bay to greet their visiting monarch and escort her into the harbour. In 1986, Prince Charles and Diana, Princess of Wales, officially opened Expo 86, arriving at the opening ceremonies in False Creek on a large yacht.

Steamships began offering trips to Alaska aboard converted World War II navy corvettes. Today Vancouver Harbour is one of North America's busiest cruise ports from May to October.

A crowd gathered when the first CPR liner arrived in Vancouver on April 28th, 1891.

Getting Around

Canada Place Cruise Ship Terminal is located in the heart of downtown Vancouver. It's a city landmark with large white sails crowning a complex containing a Pan Pacific Hotel and IMAX 3D Theatre. Long-term parking is available here (visit www.portmetrovancouver).

The Vancouver International Airport is about a 30-minute taxi ride to downtown; the set fare from the airport to Canada Place Cruise Terminal is $35. SkyTrain's Canada Line provides rapid rail service (25 minutes) to downtown's Waterfront Station.

Seattle-Tacoma International Airport is a distance of 160 miles to Vancouver's cruise piers (driving time of about three hours plus the wait at the border crossing).

A view of Canada Place from Stanley Park's cricket pitch.

Vancouver's **Ballantyne Pier** served as an overflow cruise terminal when Canada Place was full but was retired as a cruise facility at the end of the 2014 Alaska cruise season.

The downtown core is easy to explore on foot, starting at the Tourist Info Centre (200 Burrard Street, Waterfront Centre) beside the Canada Place Cruise Ship Terminal. Maps, brochures, bus and ferry schedules, and other information are available here.

Local tours include those operated by trolley car and double decker bus on a narrated loop tour that covers the city's highlights, such as Stanley Park, Chinatown, Yaletown and Granville Island.

These hop-on/hop-off tours are operated by Vancouver Trolley Company. They begin in Gastown at the Steam Clock but can be boarded anywhere along their route, with a trolley car or bus departing every 15 minutes and making numerous stops along the way. Tickets can be bought from the driver.

False Creek can be toured by small passenger ferries (described further in the False Creek section of this chapter).

Stanley Park can be reached by bus (#19 'Stanley Park' from downtown) and a shuttle operates within the park.

Vancouver is a safe, walkable city, although visitors should avoid venturing on foot east of Carrall Street in Gastown at night.

Car break-ins are a problem, so park only in well-secured lots and never leave valuables in an unattended vehicle.

Shopping

Shopping complexes within easy walking distance of the Canada Place Cruise Terminal include the **Sinclair Centre** and The Landing, both of which are restored heritage projects housing

An aerial view of Canada Place Cruise Ship Terminal.

upscale shops and fashion boutiques. One of Canada's oldest jewelry store chains is Birks and this company's Vancouver flagship store is housed in a heritage building at Granville and Hastings, opposite the Sinclair Centre. **The Landing** marks the entrance to **Gastown** and its gallery-lined **Water Street.**

Vancouver is a pre-eminent centre for acquiring contemporary Northwest Coast native art, and several of the city's finest galleries are located on Water Street, including Spirit Wrestler Gallery, Inuit Gallery of Vancouver (opposite the Steam Clock) and Hill's Native Art, which also carries a large collection of native crafts. (Other excellent galleries are located on South Granville Street, such as Douglas

ANNE'S JOURNAL

Although I've lived in Vancouver for decades, I never tire of walking the city's seawall. Starting at the Canada Place Cruise Ship Terminal and heading west along the Coal Harbour waterfront, the seawall winds past plazas, public art and pocket parks. One of the first landmarks is the Olympic cauldron, which stands outside the Vancouver Convention Centre's west building – a glass, terraced structure built on pilings and designed to encourage sea life below and plant life above on its six-acre roof garden. While strolling the seawall I enjoy looking at the boats moored in the marinas or pausing to gaze across the water to the North Shore mountains. Eventually I reach Stanley Park where the seawall winds completely around the park, providing sweeping views of English Bay. Some days I walk for miles, and other times I turn around and retrace my route to the Pan Pacific Hotel at Canada Place where I head up the escalator to the Cascades Lounge overlooking Coal Harbour. This is my favourite spot to enjoy a glass of wine while watching boats come and go, and floatplanes land or take off. I always savour this everchanging scene.

Reynolds Gallery where Damien Hirst has acquired several pieces of Northwest Coast art).

At the corner of Georgia and Granville Streets is the **Hudson's Bay** department store where you can purchase a modern version of the iconic Hudson's Bay blanket or peruse the latest London fashions in the store's trendy Topshop. The Bay stands atop a four-block-long underground shopping mall called **Pacific Centre**, which contains dozens of stores.

Robson Street is Vancouver's busiest shopping district, especially the three blocks west of Burrard to Jervis. Lined with fashion boutiques, coffee houses and restaurants, Robson Street is where everyone goes to stroll and people-watch. The two blocks of Burrard Street lying between Robson and Georgia are considered Vancouver's luxury lane with a Hermes and Tiffany & Co. located at Burrard and Alberni, and a Gucci and Louis Vuitton located around the corner in the lobby of the Hotel Vancouver.

For unique gifts and souvenirs, check out the Gallery Store at the Vancouver Art Gallery.

Where to Stay

Close to where the ships dock in downtown Vancouver is a wide range of accommodations, including several five-diamond hotels. Adjacent to Canada Place Cruise

'Light Shed' on the Coal Harbour waterfront was donated to the City of Vancouver by Britain's Duke of Westminster.

Terminal is the luxury **Pan Pacific Hotel** and across the street is the **Fairmont Waterfront**. Other Fairmont hotels in Vancouver are the **Fairmont Pacific Rim** (1038 Canada Place), **Fairmont Hotel Vancouver** (a heritage property) and **Fairmont Vancouver Airport**. A **Four Seasons Hotel** is situated a few blocks south of the harbourfront at Howe and Georgia.

The **Wedgewood Hotel** on Hornby (near Robson Square) is a member of Relais & Chateaux and has been rated Canada's best-value hotel by the readers of several travel magazines. **Shangri-La** was the hotel of choice for George Clooney, Tom Cruise and Oprah Winfrey while in Vancouver. Others favour the resort-like **Westin Bayshore** near Stanley Park. Boutique hotels in Vancouver include the **Opus** in Yaletown and the **Loden Hotel**, near Coal Harbour at 1177 Melville. A modest Vancouver gem is the heritage **Sylvia Hotel** overlooking English Bay.

Lobby of Fairmont Waterfront.

Shore Excursions
VANCOUVER

Cruise lines offer driving tours of the city combined with an airport drop-off and these range in length from two to eight hours, the latter including a lunch stop. The highlights of a city tour are Gastown, Chinatown, Stanley Park, West End and Yaletown. Driving tours to outlying attractions usually feature the Capilano Suspension Bridge and Grouse Mountain Skyride.

Dining in Vancouver

Vancouver's thriving restaurant scene has attracted such culinary talents as Michelin-starred Jean-Georges Vongerichten, who runs Shangri-La's **Market** restaurant.

Many of the city's restaurants showcase local fare, such as Pacific salmon and Saltspring Island lamb.

Good choices for west coast cuisine include **Herons Restaurant** in the Fairmont Waterfront Hotel and **The**

Teahouse in Stanley Park with a beautiful view overlooking English Bay.

For fresh seafood, try the **Blue Water Café & Raw Bar** in Yaletown.

For Italian cuisine, **Cioppino's Mediterranean Grill** on Hamilton Street in Yaletown is highly touted, as is **CinCin** on Robson Street.

Le Crocodile on Burrard and **Bacchus** in the Wedgewood Hotel are good choices for French cuisine. For refined contemporary cuisine, treat yourself to **Hawksworth Restaurant** in the Rosewood Hotel Georgia.

Popular sushi restaurants include **Minami** in Yaletown (frequented by George Clooney) and **Miku** on the waterfront near Canada Place Cruise Terminal.

Asian restaurants are numerous and Vancouver's best known Japanese restaurant is **Tojo's** at 1133 West Broadway.

For casual fare, the innovative dishes of Rob Feenie, the first

The Teahouse in Stanley Park has one of the best views in Vancouver, especially at sunset.

Canadian to win Iron Chef America, can be enjoyed at one of several **Cactus Club Café** locations including one opposite the Olympic Cauldron in Jack Poole Plaza.

Gallery Café in the Vancouver Art Gallery is a lovely spot for a casual lunch on the piazza-like patio.

And just a few blocks from Canada Place on Howe Street is **Scoozis** – a casual Mediterranean restaurant run by the Stamoulis family of Greece.

Local Attractions

1 **Gastown** – The cobblestone streets of Vancouver's original townsite are today lined with restaurants, art galleries and design studios. A statue of Gassy Jack stands in **Maple Tree Square** (where he first established a hotel in 1867) and at the corner of Water and Cambie Streets is a **chiming steam clock** which was designed to look like it was built in the 1890s. The clock, which sounds every quarter of an hour, was built in 1977 and is powered by gravity pulling down its steel balls and steam blowing the whistles. Behind Maple Tree Square is Gaoler's Mews, the site of Gastown's first jail and now a cluster of offices. Guided walking tours of Gastown are available from June through August.

2 The Lookout! – Take a glass elevator to the top of Harbour Centre Tower where a circular, enclosed viewing deck provides a 360-degree view of Vancouver and its surrounding scenery. American astronaut Neil Armstrong, the first man on the moon, was the guest celebrity at this popular attraction's grand opening in 1977. Informative plaques and historical displays help first-time visitors orient themselves with Vancouver from a bird's-eye perspective.

Some landmark buildings to look for include the **3 Marine Building** – Vancouver's finest example of art deco architecture. Completed in 1930 at the corner of Burrard and West Hastings, its architects described this 25-storey structure as "some great crag rising from the sea, clinging with sea flora and fauna, tinted in sea-green, touched with gold." The building's brass doors open into a muraled lobby where terra cotta panels pay tribute to Coal Harbour when its shorefront was a gritty industrial area of mills and rail lines.

The Marine Building is Vancouver's finest example of art-deco architecture.

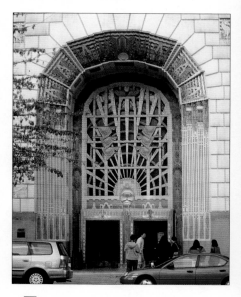

4 Vancouver Art Gallery – Located on Georgia Street and entered off **Robson Square**, this former court house was designed by British architect Francis Rattenbury, whose other turn-of-

the-century designs included Victoria's Legislative Buildings and The Empress Hotel. When the Law Courts opened on Robson Street in 1979, Rattenbury's neo-classical court house became Vancouver's art gallery, housing a permanent collection of works by Canadian artist Emily Carr. The building has appeared in numerous film and television productions, including *Night at the Museum: Battle of the Smithsonian*.

The art gallery's main entrance faces Robson Square and the **Law Court**s – an unusual court house design by Vancouver architect Arthur Erickson with its long, low profile, sloped glass roof and streaming waterfalls.

Next door to the Vancouver Art Gallery, on Georgia Street, is the green-roofed **5 Fairmont Hotel Vancouver** – a grand railway hotel that was completed in 1939, its features including a steeply pitched copper roof, extravagant window dormers and carved gargoyles.

Across the street, opposite the Vancouver Art Gallery, is the **Rosewood Hotel Georgia**, which first opened for business in 1927 and recently underwent a four-year, $120-million restoration. Next door, in the HSBC Building, is the **Pendulum Gallery** – a seven-storey glass atrium lobby where an enormous pendulum (a kinetic sculpture by Alan Storey) swings freely above the public gallery's exhibits.

Christ Church Cathedral, constructed in the 1890s, stands at the corner of Georgia and Burrard, and is where the British

The Vancouver Art Gallery overlooks Robson Square with the Fairmont Hotel Vancouver visible in the background.

Royal Family worships when visiting Vancouver. A block up from Georgia Street, on Hornby Street, is the **6 Bill Reid Gallery of Northwest Coast Art**. This museum/art gallery showcases exquisite jewelry and iconic carvings by this acclaimed artist as well as exhibitions of other West Coast aboriginal art.

At the far end of Georgia Street is **7 Library Square** – a colosseum-like structure housing Vancouver's main library. It was

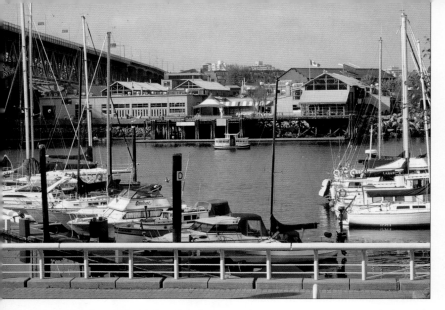

A view from the False Creek seawall, looking toward Granville Island.

designed by Moshe Safdie and was modeled on the classical forms of ancient Rome.

Vancouver's **Chinatown,** **8** the second-largest in North America, is filled with restaurants, shops and pagoda phone booths. One of Vancouver's oldest districts and declared a historical site in 1971, Chinatown is home to the **Dr. Sun Yat-Sen Classical Chinese Garden,** the first authentic full-sized classical Chinese garden built outside of China. Surrounded by high white walls, this garden is an oasis of tranquillity, its courtyards duplicating the private Ming Dynasty. Next door is the Chinese Cultural Centre, which conducts walking tours of Chinatown.

False Creek bustles with year-round activity, its shores lined with marinas, waterfront parks and condominium towers.

Kayakers and scullers share its waters with barge-towing tugboats and recreational boats of all sizes. Throughout the day and early evening, the blue-colored False Creek Ferries and the multi-colored Aquabus ferries criss-cross False Creek, carrying foot passengers to Granville Island and other creekside attractions, including **Science World** – a science center housed in a silver geodesic dome at the head of False Creek.

The Aquabus ferry also stops at **Yaletown,** a 19th-century warehouse district where red-brick buildings have been converted into New York-style artists' lofts, galleries, antique shops, trendy restaurants, and offices occupied by graphic designers and film production companies.

Granville Island **9**, is the centerpiece of False Creek. An artisans' enclave with an art college and crafts studios, Granville Island is home to one of North America's most successful public

Passenger ferries provide easy access to False Creek's shoreside attractions.

markets, where locals shopping for fresh produce mix with out-of-town visitors strolling past the crafts stalls.

Granville Island also contains a community centre and children's waterpark, in addition to boutiques, restaurants and live theatre. Eagle Spirit Gallery, offering Northwest Coast Native and Inuit art, is located on Maritime Mews. A visitor information centre is located opposite the Public Market.

Scenic **Vanier Park** 10, with shoreside views across English Bay to the West End, can be reached on foot from Granville Island via the seawall, or from downtown Vancouver by boarding a False Creek passenger ferry at Sunset Beach (the bottom of Thurlow Street). Vanier Park is popular with dog walkers, kite flyers and model boat owners who gather at its ornamental lake on Sunday mornings.

Several museums are located in Vanier Park, including a **Maritime Museum**, which houses the historic *St. Roch* – an Arctic

Upscale floathomes line the False Creek waterfront.

supply and patrol vessel that was the first to navigate the North West Passage from west to east in 1940-42. Outside the museum is Heritage Harbour where traditional wooden vessels are moored and visiting tall ships dock.

Nearby is a complex housing the **Vancouver Museum and Pacific Space Centre**, which features a planetarium beneath its white circular roof.

Prospect Point

Restaurant

LIONS GATE BRIDGE

Park/
Picnic area

STANLEY PARK

Siwash Rock

Hollow Tree

Seawall & Park Trails -------

0   1/4

Miles

Third Beach

Ferguson Point

The Teahouse
Restaurant

Beaver Lake
Ducks

Pipe Line Road

Miniature Railroad

Burra
Inle

Girl in a
Wet Suit

Police
Paddocks

Vancouver
Aquarium

Gardens

Brockton Point Light

Rose
Gardens

LIONS GATE BRIDGE CAUSEWAY

Lost Lagoon

Totem
Poles

Second
Beach

Pool/
Playground

Fish House
Restaurant

Ducks &
swans here

Park
Entrance

Vancouver
Rowing Club

RVYC

Deadman's
Island

PARK

CHILCO

Bike Rentals

English Bay

DENMAN

NELSON

ALBERNI

ROBSON

GEORGIA

English Bay
Beach

BEACH

DAVIE

JERVIS

BUTE

HASTINGS

PENDER

CORDOVA

Vancouver Convention Centre

Stanley Park

Stanley Park, the largest urban park in Canada, is an oasis of northern rainforest criss-crossed with hiking trails and encircled by a pedestrian seawall. It originated as a 1,000-acre military reserve in the mid-1800s on land set aside to guard the entrance to Vancouver Harbour (the 12-pound muzzle loader installed near Brockton Point still booms across the water each evening at nine o'clock).

This undeveloped military reserve became Stanley Park in 1888. Its layout is based on the planning principles of American landscape architect Frederick Law Olmsted, who designed New York City's Central Park – which made a gift of eight pairs of grey squirrels to Stanley Park in 1909. Their descendants are today flourishing, along with the resi-dent raccoons and rabbits. Bird life is abundant along the shores of Lost Lagoon.

Stonemasons first began working on Stanley Park's retaining wall in 1914, which eventually became the pedestrian seawall and is now 5.5 miles (8.8 km) in length and completely encircles the park. Trails crisscross the park's 1,000 acres (405 hectares) and are patrolled by a mounted squad of Vancouver police officers.

Attractions within the park include the **Vancouver Aquarium Marine Science Centre**, Canada's largest marine mammal rescue and rehabilitation center. It is home to Steller sea lions, beluga whales and sea otters (some were brought here following the *Exxon Valdez* oil spill in Alaska's Prince William Sound in 1989).

SS BEAVER

The S.S. *Beaver* was a famous steamship employed by the Hudson's Bay Company during the fur trade. In 1888, while departing Vancouver Harbour, the ship was gripped not by tidal rips and back eddies but by a sense of panic in her crew when they discovered their liquor supply had been left behind in port. They turned the ship sharply around and accidentally grounded her off Prospect Point. A few years later, the luxurious new CPR liner *Empress of India* visited Vancouver Harbour on her maiden voyage.

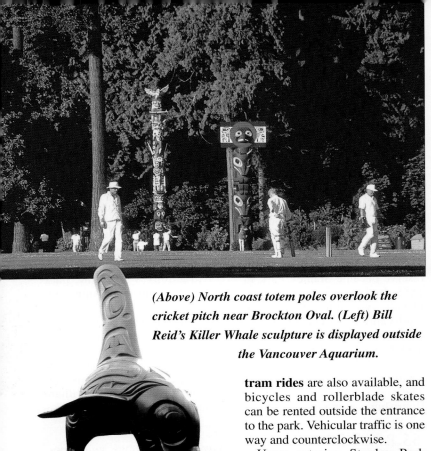

(Above) North coast totem poles overlook the cricket pitch near Brockton Oval. (Left) Bill Reid's Killer Whale sculpture is displayed outside the Vancouver Aquarium.

Several **restaurants** are located in Stanley Park, including The Teahouse at Ferguson Point (with lovely views overlooking English Bay) and the Fish House (located near the southwest entrance of the park). Take-out food stands are at Third Beach and Second Beach.

Vancouver Trolley Co. operates **park shuttle buses** daily throughout the summer from 11 am to 6:30 pm. They circle the park with stops at 15 locations; the fare is $10 for adults. **Horse-drawn**

tram rides are also available, and bicycles and rollerblade skates can be rented outside the entrance to the park. Vehicular traffic is one way and counterclockwise.

Upon entering Stanley Park from Georgia Street, the road paralleling the seawall veers to the right and traces the shoreline of Coal Harbour where you will see the Vancouver Rowing Club, the Royal Vancouver Yacht Club and **Deadman's Island**, which was a traditional burial ground of the Coast Salish natives who lived in the area when British colonists first arrived. A naval base – HMCS *Discovery* – was built on Deadman's Island during WWII.

As you approach the park's most easterly point of land – **Brockton Point** – you will pass (on your left) a large display of Northwest Coast native totem poles and welcome gateways (the

Stanley Park Shuttle stops here and there is also ample parking). After rounding Brockton Point, doing a 180-degree turn and doubling back, you pass the cricket grounds and Brockton Oval to the left. A bit further along, sitting on a rock near shore, is *The Girl in a Wetsuit*. Frequently compared to Copenhagen's *Little Mermaid*, this bronze sculpture is the work of Elek Imredy, who came to Vancouver from Budapest, Hungary in 1957 following an uprising in his homeland.

Just beyond Lions Gate Bridge is **Prospect Point** where a viewpoint overlooks the bridge. In the winter of 2006, gale-force winds battered a swath of forest between Prospect Point and Siwash Rock, snapping branches and toppling trees. The park's oldest tree, a 1,000-year-old red cedar which has been featured in *National Geographic* magazine, survived the devastation only to topple a year later because of root rot.

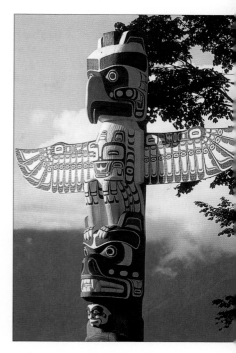

(Above) Thunderbird sits atop this totem pole near Brockton Point. (Below) A pleasure craft cruises past Brockton Point.

The famous **Hollow Tree** – a giant cedar snag that's hollow inside – has been a city landmark for more than a century and a popular photo stop for park visitors. So when the massive stump started to lean and had to be braced, a lengthy debate ensued about its future. In the end, the Hollow Tree Conservation Society lobbied the parks board not to cut it down, and raised enough money to pay for engineering work to straighten and stabilize the stump. Nearby, on the seawall, is **Siwash Rock** – a sea stack formed over time from surf eroding a cliff but leaving a resistant portion standing.

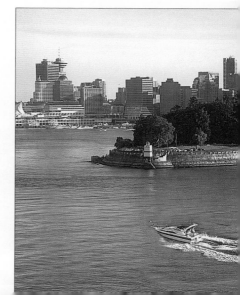

Vancouver's other famous park attraction is **Queen Elizabeth Park**, located south of the downtown core on Cambie and 33rd. Its 130 acres of gardens and grounds occupy a reclaimed quarry situated on the highest point in Vancouver. Offering beautiful views of the city skyline, the park's landscaping is a pleasing mix of native and exotic trees and shrubs, with seasonal floral displays in the Quarry Garden. Within the park is the **Bloedel Floral Conservatory**, a 'garden under glass' containing a dazzling display of exotic plants and tropical flowers. A bronze sculpture by Henry Moore, *Knife Edge Two Piece*, stands beside the dancing fountain in the park's plaza. Lunch or dinner can be enjoyed at Seasons in the Park Restaurant.

Excellent food and city views can be enjoyed at Seasons in the Park in Queen Elizabeth Park.

Southeast of downtown on the University of British Columbia campus is the **Museum of Anthropology** (MOA), housing one of the world's finest displays of Northwest Coast native art and the largest collection of works by acclaimed Haida artist Bill Reid. Showcased here is Reid's famous cedar sculpture *The Raven and the First Men* depicting the Haida people's creation myth. The building itself, an award-winning design by Vancouver architect Arthur Erickson, is set on an ocean bluff overlooking the Strait of Georgia. The Great Hall, a concrete structure of soaring glass inspired by the traditional post-and-beam construction of native longhouses, provides a stunning venue for the museum's collection of totem poles, canoes and feast dishes. Masterpiece Gallery displays intricately handcrafted works in silver, gold and argillite. Outside on the grounds is a replica Haida coastal village.

The North Shore

Vancouver's North Shore can be reached from downtown Vancouver on the **SeaBus** – a 15-minute boat ride departing regularly from the station located immediately east of Canada Place Cruise Terminal. The SeaBus docks at **Lonsdale Quay Market**, which features an assortment of shops and restaurants, and provides good views across the water of downtown Vancouver. Much of the North Shore's waterfront is industrial, with freighters loading lumber, wheat, coal and piles of yellow sulphur.

By road, the North Shore is reached via the **Lions Gate Bridge** – built in 1938 by the Guinness brewing family of Ireland to provide access to their new North Shore subdivision, called British Properties. This suspension bridge was named for The Lions – twin mountain peaks visible from the bridge. Its span is outlined at night by a string of lights which were a gift from the Guinness family to commemorate the city's 100th birthday in 1986.

One of the North Shore's most popular attractions is the **Grouse Mountain Sky Ride** – a ride in this aerial tramcar is one of the easiest ways to experience British Columbia's famous mountain scenery. The Sky Ride is one of North America's largest aerial tramway systems, whisking passengers 3,700 feet (1,100 m) above sea level to a mountain plateau where you can enjoy panoramic views of the city, sea and mountains. Snowcapped Mount Baker, in Washington State, can

Grouse Mountain Skyride

VANCOUVER & AREA

CRUISE ROUTES

MAIN ROUTES: - - - - - - -
ALTERNATE ROUTES: - - - - - - - - -
FERRY ROUTES: - - - - - - - - - - -

Howe Sound

Horseshoe Bay *(Ferry Terminal)*

Grouse Mountain

Capilano Suspension Bridge

Bowen Island

Pt. Atkinson

North Vancouver

Stanley Park

Burrard Inlet

Vancouver

HASTINGS

University of British Columbia

GRANVILLE OAK CAMBIE

Queen Elizabeth Park

LOUGHEED HWY

Strait of Georgia

Vancouver Int'l Airport

99

Fraser River

❶

Fort Langley

0   10

Steveston

N Miles

Ladner

Tsawwassen Ferry Terminal to Victoria

White Rock

CAN

U.S.A.

be seen on clear days. In summer, the Peak Chair can be ridden to the 4,100-foot summit for an even more spectacular 360-degree view. Facilities atop Grouse Mountain include three restaurants and numerous hiking trails.

Another popular North Shore attraction is the **Capilano Suspension Bridge** – the world's longest and highest suspension bridge. Swaying 25 storeys above a river gorge is a thrilling experience, but not for someone who's afraid of heights! The wood-and-wire bridge, 450 feet across, may feel rickety but its multi-strand pre-stressed cables are encased in 13 tons of concrete at either end. The original bridge was made of hemp rope and wood, and was built in 1889 by a Scotsman named George Grant Mackay using a team of horses to drag the heavy rope cables across the canyon. The year 2003 marked the opening of **Treetops Adventure** – a series of cable bridges suspended between viewing platforms that are 12 storeys above the forest floor. Capilano's newest and scariest attraction is **Cliffwalk** – a cantilevered walkway suspended from the side of a sheer granite cliff rising 300 feet above the canyon floor.

If time permits, consider a trip by road or rail to the alpine village of **Whistler**. Located 75 miles north of Vancouver, Whistler was the venue for downhill skiing, Nordic events and sliding sports at the 2010 Winter Olympics. View fabulous scenery all the way along the four-lane Sea to Sky highway or during the three-hour rail trip aboard Whistler Mountaineer to

(Above) Cliffwalk at Capilano Canyon. (Below) Whistler Village. (Facing page) The scenic Sea to Sky Highway.

this year-round resort. Outdoor activities include biking, zip lining, fishing and river rafting, while golf enthusiasts can choose from four championship courses. Hikers can explore the miles of valley trails or ride ski lifts up to the alpine trails. The Peak to Peak Gondola stretches a distance of 2.75 miles between two mountains. The European-style Whistler Village features pedestrian streets lined with sidewalk cafes, specialty shops and art galleries.

The **Sea to Sky Gondola** near Squamish (on the drive between Vancouver and Whistler) was popular within weeks of opening in spring 2014. Visitors enjoy a 10-minute ride from sea level up to the summit's viewing platform, lodge and hiking trails.

The Canadian Rockies

Among the array of land tours that can be combined with an Alaska cruise beginning or ending in Vancouver, an enduring favourite is the trip by road or rail to Western Canada's Rocky Mountains. Famous worldwide for their beauty, the national parks of Banff and Jasper, along with Yoho and Kootenay, encompass 7,800 square miles and three mountain ranges. Their rugged terrain was a formidable challenge to the early explorers. Aided by native guides familiar with mountain passes, they tackled the region's steep gorges and raging rivers, at times inching their way along canyon walls on rope ladders while sure-footed mountain goats watched nonchalantly from rock ledges.

Today, millions of visitors travel in comfort along the routes forged by these daring men. A transcontinental railroad was completed in the late 1800s, when Cornelius Van Horne of the Canadian Pacific Railway famously declared, "If we can't export the scenery, we'll import the tourists."

Today a leisurely rail journey can be enjoyed along winding tracks that cling to mountainsides and plunge through tunnels. For those who prefer to travel by motor coach or car, the highway is equally scenic, with the option of pulling over at scenic view-points or places of interest.

There are many highlights along this route, widely touted as one of the world's most scenic, including pristine **Emerald Lake** with views of the Burgess Shale, and **Takakkaw Falls** – one of the highest waterfalls in Canada, its water plunging from a crevice with such force that a distant viewing platform remains in perpetual drizzle.

The Great Divide is at Kicking Horse Pass, and the nearby **Spiral Tunnels** were built in 1907 to reduce the rail line's steep grade descending from the Continental Divide. On the western outskirts of the Rocky Mountain National Parks, is **Craigellachie** – named for a rock near Banffshire, Scotland (which symbolizes a call to battle) and the spot where the Last Spike was driven into Canada's transcontinental railway on November 7, 1885, joining the country from ocean to ocean.

(Above) Jasper Park Lodge
(Below) Banff Springs Hotel

Rocky Mountaineer Railtours traces the Bow River

The heart of the Rocky Mountain National Parks is **Banff**, the oldest and most visited of the four parks. In 1883, after some railway workers chanced upon the Cave and Basin hotsprings, an area was set aside as park reserve and became Canada's first national park. Initially called Rocky Mountains Park, the name was later changed to **Banff National Park** in honour of Banffshire, Scotland, the hometown of the CPR's Lord Strathcona.

Jasper National Park was established in 1907 when a second, more northerly rail line was built. The townsites of Banff and Jasper quickly became service centers for railway workers and park visitors.

Both towns contain lovely stone churches, log buildings and luxury hotel resorts. Banff's most famous man-made landmark is the baronial **Banff Springs Hotel**. Resembling a Scottish castle, this magnificent hotel was built by the Canadian Pacific Railway. The

Banff Springs golf course was considered a Stanley Thompson masterpiece when it opened in 1929, and its famous par-three Cauldron features a green bounded by a cliff rising nearly 3,000 feet.

The town of **Jasper** is smaller than Banff, but the park itself is larger. It too contains a famous railway-built resort called **Jasper Park Lodge**, which overlooks Lac Beauvert and glacier-clad Mount Edith Cavell. The Jasper Park Lodge golf course was designed in 1925 by Stanley Thompson and remains the template for present-day architects with its seamless layout amid spectacular mountain vistas and lakeside settings.

The parks' natural habitat ranges from sub-alpine meadows filled with wildflowers to valley slopes covered with stands of Douglas fir. The parks are home to dozens of species of wildlife. Moose, elk,

A morning view of Lake Louise and Victoria Glacier.

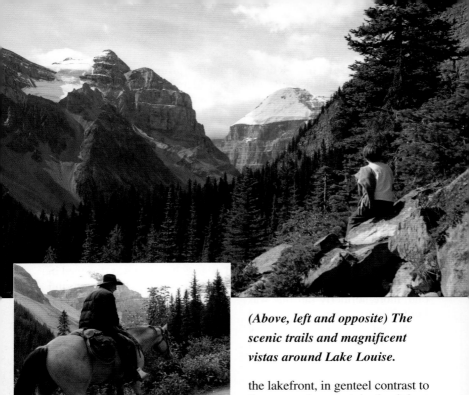

(Above, left and opposite) The scenic trails and magnificent vistas around Lake Louise.

mountain goats, bighorn sheep and deer are often seen by park visitors – most frequently in the early morning or evening. Less frequently sighted are the bears, cougars and wolves that roam the parks. Gondola rides provide sweeping views of forested valleys and snowcapped peaks.

Summer weather in the Rockies is pleasantly warm with occasional hot spells. Throughout the summer, the parking lot at **Lake Louise** in Banff National Park is filled with cars bearing license plates from across North America. Described by many as the most beautiful place on earth, turquoise-hued Lake Louise is a soothing sight. Lawns and flowers border the lakefront, in genteel contrast to the rugged mountain backdrop which is dominated by Victoria Glacier. Chateau Lake Louise, another railway-built resort, overlooks the lake and provides access to canoe rentals and hiking trails.

The highway connecting Banff and Jasper is called the **Icefields Parkway**, and it snakes through the highest, most rugged mountains in the Canadian Rockies. They form the Great Divide and contain the **Columbia Icefield**. Snowcoach tours prompt many travellers to pause in their journey and take a ride on a glacier, or visit the new **Glacier Skywalk** with its glass-bottomed viewing platform that extends from a cliff, high above the Sunwapta Valley.

The majority of tours to the Rockies run between Vancouver and Calgary, by road or by rail. The scenery ranges from alpine to the arid ranchland and vineyards of British Columbia's interior. The rail line and highway skirt the edge of the Fraser River canyon where, at its narrowest point, is a deep gorge called **Hell's Gate**. The Fraser River drains a watershed the size of Britain and the whitewater rushing through Hell's Gate can be viewed from an aerial tramway that descends 500 feet down to water level.

The city of **Calgary**, situated in the rolling foothills of Canada's Rocky Mountains, enjoys a location of remarkable contrast. The western horizon is dominated by the snowcapped peaks and timbered slopes of the rugged Rockies. To the east, stretching as far as the eye can see, is a vast grass-covered plain where herds of buffalo once roamed. This is cattle country, and Calgary's cowboy heritage is displayed throughout the city, its western hospitality symbolized by a white Stetson, the wide-brimmed hat long favoured by cowboys. Each summer the city hosts the Calgary Stampede, and the roof of the city's sports arena – built for the 1988 Winter Olympics – is shaped like a giant saddle.

(Below) Chateau Lake Louise

The city began as a fort, built at the confluence of the Bow and Elbow Rivers in 1875 by the North West Mounted Police to maintain law and order among the region's whiskey traders and buffalo hunters. They named it Fort Calgary after a bay on the Isle of Mull in Scotland. Today Calgary is the administrative center of Alberta's oil and gas industry and a transportation gateway for Banff National Park, just an hour away by road.

CANADA'S INSIDE PASSAGE

Vancouver to Prince Rupert

There are many scenic waterways in this world, but there is only one Inside Passage. Stretching northward from Puget Sound in Washington State to Glacier Bay in Southeast Alaska, this vast and intricate coastline of winding channels, forested islands and turquoise fjords is unsurpassed in scenic beauty. The Canadian portion of the Inside Passage spans 500 nautical miles, from the southern tip of Vancouver Island to the exposed waters of Dixon Entrance – where the border lies between British Columbia and Alaska.

Cruise ships departing from Vancouver head northward up the Strait of Georgia, a major body of water that is busy with commercial traffic, including car ferries, freighters, fishing boats, tugs towing barges and, from May through September, cruise ships. The southern Strait of Georgia is dominated by the **Fraser River**'s outflow, especially from May to early August when the freshet is running. This green, silt-laden freshwater is run-off from mainland mountains which flows into the Fraser River and eventually drains into the Strait of Georgia.

The Fraser River is British Columbia's most important waterway. It originates in the Rocky Mountains, at Yellowhead Pass, and meanders for nearly 900 miles before emptying into the Strait of Georgia. Along the way, the Fraser's tributaries drain a watershed encompassing nearly one-third of the province. Its basin, which supports half of the province's agricultural land, is home to two of every three B.C. residents. Thousands of waterfowl nest annually on the river's delta and migrating salmon return regularly to the mouth of the Fraser, which contains North America's chief spawning grounds for the Pacific salmon.

A northbound cruise ship approaches Texada Island in the Strait of Georgia.

The fishing village of Steveston lies near the mouth of the mighty Fraser River.

Lying opposite the mouth of the Fraser River is **Vancouver Island** – a single, mountainous island nearly 300 miles in length which is named for the British sea captain who first circumnavigated it in 1792. Vancouver Island buffers the southern Inside Passage from swells rolling in from the Pacific Ocean, but there's one thing it can't stop from reaching these protected waters – the tide. Controlled by the gravitational pull of the moon, a rising tide rushes with cyclical predictability around both ends of Vancouver Island and pours into the straits and channels of the Inside Passage. When this onslaught of water is compressed through narrow passes and channels, bottlenecks occur. But, unlike car traffic which comes to a standstill in such circumstances, water does the opposite – it turns into churning rapids complete with whirlpools, back eddies and rip tides.

The numerous channels that weave through the islands clogging the Inside Passage are all affected by tidal currents. Mariners pay special attention to the area's tide tables (published annually by the Canadian Hydrographic Service) in order to reach a pass when the water is slack and presents no danger. Even large cruise ships time their transit of **Seymour Narrows** – one of the swiftest tidal passes of the Inside Passage – to coincide with slack water. Upon leaving Vancouver Harbour to commence a northbound cruise, ships will sometimes take an unexpected detour into the scenic waterways of Howe Sound. This is not just to provide passengers with a lovely porthole view during dinner, but to delay the ship's arrival at Seymour Narrows. The side trip ensures a safe passage through the Narrows – especially if a large tide is running.

Howe Sound was once the world's largest log booming ground and recreational boats often tied to these log booms, their skippers hammering a couple of 'dogs' (metal eye hooks) into the outer log for attaching the mooring lines. The only drawback to docking at a log boom was the possibility of a tug arriving in the middle of the night to tow the 'dock' away, complete with attached boats. These log booms featured prominently in *The Beachcombers*, a popular TV show which ran for 370 episodes and gained an international audience. Most logs are now sorted and stored on dry land.

Nanaimo

Lying across the Strait of Georgia, on Vancouver Island, is the small city of Nanaimo. This emerging cruise port began as a coal-mining town in the 1850s. With today's population of about 73,000, Nanaimo has retained a small-town ambience, and cruise passengers disembarking here will find numerous attractions within walking distance of the

Howe Sound is the first inlet a northbound ship passes on its way to Alaska.

Shore Excursions
NANAIMO
Shore excursions offered in Nanaimo include a heritage walking tour and driving tours to outlying attractions such as a raptor center and Cathedral Grove Provincial Park where a protected stand of old-growth forest contains towering Douglas Fir trees that are more than 800 years old. Other places visited from Nanaimo include Qualicum Beach Village, the historic towns of Ladysmith and Chemainus, and the scenic drive to Port Alberni for a ride in rail cars pulled by a vintage steam locomotive.

tender dock. A visitor infocentre is housed in The Bastion – a wooden military bastion built in 1853 by the Hudson's Bay Company to protect British settlers who came to work in the local coal mines. They called their new home Colville Town, but the native name of Nanaimo, which means 'big strong tribe' in reference to five villages located in the area, has endured. The city's museum, featuring historic coal mining exhibits, is located nearby on a hill overlooking the waterfront.

A pedestrian seawall winds along the harborside, past the Boat Basin's fishboat docks and seafood stands where you may just sight a river otter. These furry animals have become regular (albeit non-paying) customers at Trollers Fish & Chips – a popular floating restaurant where the otters come up through a hole used for discarding fish guts. The waterfront promenade leads to **Maffeo Sutton Park** and its man-made tidal pool called Swy-A-

The waterfront promenade in Nanaimo, on Vancouver Island.

Lana Lagoon. A foot passenger ferry departs here on regular 10-minute crossings to nearby **Newcastle Island** – Nanaimo's equivalent of Vancouver's Stanley Park. The entire island is a provincial park, with a visitor pavilion located near the ferry dock and miles of hiking trails encircling and crisscrossing the island, which is home to blacktail deer, beavers, river otters, rabbits and raccoons. **Protection Island**, best known for its Dinghy Dock Pub, is also serviced by a passenger ferry that departs from the Boat Basin.

In the waters due north of Nanaimo there lies a military test range called **Area Whiskey Golf** which, during the Cold War, gained an ominous reputation. Tales circulating through waterfront pubs ranged from the believable to the bizarre, including one that the mountain behind the military base at **Nanoose Bay** had been hollowed out to hold nuclear submarines. In actual fact, the range is strictly a testing facility, under the command of Canadian military personnel who watch over Area Whiskey Golf from Winchelsea Island Control. The test site, established in 1967, is owned and operated by the Canadian government. It was chosen because its bottom topography is perfectly suited for technical acoustic testings, and most of the tests are conducted by Canadian and American surface ships and submarines. Whenever Whiskey Golf is being used for testing non-explosive torpedoes, sonobuoys or sonars, vessels are not allowed to pass through the 'active' portion of this restricted area, and any boats caught wandering through the restricted zone are escorted to safer waters. Public safety is the reason for this no-trespassing policy, and even a killer whale passing through will result in a test being cancelled.

The **Sunshine Coast**, which stretches from Howe Sound to Desolation Sound, has been attracting visitors since the late 1800s, when steamships ran excursions to summer resorts along this scenic section of coastline. One of the prettiest anchorages is **Smuggler Cove**. It's now a marine park but during Prohibition in the 1920s it was a storage area for bootleg whiskey that was smuggled by boat into the U.S.A. American yachtsmen who visited Smuggler Cove in those days had a favorite song which went like this:

Smuggler Cove is one of many small-boat anchorages found along B.C.'s Inside Passage.

Four and twenty Yankees feeling rather dry,
Sailed into Canada to have a drink of rye,
When the rye was open they all began to sing,
God bless America, but God Save the King!

The Sunshine Coast is today renowned for its scenic cruising which includes **Princess Louisa Inlet** – one of Canada's most spectacular fjords. Three steep-sided reaches twist inland past hanging waterfalls before culminating at Princess Louisa Inlet where the Chatterbox Falls, fed by glaciers and lakes, plunge 1,800 feet down granite cliffs into the still water. Erle Stanley Gardner, the American writer who created Perry Mason, wrote in his *Log of a Landlubber* that he didn't need to see the rest of the world after seeing Princess Louisa Inlet. "One views the scenery with bared head and choking feeling of the throat," he wrote. "It is more than beautiful. It is sacred."

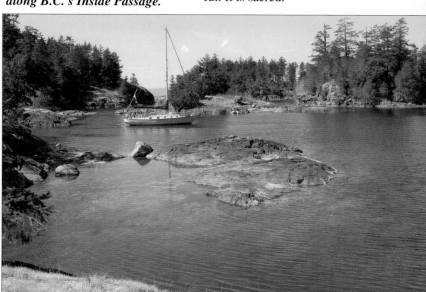

The natives called the inlet Suivoolot, meaning warm and sunny. When James (Mac) Macdonald, a Nevada prospector, laid eyes on 'The Princess' in 1919 he instantly succumbed to her charms, obtained land by the falls and built a log cabin. After years of welcoming mariners to his very own Yosemite Valley and fjords of Norway, Mac turned this prized property over to the newly formed Princess Louisa International Society to preserve the inlet "as God created it, unspoiled by the hand of man" so that "all may enjoy its peace and beauty." The Society has chapters in Renton, Washington, and Victoria, British Columbia, and it functions in cooperation with BC Parks to maintain the visitor floats, wharves and picnic shelter.

Ships departing from Vancouver spend a relaxing first day at sea, cruising the scenic waters of Canada's Inside Passage.

Texada Island is a large island lying in the middle of the Strait of Georgia, often passed by northbound cruise ships as the summer sun is setting to the northwest. It was on Texada that a large whiskey still produced the bootleg liquor that reached thirsty Americans via Smuggler Cove. Before that, in the 1870s, whaling was a profitable enterprise, with processing operations set up in Blubber Bay at the island's northern tip. The next island over, called **Lasqueti**, is home to domestic and wild sheep which wander the rugged hillsides and cliff-edged shorelines. In rocky coves oysters grow in abundance, the commercially farmed ones shipped to gourmet restaurants in faraway cities. The pace of life on Lasqueti is tranquil and the island residents carefully guard their isolation. No car ferry calls at Lasqueti, so motor vehicles and other large items must be brought in by barge. Nearby Jedediah Island was donated to the provincial government for a marine park.

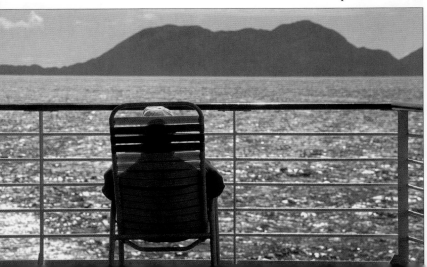

Also nearby is **Desolation Sound Marine Park**, a very popular destination for recreational boaters from Vancouver and Seattle. Named by Captain Vancouver in 1792, Desolation Sound is anything but desolate during the summer months when sunny weather transforms this wilderness park, unreachable by road, into a popular destination for boaters and kayakers who anchor or beach their craft in one of numerous stream-fed anchorages where trails lead past cascading falls to pristine mountain lakes. There is little tidal current in the Desolation Sound area, so the seawater is warm enough for swimming in summer. The same cannot be said of the waters in nearby Discovery Passage (part of the cruise ship route), where tidal currents are extremely swift.

A small cruise ship steams past the entrance to Desolation Sound – a popular destination for recreational boaters.

Campbell River

If any port along the British Columbia coast can lay claim to being the heart of the Inside Passage, it might well be the small city of Campbell River. A steady stream of vessels, from kayaks to cruise ships, passes by Campbell River throughout the summer, traveling this main artery of the Inside Passage. They are following the route first charted by Captain George Vancouver in 1792 as they pass beneath the white cliffs of **Cape Mudge** at the southern entrance to Discovery Passage.

A full century later, a rush of steamships carrying Klondike-bound prospectors headed north up **Discovery Passage**, past the mouth of the Campbell River. Passing beneath their keels were huge runs of salmon, which thrive in the cold, swift-flowing waters of Discovery Passage and have earned Campbell River the right to proclaim itself Salmon Capital of the World. Five species of salmon migrate up the Campbell

River, but it's the prized chinook (called King in Alaska) that first caught the world's attention when, in 1896, Sir Richard Musgrave wrote an article for *Field* magazine in which he praised his native guides' simple yet skillful method of catching these fighting fish from dugout canoes.

In the 1920s, a boatbuilder named Ned Painter and his wife June began renting wooden rowboats at the mouth of the Campbell River. This modest operation evolved from fishing camp to cottage resort to the opening of **Painter's Lodge** in 1938. This historic resort (which burned in 1985 and was replaced with a modern facility) achieved worldwide fame as a sportfishing retreat and attracted many a celebrity to Campbell River, including Bing Crosby and Bob Hope. **April Point Lodge** on

Carnival Spirit cruises along Discovery Passage, past Campbell River.

Quadra Island, established in 1945 by the Peterson family of San Francisco, also became a popular sportfishing retreat.

The salmon caught in Discovery Passage are returning from the open ocean to their spawning rivers. Salmon like the cold, swift-flowing waters that race down the east side of Vancouver Island, and experienced fishing guides learn how to read the tides and currents in their area to figure out where the best fishing is each day.

In addition to its world-class sportfishing, Campbell River is a base for ecotourism. **Shore excursions** include sportfishing, kayaking, hiking and even snorkeling with the salmon. Wildlife viewing is also offered, as are tours to Canyon View Trail in Elk Falls Provincial Park and to the alpine resort at Mount Washington. The ships dock at the new **Wei Wai Kum Cruise Ship Terminal**, where disembarking passengers can visit a traditional native village showcasing local art and crafts.

The Ripple Rock Trail provides a close look at **Seymour Narrows**, which lies six miles north of Campbell River, at the narrowest part of Discovery Passage. This is where infamous **Ripple Rock** – a two-headed pinnacle rock in the middle of the Narrows – used to lie just nine feet below the water's surface at low water. It caused the sinking of more than 100 vessels before its top was blown off in 1958. Explosives were inserted into the core of Ripple Rock via an underwater tunnel that connected with Maud Island. When the world's largest non-atomic explosion was over, the top of Ripple Rock lay a safe 45 feet below chart datum.

Even with that hazard removed, Seymour Narrows can generate more than 13 knots of mid-channel current on a large tide. When this jet-like stream rubs against the nearly motionless peripheral waters, it produces a line of whirlpools down both sides of the pass. Most passengers will be spared this impressive sight because ship captains usually time their transit of the Narrows to coincide with slack water.

It's worth stepping out on deck to watch as your ship glides under the power line spanning Seymour Narrows. The vertical clearance used to be 161 feet – just high enough for cruise liners to pass beneath it at high water. Then, in 1995, Royal Caribbean Cruises positioned its new megaship *Legend of the Seas*

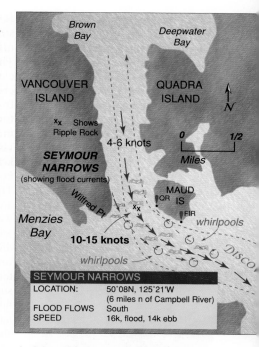

SEYMOUR NARROWS	
LOCATION:	50°08N, 125°21'W
	(6 miles n of Campbell River)
FLOOD FLOWS	South
SPEED	16k, flood, 14k ebb

A rising tide is squeezed through Seymour Narrows, creating swift currents and churning whirlpools. Twin X's mark the location of Ripple Rock.

on an Inside Passage itinerary and the hydro line had to be raised by about 20 feet. The perspective when looking skyward from a ship's deck makes the wires appear unnervingly close to a ship's superstructure.

Chatham Point marks the intersection of Discovery Passage with **Johnstone Strait** – the most direct route through the Inside Passage and the one used by commercial traffic. It was named in 1792 for Lieutenant James

Johnstone, an officer in charge of survey parties under the command of Captain Vancouver. These survey expeditions were carried out in open boats, and crewmen would draw on the oars from dawn until dusk and sometimes well into the night. Stowed in the boats were two weeks' provisions, survey instruments, muskets for shooting game, and trinkets for trade with the natives. These expeditions were not pleasant jaunts. The climate then was wetter and cooler than it is today, and the men were constantly drenched by rain. They often ran low on food when an expedition took longer than anticipated so, to supplement their provisions, they hunted, fished and bartered with natives. At night they camped on shore while the men on watch cooked the next day's food over open fires. If the forest above the highwater mark was impenetra-

(Left) The top of dreaded Ripple Rock, in the middle of Seymour Narrows (shown below), was finally blown off in 1958.

ble, they were forced to sleep in the boats. This was something the men detested and some preferred to take their chances on shore. On one occasion, when swamped by a rising tide, an oarsman was so tired he didn't wake up and was floating away when roused by his companions.

Johnstone, a talented young officer, was pushing his survey party to its limit as they made their way north in search of a northwest passage. They tried in vain to row through one set of rapids and had to haul the boat through with ropes. Some natives were watching all this activity from shore and lent a hand.

Johnstone's first clue to the existence of Vancouver Island came with the tide. While he and his men were sleeping on shore one night, they were unexpectedly swamped by a tide that was rising instead of falling. This meant the tide was coming in through a northern entrance and this revelation diverted Johnstone's attention from tracing the continental shoreline to locating a seaward passage at the top of Vancouver

Island. Johnstone Strait is now a marine highway traveled by ships, tugs and fishboats. Much of the forested land viewed from your ship is Crown Land (owned by the provincial government) and tree farm licenses are granted to forestry companies which harvest the timber. Considerable controversy surrounds a common logging practice called clearcutting, which is outlawed in sensitive areas such as alongside salmon streams.

A century ago, logging was done by hand. Men would fell a tree with axes while standing on spring boards wedged into tree trunks. The timber was hauled out by oxen along skid trails to the local mill. In 1889 the Union Steamship Company was established to service remote coastal settlements, many of which were built on floats and could move from one sheltered cove to another. Initially these logging camps were a collection of bunkhouses,

The cruise ships round Chatham Point when entering or leaving Johnstone Strait.

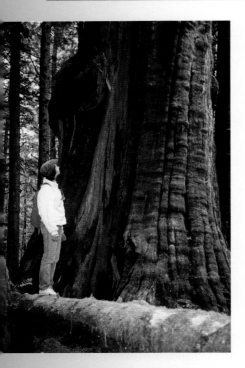

(Above) A cedar snag left standing by hand loggers at the turn of the 19th century, when loggers and their families often lived in floating villages (below).

cookshacks and equipment sheds, but with the growing number of women in the camps – hired to cook or accompanying their husbands – tidy floathomes became a common sight. Picket fences, split from cedar, would prevent small children from falling in the water, and some floats were large enough to hold a garden. If the collection of floats included a large empty one, this would serve as a communal tennis court or baseball diamond. One logging camp evolved into a floating village with a store, community hall, post office and school.

Those built on land included **Blind Channel** on West Thurlow Island, where a sawmill was built in 1910. The community became a center for nearby logging camps, with a hotel and dock built to accommodate the Union Steamship boats that called with freight and passengers. A one-room schoolhouse at Blind Channel served the area, and children not living on West Thurlow Island were rowed to school by their mothers. By 1918 the popu-

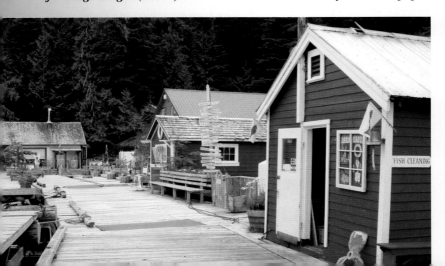

lation at Blind Channel had soared to 120, with a cannery and shingle mill in operation. The mill's boiler usually had enough steam left at the end of the day to power a generator that lit up everyone's home with a recent invention called the light bulb. A gas engine provided auxiliary power on Saturday nights when the dance hall was lit. Loggers from nearby camps would descend on Blind Channel and forget their worries as they kicked up their heels and "skidded the ladies across the floor."

World War II brought changes to the British Columbia coast. Following Japan's attack on Pearl Harbor, blackouts went into effect and the coast darkened. Lighthouses were covered, vessels traveling at night couldn't use running lights and no weather reports were issued. People of Japanese descent living on the coast were relocated to the interior and their fishing vessels were impounded. To protect against Japanese invasion, flying boat stations were established and a reserve unit of fishermen within the Royal Canadian Navy – dubbed the Gumboot Navy – was formed to patrol the coast. **Yorke Island**, at the junction of Johnstone Strait and Sunderland Channel, became a military outpost designed to detect and destroy any enemy ships approaching Vancouver from the north with its searchlight and 6" turret guns. Yorke Island never came under attack and the last firing practice took place on August 10, 1945. The troops were coming home, the Gumboot Navy had

disbanded and the British Columbia coast, like the rest of the world, entered a new era.

A shortage of skilled tree fallers on the coast during the war years had spurred the development of gasoline-powered saws. Following the war, improved machinery, centralization of sawmilling operations and the use of floatplanes to fly logging crews in and out of camps, all contributed to the decline of coastal logging communities. Once a working coast, its scenic waterways began attracting recreational boaters and, eventually, eco-tourists who fly to the area's remote wilderness lodges.

Johnstone Strait has become famous for its population of resident killer whales, which feed here on salmon and are frequently sighted in the vicinity of **Robson**

A World War II ammunition bunker on Yorke Island.

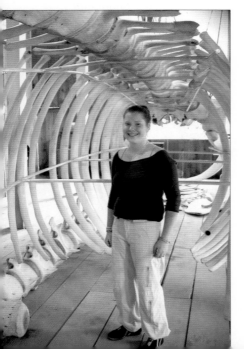

(Above) Yorke Island guns guarded the B.C. coast from enemy invasion during World War II. (Below) A fin whale skeleton displayed in the Telegraph Cove Museum.

Bight. In 1982 this bight was protected as an ecological reserve to prevent vessels from entering and disturbing the **killer whales** that linger here to rub against rounded pebbles in the bight's rocky shallows. The nearby boardwalk village of **Telegraph Cove**, founded in 1912 as a one-room telegraph station, has become a popular base for whale-watching tours in Johnstone Strait, while serious students of whale behavior set up camp on a bluff of West Cracroft Island, directly opposite Robson Bight. The whales often travel between Johnstone Strait and Blackfish Sound via Blackney Passage, which is the route taken by northbound cruise ships, and the Pacific Killer Whale Foundation monitors underwater whale vocalizations from Hanson Island. The whale museum in Telegraph Cove houses a killer whale interpretation center and displays the skeleton of a 66-foot-long fin whale discovered on top of the bow bulb of the cruise ship *Galaxy* in the summer of 1999.

ROBSON BIGHT
Killer Whale routes: ·······
Cruise Routes: - - - - -

Southbound cruise ships often follow Broughton Strait past **Alert Bay** on Cormorant Island (named for the British naval survey ships *Alert* and *Cormorant*). Alert Bay is a major port for the commercial fishery and a cultural and commercial center of the Kwakwaka'wakw.

At one end of town, along the waterfront, is the 'Namgis Burial Grounds where the first of its totem poles was raised in the late 19th century. At the other end of town is the **U'mista Cultural Centre**, a modern museum built in the traditional plank-and-beam style. Inside is a collection of

(Above) Killer whales inhabit Johnstone Strait from spring through fall. (Below) A welcome gate greets visitors to Alert Bay.

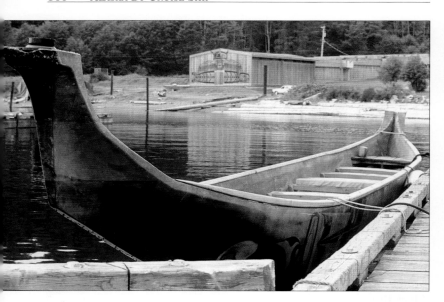

(Above) A dugout canoe bobs on its moorings in front of the U'mista Cultural Centre at Alert Bay. (Below) Totem poles at the town's burial grounds.

elaborate masks, rattles and whistles that are used at Kwakwaka'wakw potlatch celebrations of feasting, dancing and gift giving.

A hike up the hillside behind the museum, along residential streets, takes visitors to the Big House. A community center, it is primarily used for potlatches. A two-day potlatch was underway in August 2007 when **Oprah Winfrey** arrived by private yacht at Alert Bay and paid a visit to the Big House where she was given the honorary name Noxsolaga, meaning 'wise woman.'

Standing near the Big House is the **world's tallest totem pole**, at 173 feet high. Raised in 1973, the pole displays various crests and is crowned with Sun Man, crest of the Quatsino. This pole has become a point of interest for passing cruise ships, which glide slowly past Cormorant Island before entering Johnstone Strait.

At the western end of Broughton Strait is the logging town of **Port McNeill**, named for a Boston-born captain hired by the Hudson's Bay Company during the fur trade. Across the water from Port McNeill, on Malcolm Island, is the fishing port of **Sointula** (a Finnish word meaning 'harmony') which was founded at the turn of the last century by pioneer farmers from Finland.

The lighthouse at Pulteney Point on Malcolm Island is one of numerous **lighthouses** built after gold was discovered on the Klondike in 1896 and steamship traffic increased dramatically as prospectors rushed north along the Inside Passage. A network of lighthouses, buoys and beacons helped keep many, but not all, vessels off the rocks.

When a steamer ran aground in 1916 off **Scarlett Point**, the lighthouse keeper who rowed out to retrieve the crew was greeted by the ship's captain. "I know all the rocks around here. And this," he said, gesturing to the one that had just ripped a hole in his keel, "is one of them." The steamships of a century ago have been replaced with today's cruise liners. Also plying these waters are car ferries. Those of the Alaska Marine Highway travel the Inside Passage between Alaska and Bellingham, Washington, while the BC Ferry Corporation provides service to British Columbia's north coast out of **Port Hardy.**

Port Hardy is a fishing and forestry town, and its local museum features **Edward Curtis**'s epic film *Land of the War Canoe*. A self-taught photographer from Seattle, Curtis devoted three decades of his life to producing a 20-volume collection of photographs and a film about the Kwakwaka'wakw called *In the Land of the Head Hunters*, which premiered in New York in 1914 and has since been renamed *Land of the War Canoe.*

A Disney ship cruises past the fishing town of Port McNeill.

Ketchikan

ALASKA
BRITISH COLUMBIA

DIXON ENTRANCE

U.S. pilots are picked up
in this area for Ketchikan
bound ships.

Khutzeymateen
Inlet

Cruise ships stop briefly
in this area to pick up or
drop off Canadian pilots.

Dundas I

*Green
Island*

Old
Massett

*Triple
Island*

Metlakatla
**Prince
Rupert**

Tyee

HAIDA

Porcher
Island

Grenville Channel

KITIMAT

GWAII

*Bonilla
Island*

(formerly Queen

*Captain
Cove*

Banks
Island

Pitt
Island

Charlotte

Hartley Bay

H E C A T E

*Wreck of
Queen of the North*

Islands)

Butedale
(aband.)

P A C I F I C   O C E A N

Campania
Island

S T R A I T

**Princess
Royal Island
(Great Bear Rainforest)**

Anthony
Island (Ninstints)

Aristazabal
Island

*Boat
Bluff
Light*

Klemtu

**Cruise ship route
from Seattle**

**Cruise ship route
from Vancouver**

Ivory I

*Laredo
Sound*

*Dryad
Pt. Light*

HAIDA GWAII

Bella
Bella

CRUISE ROUTES

MAIN ROUTES: - - - - -
ALTERNATE ROUTES: ·········
NATIVE SETTLEMENTS: ●

**Hakai
Recreation
Area**

●Namu

*Queen
Charlotte
Sound*

Calvert
Island

*Fitz Hugh
Sound*

Egg I

0   40

N

Miles

*Course of Sway
(See Anne's Journal)*

Pihe I.

Scott Islands

*Triangle
Island*

Scarlett Pt.

Pine Island stands like a lonely sentinel at Queen Charlotte Strait's western entrance, bearing the full brunt of Queen Charlotte Sound's winter storms, Until 1907, when a lighthouse was erected, Pine Island's only visitors were the seabirds who nest here, including the Rhinoceros Auklet. These nocturnal seabirds tend to make ungraceful landings when flying back from sea after dark. Veering in for a landing, they often hit a tree and fall with a thud to the ground, which is where they burrow anyway. Pine Island is today a pilot station where cruise ships pause to embark or disembark Canadian pilots.

Ships that are tracing the inner channels of British Columbia's north coast will have pilots on board, while those transiting the open waters of Hecate Strait will not. The inner route is along **Fitz Hugh Sound**, which is a long, wide channel that hugs the mainland coast and is shielded by islands from the open ocean. On

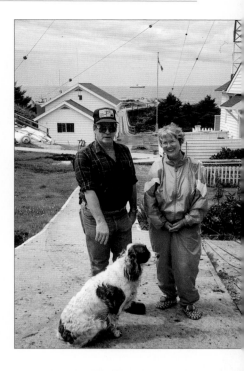

(Above) The lighthouse keepers at Egg Island. (Below) A purse seiner sets its net in the waters of Fitz Hugh Sound.

Anne's Alaska Journal

Few bodies of water have a more notorious reputation than Queen Charlotte Sound. Winter storms here are ferocious, one of which Jack London describes in *The Call of the Wild* when Buck is on a ship bound for Alaska.

Fortunately it was summertime when Bill and I sailed our 35-foot sloop *Sway* across Queen Charlotte Sound to Haida Gwaii. There are easier ways to get to these isolated islands, but we decided to sail directly from the north end of Vancouver Island, across 140 miles of open water.

We had taken our Scottish terrier for his last walk ashore and fresh coffee was in the thermos when we raised anchor at 0700 hours on a cloudless July morning and headed into the Sound (see map page 168). A pod of dolphins swam alongside our boat as we rode the swells, our bow climbing to the top of each crest, then plunging into the trough on the other side. The wind, a moderate northwesterly, stayed on our nose

Dreaded McEwan Rock on the edge of Queen Charlotte Sound.

as we beat to weather across Cook Bank.

With Cape Scott off our port, we tacked away from land, our stalwart craft pounding through the steep seas. Eventually, my stomach protested. Following my third trip to the lifelines, I retired to the cabin and lay on the settee, a nervous dog lying on top of me.

By mid-afternoon the wind was blowing 25 knots and the waves were climbing to 15 feet. Spray shot across the decks as our boat slammed into wave after wave. Seawater seeped down the navel pipe and along a forepeak bulkhead onto the cabin sole where it formed a sloshing puddle. At one point, the latch on a hanging locker ripped off and the freely-swinging door began bashing against a bulkhead.

Occasionally I relieved Bill at the helm. As twilight approached we decided to reef the mainsail in case the wind hardened further during the night. We hove to and, lying broadside to the swells, *Sway* rocked in front of an amber sky. Then, with the main reefed, we pointed her bow back into the wind and waves.

By nightfall we had covered 50 miles. The waves kept coming, and Bill and I now wore harnesses clipped to a padeye in the cockpit. Our dog Tuck wore a life jacket and was attached to me with a line. The three of us sat in the forward corner of the cockpit watching the loran as if it were television. It was a reassuring presence, constantly telling us our position and speed over ground. The sky was filled with stars.

We switched to a port tack just before midnight and the ride became more comfortable. Bill went below for a nap but before he could lie down I had him back on deck to check out a boat a few miles off our starboard bow.

"It's a seiner fishing," Bill said. "He's been motoring back and forth for the past hour."

A minute later I called down to Bill that we were on a collision course. He came up again. I suggested we tack away. He suggested we hold our course. A minute later we crossed the bow of the slow-moving seiner and Bill was finally able to catch some sleep. But then I saw another boat off our starboard bow. It looked like a large white fishboat coming straight at us. "I see another boat out here," I called down to Bill. He popped his head out of the hatch.

"It's just the moon," he said. The moon? I looked at it for a while.

Sure enough, the rising moon had cast light onto a low cloud bank and, with no land to lend perspective to this apparition, it looked like a large white boat.

Throughout the brief northern night, shearwaters and storm petrels circled the boat. At dawn, we shook the reef out of the main and shortly after that we started the engine and motorsailed. We lit the diesel stove and made some breakfast. I was ready to try a cup of chamomile tea and Tuck was interested in food and water.

By dinnertime the islands of Haida Gwaii (formerly known as Queen Charlotte Islands) had appeared on the horizon. We were in the homestretch now. The sun was setting as we drew near the volcanic mountains of Kunghit Island standing black against a fiery sky.

We slipped through still waters and anchored in Balcom Inlet under the watchful eyes of a raven, its call the only sound in the silent night. The next day we would explore the anchorage's moss-carpeted forest, and picnic beside a clear mountain stream. But first we would sleep.

Anne sailing among the pristine islands of Haida Gwaii.

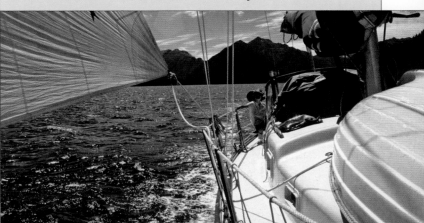

the mainland shore of Fitz Hugh Sound is the historic cannery town of **Namu**, its boardwalks leading past weatherbeaten buildings supported on pilings. Namu in its heyday was a bustling place during the salmon season, when tins of salmon rolled off the assembly lines and were shipped to markets in North America and abroad. The nearby Koeye River attracts grizzly bears in summer with its large salmon runs.

Also accessed off Fitz Hugh Sound is **Hakai Luxvbalis Conservancy** – the largest marine protected area on the British Columbia coast, its scrub-forested islands providing boaters with sheltered anchorages and access to miles of ocean beaches. Most of the park is wilderness, with floating fish camps operating in these waters each summer.

Ships following Fitz Hugh Sound will sometimes proceed along narrow Lama Pass and cruise past the Heiltsuk community of **Bella Bella** on Campbell Island. In the summer of 1993, this remote village hosted a week-long festival and its population doubled when people from 30 different native groups converged on Bella Bella. Many arrived in traditional dugout canoes they had paddled from as far away as Washington State.

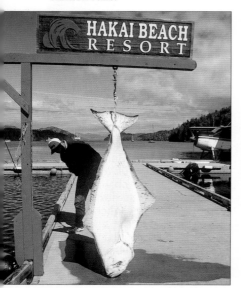

(Left) A halibut caught in Hakai Recreation Area is weighed in. (Below) A small cruise ship pulls into Captain Cove on B.C.'s north coast.

Just north of Bella Bella is **Dryad Point Lighthouse**. Ship passengers are treated to a close look as the ship makes a tight turn around this point. The lighthouse, like many others along the Inside Passage, was established during the Gold Rush to aid steamships following this maze-like route to the Klondike.

The lighthouse on **Ivory Island**, at the other end of Seaforth Channel, was built a year earlier – in 1898. Completely exposed to the open ocean, it bears the brunt of winter storms rolling in from the Pacific. Farther along the meandering maze of interconnecting waterways is **Boat Bluff Lighthouse**. This scenic lighthouse overlooks Sarah Passage and sits on an island inhabited by wolves. One former keeper, fearing for the safety of his small children, asked for a transfer from this lighthouse.

(Right) Dryad Point Lighthouse near Bella Bella was built in 1899. (Below) Boat Bluff Lighthouse.

The natives were always wary and respectful of wolves. In her *Klee Wyck* stories, published in 1941, the artist Emily Carr wrote of an elder who, upon seeing her about to enter a forest, "ran and pulled me back, shaking his head and scolding me . . .   The Indians forbade their children to go into the forest, not even into its edge. I was to them a child, ignorant about the wild things which they knew so well."

Wild things are found throughout the Inside Passage of British Columbia, and a huge tract of northern coastal land has come to be known as the **Great Bear Rainforest**. Lying within this remote and relatively uninhabited area is Princess Royal Island, home to a rare type of black bear called a kermode. A genetic mutation has given this black bear a fur coat that is not black, brown or cinnamon – but pure white. These rare bears are not easy to find in the old-growth forest of an island the size of Princess Royal, but biologists with the Valhalla Wilderness Society have been conducting research here since 1990 to determine the bears' population and habitat. The Society proposed that a kermode sanctuary be established on Princess Royal Island to save the white 'spirit' bears that live here and, in 2001, a logging moratorium was imposed by the provincial government. When a Canadian

An Alaska-bound tug heads up
Princess Royal Channel.

schoolboy named Simon Jackson decided to found the Spirit Bear Youth Coalition, his impassioned activism sparked Hollywood's interest which resulted in the independent production of an animated feature film called *The Spirit Bear*, its profits helping to preserve the kermodes' habitat.

The narrow reaches of **Princess Royal Channel** are lined on either side with cliff-hanging waterfalls that vary from single strands to tumbling cascades. Halfway along this watery corridor a small island splits the channel. Ships often steer to the south of Work Island, affording passengers a full view of the abandoned cannery at Butedale on Princess Royal Island. To the right of the weatherbeaten cannery is a spectacular waterfall.

Of all the channels of sheer cliff and clinging cedar that comprise the Inside Passage, none is more impressive than **Grenville Channel** – squeezed between the mainland and Pitt Island. Not only do the precipitous sides of this channel rise from watery depths of 1,600 feet to forested heights of 3,500 feet, they form such a narrow corridor that large ships entering from the south look like they're going to get stuck in the first bend. This is of course an optical illusion, but the channel is, at its narrowest point, only a fifth of a mile wide.

On March 22, 2006, shortly after midnight, *Queen of the North* (operated by BC Ferries) was emerging from the southern end of Grenville Channel when the vessel's bridge crew failed to make a required course change. The ferry ran into Gil Island and promptly began taking on water as it listed to starboard. While the crew and passengers abandoned ship, residents of the nearby native village in **Hartley Bay** rushed to their fishboats and headed into the darkness to retrieve the survivors drifting in lifeboats. Of the 101 people on board the ferry, two were never found and presumably went down with the ship.

Queen of the North isn't the only wreck lying on the sea bottom of these deep channels. The U.S. Army transport ship *General Zalinski* sank near the south end of Grenville Channel one night in September 1946 when, in driving rain, the vessel struck some rocks off Pitt Island. The stricken ship's 48 army personnel were rescued by a tug and a passenger steamer.

Today's cruise ships often bypass Grenville and Princess Royal Channels, following instead a more direct route along Principe and Laredo Channels past **Campania Island**, which is a striking sight with its high barren mountains and dome-shaped summit. More and more ships are bypassing the north coast's inner channels altogether and traveling entirely along **Hecate Strait**, a wide body of water separating the mainland islands from the **Haida Gwaii** archipelago. Formerly called the **Queen Charlotte Islands,** their name was officially changed in 2010 to Haida Gwaii, meaning Islands of the People.

A northbound cruise ship steams up Laredo Sound.

These islands are the peaks of a submerged volcanic ridge of the continental shelf. When the last Ice Age glaciers advanced, parts of this 175-mile long archipelago were left untouched, which is why the islands contain species of plants and animals found nowhere else in the world. Others that thrive here are rare, such as a type of moss found only in the Himalayas and Scotland.

Helping to preserve the unique biology of these 'Canadian Galapagos' is their isolated location. For centuries the only sea-farers who plied the shallow, choppy waters of Hecate Strait were the Haida. Traveling in canoes carved out of cedar logs, these skilled mariners established villages throughout what they called **Gwaii Haanas**, meaning Islands of Wonder.

The southern islands are a wilderness park reserve and are reached only by boat or float-plane. Visitors can wander in solitude through moss-carpeted forests of spruce and cedar, the top-

(Above) A sunset over Haida Gwaii. (Below) The abandoned Haida village of Ninstints.

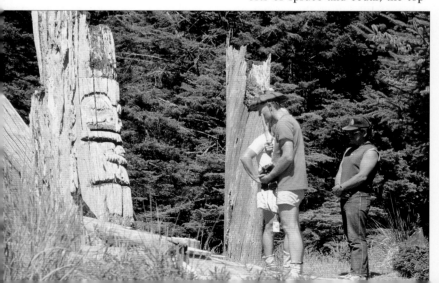

pled ones now 'nurse' logs to seedlings which sprout from their trunks.

Near the southern tip of the archipelago is Anthony Island, a small island exposed to the Pacific. On it stands the abandoned village of **Ninstints** which was declared a World Heritage Site in 1981. The village is named for a wealthy chief who was head of the Kunghit Haida when they had settlements throughout the southern islands. Some of the totem poles are still standing at Ninstints, where they overlook a lagoon protected by an islet. In summer, Haida caretakers live in a nearby cabin and keep these cedar monuments – now bleached by the elements – free of moss to prevent further rotting.

A car ferry connects the northernmost island of the Queen Charlottes – Graham Island – with the mainland, sailing between Skidegate and Prince Rupert, which is BC Ferries' northern terminus. An Alaska state ferry also docks in Prince Rupert.

Prince Rupert

Prince Rupert is located at the mouth of the Skeena River on Kaien Island. The townsite was once a gathering place for the Tsimshian and Haida. It eventually became a gathering place for European settlers when they realized the location's potential as a deepsea port. Railway magnate Charles Hays, general manager of the Grand Trunk Pacific Railway, envisioned a shipping port here that would rival Vancouver and Seattle with its boast of being a day or two closer in shipping time to the markets of the Orient.

A competition was held in 1906 to choose a namesake for the new port. The winner, chosen from history, was Prince Rupert – a cousin of Britain's King Charles II and first governor of the Hudson's Bay Company. The first sod was turned in 1908, followed by a hydrographic survey of the harbor and its approaches so that

Prince Rupert's cruise pier

lighthouses and navigational beacons could be installed to guide steamships arriving at night or in fog. All that remained to establish Prince Rupert as a major port was construction of a rail line.

Charles Hays, the man who masterminded the founding of Prince Rupert, set off for England to raise investment capital for completion of his railway's western terminus. He decided to do some networking on the return trip and chose the ill-fated maiden voyage of the *Titanic*. His life (and vision for Prince Rupert) was lost along with 1,500 others.

A railway terminus was completed a few years later but commercial fishing became the town's main industry. With the outbreak of World War II, Prince Rupert received an economic boost as thousands of American troops passed through on their way to the Aleutians and the Pacific. The port also handled freight and equipment for construction of the Alaska Highway. Today Prince

Rupert is a major port handling overseas shipments of coal, pulp and grain.

Large cruise ships calling at Prince Rupert dock at the **Northland Terminal** and small ships dock next door at the **Atlin Terminal** – a converted fish plant which houses the Visitor InfoCentre. Within walking distance of both terminals is the local museum, and the shops and restaurants at historic **Cow Bay**, named for the first herd of dairy cows that arrived in 1906 and swam ashore. Along the waterfront, at 113 Cow Bay Road, is **Smiles Seafood Cafe** – a town landmark since 1934. During World War II, Smiles stayed open 24 hours a day to serve Canadian and American troops stationed in Prince Rupert. The cafe's famous halibut and chips are still a favorite with locals and visitors.

The border between British Columbia (Canada) and Alaska (USA) lies north of Prince Rupert along an open body of water called Dixon Entrance. This international border, lying as it does on water, and is not as easy to pinpoint as one on land. Set in 1903, it runs from Cape Muzon to the entrance of Pearse Canal, then follows Portland Canal to its head. Depending on a ship's exact route, two Canadian pilots embark or disembark on the south side of Dixon Entrance and two American pilots do likewise on its north side.

One of the best locations to see grizzly bears is at the Khutzeymateen bear sanctuary.

Shore Excursions

PRINCE RUPERT

Shore excursions offered in Prince Rupert cover an array of ecotours, including sport-fishing, river rafting, coastal kayaking, seaplane adventures and rainforest walks. A visit to an ancient native village site and salmon barbecue in a traditional longhouse is also offered. Also featured is a visit to the outlying North Pacific Cannery Village at Port Edward, its boardwalk buildings (erected in 1889) now containing exhibits on the history of west coast fishing. Visitors can rent rods and tackle, and try angling for salmon, halibut and cod off the dock.

Whalewatching boat tours are also available, as are boat trips to the Khutzeymateen River valley north of Prince Rupert, the site of Canada's first grizzly bear sanctuary. Each summer, grizzlies emerge from the mountains and gather on the banks of the Khutzeymateen River to gorge on pink salmon. Grizzlies will gather in close proximity to one another only if there is an easy food source, such as the spawning salmon stream which exists at the head of this uninhabited inlet. This dense concentration of grizzly bears (about 60) prompted the British Columbia provincial government, in 1994, to protect 110,000 acres of the valley.

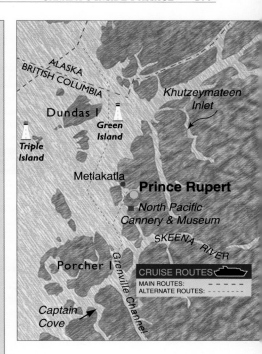

(Below) Green Island Lighthouse can be viewed on a Prince Rupert shore excursion.

Petersburg

Mitkof I

Snow
Passage

Zarembo I

Wrangell

CRUISE ROUTES

MAIN ROUTES: – – – – –
ALTERNATE ROUTES: · · · · ·
NATIVE SETTLEMENTS: ●

KETCHIKAN

POPULATION: 13,500
ANNUAL RAINFALL: 151 inches
DISTANCE TO JUNEAU: 324 miles
DISTANCE TO SKAGWAY: 420 miles

Etolin I

Clarence Strait

Coffman
Cove

PRINCE OF WALES ISLAND

Thorne Bay

Yes Bay

Neets Bay

Meyers
Chuck

Traitors
Cove

Kasaan

Behm
Canal

Loring

Hollis

Guard I

REVILLAGIGEDO
ISLAND

Rudyerd
Bay

Hyder

Ste

Portland Canal

Misty Fjords
National
Monument

KETCHIKAN

Gravina
Island

REVILLAGIGEDO CHANNEL

Behm
Canal

Nichols
Passage

Annette I

Duke I

ALASKA

Pearse Canal

Cape
Muzon

Cape
Chacon

Cape Fox

USA
CANADA

DIXON ENTRANCE

BRITISH COLUMBIA

Triple I

Green I

Port
Simpson

0   30

Miles

N

Prince Rupert

KETCHIKAN
& Misty Fjords National Monument

During the steamship days, Ketchikan was dubbed 'Alaska's First City' because it was the first Alaskan port of call to receive mail and supplies from the south. Ketchikan is still the first stop for Alaska State Ferries arriving from Bellingham and Prince Rupert. The town stretches along the west shore of Revillagigedo Island at the base of Deer Mountain and is reached only by sea or air. An airport lies opposite on Gravina Island and the narrow channel in between – Tongass Narrows – is busy with boats and floatplanes.

Ketchikan began with a saltery in 1883, followed by a cannery a few years later. As more canneries were built, a boardwalk town sprung up along the waterfront straddling Ketchikan Creek, which is a major spawning river for salmon. In 1903 the new sawmill began making boxes for the cases of salmon being shipped out of local canneries and by the 1930s – the industry's heyday – more than a dozen canneries were packing two million cases of salmon annually.

Ketchikan was a rowdy town where local fishermen, miners and loggers spent much of their free time drinking, gambling and visiting the madams of Creek Street, whose houses were built on pilings and connected by boardwalks. Business didn't slow during Prohibition when bootleg whiskey was smuggled into

Ketchikan's Creek Street

Aerial view of Ketchikan's harbor

Ketchikan. It was delivered by skiff at high tide and lifted through trap doors in the madams' floors.

Ketchikan's lumber industry flourished during World War II, its mills providing Sitka spruce – a strong and lightweight wood – for the construction of fighter planes. In the 1950s Ketchikan's wood products industry overtook its declining salmon industry, which nearly collapsed in the '70s due to overfishing. Only two canneries are currently in operation but a few million pounds of fresh seafood are now airfreighted annually. The Deer Mountain Hatchery, built on Ketchikan Creek in 1954, currently releases 300,000 salmon a year.

Another thriving industry in Ketchikan is tourism. The town has become a showpiece for Tlingit culture, with totem poles and other native art on display at local museums, parks and nearby villages. The name Ketchikan is based on a Tlingit word which, loosely translated, means 'thundering wings of an eagle' and the Tongass National Forest is named after a Tlingit clan. (The island on which Ketchikan is located was named by Captain Vancouver in 1793 for Spain's Viceroy to Mexico whose title was Count of Revilla Gigedo.)

Ketchikan's numerous church spires serve as perches for eagles attracted to the salmon in Ketchikan Creek, at the mouth of which residents often gather on a summer evening for a bit of fishing off the Stedman Street Bridge. Creek Street is also a popular swimming hole for local children.

Getting Around

A Travel Information Office is located on the Cruise Ship Dock where you can pick up tourist information, including a walking map of Ketchikan. Enquires can be made here about reserving a taxi; the standard fare is about $55 per hour. You can also book local and out-or-town excursions, but these are often fully booked if several ships are in port that day.

Downtown attractions can be reached on foot or by taking the free Downtown Loop Shuttle that serves all of the cruise ship berths on a 20-minute loop with stops at the Discovery Center, Creek Street, Totem Heritage Center and Fish Hatchery.

One way to reach Saxman Village (three miles south of town) is by taking the Silver Line South bus ($1 each way). You can also walk along the waterfront but

Ketchikan's welcome arch over Mission Street greets cruise passengers strolling along Front Street. (Below) A horse-drawn trolley tour is one way to see the local sights.

it takes close to an hour. Entry to the Village is $5, which provides access to its fascinating collection of totem poles. (To attend a potlatch, you must book a tour.)

The public bus system also provides transportation to Totem Bight Park (10 miles north of town). Take the Silver Line North bus ($1 each way). Admission to the park, featuring forest trails, totem poles and a long house, is free.

Shopping

Ketchikan's streets are lined with shops selling Alaskan souvenirs and galleries featuring Alaskan art. Tongass Trading Co. is a good place to purchase rainwear and other clothing suitable for Alaskan weather. Alaska Totem Trading, at the entrance to Totem Bight Park, carries a great selection of hand-carved yellow cedar totem poles in a variety of sizes.

Shore Excursions
KETCHIKAN

Misty Fjords is the premier wilderness attraction in Ketchikan and a must-see for first-time visitors, either on a flightseeing excursion (2 hrs) or a combination flightseeing/boating excursion (4 hrs). Other guided tours worth considering in Ketchikan include sportfishing for salmon, canoeing on an alpine lake, mountain biking, and sea kayaking. Rainforest hikes with naturalists as guides are also offered, as are bear-watching excursions to Neets Bay and Traitors Cove, where black bears gather to feed on salmon. These outlying wilderness sites are usually reached by float plane, although some entail boarding a motor coach, then transferring to a tour boat to visit outlying resorts and canneries. Sightseeing in Ketchikan can be done on foot, by horse-drawn trolley or aboard the DUCK – an amphibious vehicle which travels both the streets and the harbor of Ketchikan. Undersea viewing is offered aboard a Nautilus semi-submersible vessel, as is snorkeling (thick wetsuits are provided). If you would like to swing across a forest canopy, try the Rainforest Ropes & Zipline Challenge with its aerial bridges, tree-viewing platforms and zip lines which are suspended 135 feet above the forest floor.

Ziplining near Ketchikan

A Walking Tour of Downtown

Many of Ketchikan's attractions are best seen on foot and a stroll along its streets, even in the rain, is a pleasant way to acquaint yourself with the town.

A popular local attraction right on the waterfront is the **Great Alaskan Lumberjack Show**, held in an open-air amphitheater **1**. This site is where the Ketchikan Spruce Mill, one of the largest in the world, stood until it shut down in the 1970s. The lumberjack show features skilled woodsmen pitted against one another in log rolling, pole climbing and other competitive events. Tickets can bought through your ship's shore excursion office.

Another attraction near the waterfront is the **Southeast Alaska Discovery Center 2**. Built in the cannery style, this modern center contains impressive exhibits on the area's natural environment, wildlife and native heritage.

Nearby is **Whale Park 3** where flower gardens and benches create an inviting setting for Ketchikan's historic Knox Brothers Clock and a replica of the Chief Kyan Totem Pole, carved by Stanley Marsden in 1964. It was first erected beside Ketchikan Creek where the Tlingit Chief Kyan held rights to a summer fish camp.

Kitty-corner to Whale Park, on Mission Street, is **4 St. John's Episcopal Church** – built in 1903 and the oldest standing church in Ketchikan, its interior built with red cedar. The Seamen's Center

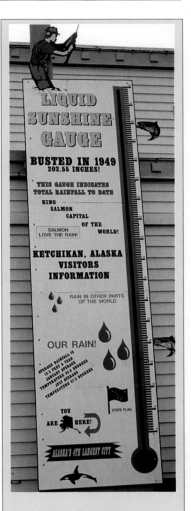

Sunshine Gauge

Southeast Alaska's abundant moisture doesn't go unnoticed in Ketchikan, where a Liquid Sunshine Gauge is displayed on the cruise ship dock. This gauge measures the inches of rain the town receives annually – an impressive 150 inches on average. If the sun is shining when your ship pulls into Ketchikan, consider yourself lucky.

was built a year later as a hospital and is now a gathering place for marine workers.

From Whale Park you can see the pink-colored **U.S. Forest Service building** **5** which contains displays and information on the Tongass National Forest.

Standing opposite the Forest Service building is the **Chief Johnson Totem Pole** **6**, carved by Tlingit artist Israel Shotridge and raised in 1989. It's an exact replica of the original pole raised in 1901 by Chief Johnson, which is now housed in the Totem Heritage Center.

Follow Stedman Street to the bridge spanning the mouth of Ketchikan Creek. Look down and you might see salmon milling about while they adjust to fresh water before beginning their uphill swim to their spawning grounds. During openings, locals often fish below this bridge.

(Above) The Great Alaskan Lumberjack Show and (inset) gift shop. (Below) A replica of the Chief Johnson Totem Pole stands near the Creek Street footbridge.

Carry on along Stedman, past picturesque **Thomas Basin** with its small-boat marinas. In the early part of the last century, before a breakwater was built, the basin's long tidal flats were used as a baseball park. The game was called when a rising tide started flooding the outfield. On the far side of Thomas Basin is a wood-plank street built over the water. Called **Thomas Street 7**, its historic buildings were once part of the New England Fish Co. cannery. A viewing walkway extends to the end of the breakwater.

Retrace your steps along Thomas and Stedman Streets, past The New York Hotel & Cafe,

Dolly's House is a major attraction on Creek Street.

to Ketchikan's famous **Creek Street 8**. This former red-light district is now a respectable part of town and a major tourist attraction. This boardwalk set on pilings takes you along the shores of Ketchikan Creek, past shops and a museum called **Dolly's House**. Dolly was the town's most successful madam and her house has been preserved, complete with furnishings and other memorabilia.

About halfway along Creek Street is a tramway car that whisks passengers (for a small charge) up the hill to the Cape Fox Lodge and **Ted Ferry Civic Center 9**. Here you have a sweeping view of downtown Ketchikan and Tongass Narrows.

Back down on Creek Street, pause at the footbridge where again you may see salmon heading upstream to the salmon ladder (the Married Man's Trail runs alongside the creek).

On the other side of the footbridge is the **Tongass Historical Museum and Public Library 10**. Here you can view exhibits depicting Ketchikan's earlier days. Standing outside is the Raven Stealing the Sun Totem Pole by

Tahltan-Tlingit Dempsey Bob.

Dock Street leads from the Museum back down to Front Street. On the way you will pass the foot of Edmond Street, which is a long set of wooden stairs going up the hillside. A stroll along Front Street takes you past the historic **Gilmore Hotel** 11 (on the National Historic Register) to the tunnel under **Knob Hill**.

The tunnel was built in 1954 so that historic homes on Knob Hill could be preserved. Had a road been built, part of the hill would have been blasted away and the houses demolished. Many stories are told to visitors regarding this tunnel's construction, the best one being that federal funds were available at the time for building a bomb shelter, so Ketchikan built one with two entrances and a road running through it.

If you carry on along Front Street, you'll reach **Harborview Park** 12 overlooking Ketchikan's main boat basin. Benches here provide both a resting spot and a view of the busy harbor's fishboat and floatplane activity.

An Extended Walking Tour

Ketchikan is built on the slopes of Deer Mountain, so to see more of the local sights on foot involves a bit of climbing. Recommended is a hike up Front Street's steps to Cedar Street where you can overlook the waterfront. Take the Main Street stairs back down to Pine Street. At the corner stands the **Burkhardt House** (a.k.a. **Monrean House**) 13 – built in 1904 for one of the town's lead-

(Above) The Married Man's Trail leads from Creek Street to the Salmon Ladder. (Below) The heritage homes of Knob Hill straddle Water Street Tunnel.

(Above) Deer Mountain Trail
(Below) Totem Bight Park.

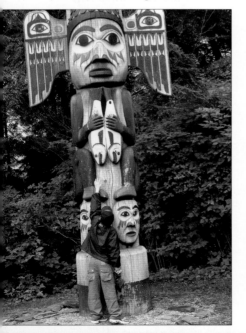

ing businessmen. Preserving the Queen Anne style so popular at the turn of the last century, this house is on the National Register of Historic Places. Continue along Main Street, turn left at Grant and at the next block turn right on Edmond. Now you're at the top of the long wooden staircase leading down to Dock Street.

At the bottom of the stairs, turn left on Dock Street, then left again on Bawden. Stay with Bawden until you reach Park Avenue, which veers to the right across Ketchikan Creek. A concrete salmon ladder is located here and the Married Man's Trail branches off Park and leads to Creek Street.

Stay on Park and follow it the **Deer Mountain Tribal Hatchery & Eagle Center 14** which backs onto a peaceful park containing ornamental ponds once used by the town's first hatchery. Here you can learn about salmon and view a pair of resident bald eagles. A footbridge leads between the hatchery and the **Totem Heritage Center 15** which houses a major collection of authentic totem poles. Outside on the grounds is a self-guided nature path.

A good hike can be taken up **Deer Mountain 16** for a splendid view of the island. Follow Fair Street (at the top of Deermont Street) to Ketchikan Lakes Road which leads to the Deer Mountain Parking Lot Trailhead. The trail, which is about three miles long and ascends 3,000 feet, is suitable for moderately experienced hikers, and the first overlook is just one mile from the trailhead.

Outlying Attractions

Tlingit heritage is strong in the Ketchikan area, and is showcased in two outlying attractions. One is Saxman Native Village (described on page 192). The other is **Totem Bight State Historical Park**, located about 10 miles north of town and accessible by public bus, taxi or shore excursion. Admission is free to this former native village site where a short trail winds through the forest and opens into an old campsite containing a collection of authentic totem poles and a ceremonial clan house. For more information on the park and its many totem poles, visit dnr.alaska.gov/parks/units/totembgh.htm.

Loring, in the western arm of the Behm Canal, was a cannery site from 1885 to 1930, and pieces of the wrecked side-paddle steamer *Ancon* can be seen here at low tide. The steamer used to deliver mail, freight and passen-

(Above) A Tlingit totem pole at Saxman Village. (Below) The clan house at Totem Bight.

SAXMAN VILLAGE

One of Ketchikan's most popular attractions is Saxman Village, located two miles south of town and accessible by bus or on foot. Admission is $5 and allows you to view the totem poles but does not include a potlatch inside the clan house. If you book a shore excursion, a motor coach will take you to the village for a two-hour visit immersed in Tlingit culture. Your hosts are descendants of those who lived at Cape Fox and Fort Tongass until the late 1880s, when they were persuaded by Presbyterian missionaries to relocate to this site. Founded in 1894, the village was named for school teacher Samuel Saxman. In the 1930s, the people of Saxman returned to their original village sites to retrieve the totem poles they had left behind.

New poles have been carved since then and they stand in a semi-circle overlooking the village and Tongass Narrows. Guests arriving with a tour group at Saxman are treated to the live enactment of a Tlingit legend and are ushered into the Clan House, built of red cedar and displaying the Beaver crest on its carved corner poles. In keeping with a traditional potlatch, the Cape Fox Dancers perform a series of dances, then invite members of the audience to join them. Upon leaving, each guest is given a small packet of trading beads – in keeping with potlatch customs.

Outside the Beaver Clan House, a guide explains the stories behind some of the totem poles displayed in the park. A few minutes are allowed for visiting the gift shop before the tour concludes in the Carving Center, where the art of totem carving is explained. Anyone interested in native culture will find a visit to Saxman both enlightening and entertaining.

Wearing traditional regalia, a young Tlingit performs a potlatch dance in the Beaver clan house.

gers to Loring until one day in 1889 when an overly enthusiastic cannery worker cast off the departing ship's dock lines before an officer was ready at the controls. The steamer drifted onto a reef where it holed and sank with no loss of life – except maybe the cannery worker's!

For wildlife viewing, the salmon hatchery in **Neets Bay** attracts black bears to the nearby creek where they gather to feed. Viewing platforms have been built here to accommodate visitors, who arrive by floatplane. The cruise lines offer this sidetrip as a shore excursion.

Traitors Cove also attracts black bears, and it was here that some British sailors were attacked by Tlingits in 1793. Some of the natives were more curious than hostile, however, and one wanted to sail with Captain Vancouver to England but promptly changed his mind when he saw a British crewman being whipped.

Black bears gather at Neets Bay where visitors can watch them feeding from July through September.

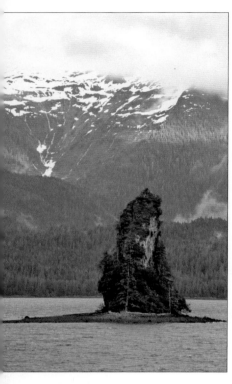

New Eddystone Rock

Ketchikan is right next door to the **Misty Fjords National Monument** – a wilderness reserve created in 1978 and, at 2.3 million acres, almost four times the size of Rhode Island. Some ships' itineraries include a scenic **side-trip** up Behm Canal to Rudyerd Bay and Punchbowl Cove. The ship slowly turns around in Rudyerd Bay and retraces its route past New Eddystone Rock as it leaves Misty Fjords National Monument to return to the main channel.

For passengers whose ship doesn't pull into Misty Fjords, flightseeing excursions are available out of Ketchikan. These excursions provide an eagle's eye view of the region's steeply treed slopes, mountain lakes, hanging waterfalls and winding fjords that were carved long ago by retreating glaciers. You may even spot some wildlife – mountain goats, bear and moose on shore; killer

THE BEAVER

One of the most common sights in Alaska – and especially in Ketchikan – is the floatplane. Used as an important link between coastal villages, remote logging camps and main ports, the floatplane has served Alaska since the 1930s. However, it was the introduction of the Beaver aircraft just after the Second World War that made short-haul air connections in Southeast Alaska inexpensive and, most importantly, safe.

BEAVER MK 1

Engine: 450 hp
Pratt & Whitney
Wing Span: 48 ft.
Length: 30 ft.
Weight: 3,000 lb.
Performance –
Maximum Speed: 160 mph
Cruising Speed: 130 mph
Rate of Climb: 1,020 ft/min
Service Ceiling: 18,000 feet

Developed by De Havilland Canada, the Beaver was designed to handle payloads over 1,000 pounds, and to take off and land in tight places, whether on land, ice, snow or water. The plane went on to become one of the most successful and long-lived designs in aviation history, with over 1,600 built. Of the 1,000 still operating, most are working along the British Columbia and Alaska coast.

Beaver floatplanes line up like taxi cabs along Ketchikan's waterfront. The Beaver has been the bush plane of choice for decades.

whales, seals and sea lions in the surrounding channels. Weather checks are made every hour but planes still fly in overcast weather; the fjords are said to be their most beautiful when mist rises off the water and wisps of cloud cling to the mountaintops.

A Misty Fjords flightseeing tour lasts about an hour and offers aerial views of the **Behm Canal**, which is about a hundred miles long and wraps right round Revillagigedo Island. Pillar-shaped **New Eddystone Rock** – a volcanic plug – juts 234 feet skyward from the middle of the canal's eastern arm. Also in the Behm Canal (but outside the National Monument) is the U.S. Navy's submarine testing facility, which is located in these remote waters to escape marine traffic noise. The submarines being tested are so quiet that navy scientists need an equally silent location to plant their rows of hydrophones and record the rhythms of the subs as they race past. Data collected from these underwater tests is analysed and used to make the submarines even quieter.

The silence of these watery canyons is revealed when your plane lands on an alpine lake or one of the inlet's upper reaches and the pilot shuts off his engine. You can climb onto one of the plane's pontoons and listen to the subtle sounds of a mountain wilderness.

Highlights of the Monument include Rudyerd Bay (a spectacular, steep-sided fjord), Punchbowl Cove (a dramatic cove of sheer cliffs), Big Goat Lake (an alpine lake containing a waterfall that plunges almost 1,000 feet), Nooya Lake (left behind by a melting valley glacier) and Granite Basin, where bare rock ridges separate a row of deep-blue alpine lakes.

Misty Fjords National Monument

(Above) Hanging waterfalls ribbon the sheer cliffs of Misty Fjords. (Right) A floatplane lands on an alpine lake in Granite Basin.

Misty Fjords National Monument lies within the 17-million-acre **Tongass National Forest**. This huge tract of forested land encompasses 90% of Southeast Alaska and was created in 1907 by President Theodore Roosevelt, an outdoorsman convinced of the need for wilderness protection after camping with John Muir at Yosemite in 1903.

About one-third of Tongass National Forest is designated wilderness. The rest is managed as a working forest, with logging and mining in operation alongside wilderness recreation and fishery management. Timber harvesting is limited and little replanting is required due to the area's temperate climate and abundant rainfall.

★ **JUNEAU**

Tracy Arm   **Sawyer Glacier**

Ford's Terror

Stikine Icefield

Seymour Channel

STEPHENS PASSAGE

Endicott Arm

ADMIRALTY ISLAND

● Angoon

Windham Bay

Hobart Bay

CHATHAM STRAIT

CANADA
USA

0   **30**

Miles

N

Pt. Gardner

FREDERICK SOUND

⌂ *Five Finger Is.*

The Brothers

Devil's Thumb
△ **(9077')**

Le Conte Glacier

KUPREANOF ISLAND

PETERSBURG ●

KUIU ISLAND

Bay of Pillars

MITKOF ISLAND

STIKINE RIVER

Wrangell Narrows

CHATHAM STRAIT

Snow Passage

WRANGELL ●

● Point Baker

↙ Zarembo I

Cape Ommaney

SUMNER STRAIT

Port Protection

WRANGELL ISLAND

Cape Decision ⌂

El Capitan Passage

Coffman Cove ●

Etolin I

Coronation Island

Warren Island

PRINCE OF WALES ISLAND

CLARENCE STRAIT

Thorne Bay ●   Meyers Chuck ●

Klawock ●

Behm Canal

Kasaan ●

Craig ●   ● Hollis

KETCHIKAN ●

⌂ *Guard I*

GULF OF ALASKA

Hydaburg ●

Dall Island

PIONEER PORTS

L and is scarce in Alaska – private land, that is. Of the state's massive land area covering 365 million acres, less than one per cent is in private hands. For almost a century Alaska's single landowner was the U.S. Government. Statehood was granted in 1959, but the complex and controversial process of land allocation is ongoing.

Millions of acres lie within national parks and wilderness refuges and, in 1971, the Alaska Native Claims Settlement Act – involving 44 million acres – was passed. Until 1995, under the state's Homestead Program a person with one year's residency in Alaska was able to acquire from 40 to 160 acres (depending on its land-use classification) but had to survey, occupy and improve the land in certain ways within set time periods in order to receive title. Today, remote recreational cabin sites on state land can be staked under legislation passed in 1997.

In Southeast Alaska the land is either national park or part of the Tongass National Forest, a 17 million acre managed preserve and the largest rainforest in the United States. Developed property in towns such as Ketchikan is scarce and expensive, with house prices considerably higher than the national average.

Yet, in spite of Alaska's land-use restrictions, the lure of the north still beckons. In 1984, the

A boardwalk leads to the local school in Port Protection.

ABC television program *20/20* featured the remote Alaskan village of **Coffman Cove**. Afterwards the residents of this tiny logging community (pop. 200), located on the northeast side of **Prince of Wales Island**, were deluged with mail from viewers who wanted to move there. The show's portrayal of Coffman Cove's wholesome lifestyle – fresh air, clean water and freedom from urban crime – appealed to many Americans living in the Lower 48. Yet Alaskans who live in outlying ports similar to Coffman Cove don't harbor any illusions about their lifestyle. Living in isolation is not for everyone. The work is often seasonal and incomes are sporadic. The winters can be long, dark and wet. Supplies must be shipped or flown into port, there are few conveniences and, for many, a trip south each winter is mandatory to their mental health. Still, most say they wouldn't live anywhere else.

Alaska breeds a hardiness in people. Early pioneers came to fish the waters, mine and log the land. Margaret Bell Wiks, well known for her children's books about Alaska's early days, was of pioneering stock. Her Scottish grandparents – James and Margaret Millar – arrived in Alaska in 1879 and established salteries on Prince of Wales Island. Their daughter Florence married a fellow named James Bell who raced his sloop against a steamer – from Puget Sound to Alaska – and won.

The Bells' daughter Margaret was born in December 1898. She was delivered by her Scottish grandmother while the doctor rested in bed. He had suffered a heart attack when the sailboat bringing him to **Thorne Bay** was caught in a storm. Margaret weighed only three pounds at birth and spent the first few weeks of her life in a shoebox on the door of an opened oven. Despite her tentative start, Margaret lived for 91 years.

Millar Street in Ketchikan is named for the family, as is the town of **Craig** on Prince of Wales Island. Craig was one of Margaret's uncles and he ran a cannery there in the early 1900s. With a present population of 1,400, Craig is home port to a substantial fishing fleet and has become the service center for Prince of Wales – the largest island in Southeast Alaska. The

Alaska's state ferries provide a transportation link between coastal communities.

island is indented with inlets and coves, many of which were fishing camps for the Haida and Tlingit before the arrival of white settlers. **Klawock** (pop. 850) was originally a Tlingit summer village, and **Hydaburg** (pop. 400) was established in 1911 when several Haida villages in the vicinity joined together. About 300 years ago Haida living in the Queen Charlotte Islands (Haida Gwaii) extended the northern boundary of their territory to encompass the southern half of Prince of Wales Island. Then their numbers, like those of other native groups, dwindled when European-imported diseases such as smallpox wiped out entire families and clans along the coast. Many villages were abandoned as survivors coalesced at central locations.

A state ferry runs between Ketchikan and Prince of Wales Island. It pulls into **Hollis**, a former mining and logging town, and each summer more and more visitors come to the island for its superb sportfishing and wildlife viewing. Extensive logging has taken place on Prince of Wales Island and logging roads connect most settlements with the Hollis ferry terminal. But the communities of **Point Baker** and **Port Protection**, at the north end of the island, don't want to be connected. When the forest service proposed extending the road system to include them, a ruckus ensued,

The boardwalk streets never get crowded in Port Protection.

with environmental organizations getting involved. The 100 residents of these two fishing ports were quite happy in their isolation. They get about in skiffs and out-of-town visitors arrive by boat or floatplane. In Port Protection, boardwalks lead past homes and the local school. A general store overlooks the fuel dock, and the men and women who live here troll for salmon in **Sumner Strait**, satisfied with a moderate day's catch.

Most cruise ships pass through Sumner Strait on their way to or from Ketchikan. Whales and dolphins also use this major channel. Its southern end is open to the Gulf of Alaska and marked by **Cape Decision** – a rocky bluff atop which sits an unmanned lighthouse. When cruise ships round Cape Decision, mountainous Coronation Island and nearby **Warren Island** lie to seaward. Both are wilderness reserves, where seabirds nest on rocky cliffs and bears feed in the streams. Tall stands of spruce inland give way to bent trees along the islands' windward shores, exposed to the open sea.

In 1793 a September storm forced Captain Vancouver's two ships to seek shelter in Port Protection before heading out to sea. That summer their survey boats had covered hundreds of miles of shoreline, including the channels that lead to the mouth of the great **Stikine River**. This river delta is one of the most productive estuaries in Southeast Alaska. Its tidal flats attract half a million migrating seabirds each year and the silt it deposits in adjacent Dry Strait prevents vessels of any size from navigating that channel.

Before the arrival of European explorers and fur traders, Tlingit natives had established a major village at the mouth of the Stikine

The American fur trading schooner **Lady Washington**

under a series of leaders named **Chief Shakes**. As the fur trade heated up, the 400-mile-long Stikine River turned into a conveyor belt for furs, with Chief Shakes and his people reaping the profits as middlemen.

In 1833 the Russian-American Company built a fort at the mouth of the Stikine to prevent Britain's **Hudson's Bay Company** from gaining a foothold in Russian territory. The HBC's main competition was from American merchant ships, so it began hiring American skippers (veterans of the coastal trade) to shadow the Boston ships and outbid the Yankee traders, who were known as 'Boston men' because almost all of them were from that port. As their profits dwindled, the Boston men gradually withdrew from the fur trade and turned their sights on whaling. Their withdrawal also meant a loss of supply ships for the Russians at Sitka. They had no alternative but to turn to the

British who had offered to supply the Russian outpost with surplus food from their forts' surrounding farms. So, in return for a reliable food source, the Russians granted the British exclusive access to coastal waters bordering the mainland. The HBC moved into Saint Dionysius Redoubt and changed its name to Fort Stikine. A brisk trade continued between local Tlingit clans and the British, who offered cloth and woolen Hudson's Bay blankets in exchange for furs.

The fur trade eventually dwindled and the British had abandoned Fort Stikine by the time a prospector named Buck Choquette discovered gold on the Stikine River in 1861. Men rushed upriver by steamer to Buck's Bar to pan for gold. A second strike was made farther upriver at Cassiar in 1874. Fort Stikine was now called **Wrangell**, named for Baron Von Wrangell, a former manager of the Russian-American Company, who had ordered the fort's initial construction.

Wrangell (pop. 2,300)

When the naturalist **John Muir** of California arrived at Wrangell by steamer in July 1879, about 1,800 miners and prospectors had already passed through that spring en route to the Cassiar gold mines. This was Muir's first visit to Alaska and his initial impression of Wrangell was that "no mining hamlet in the placer gulches of California, nor any backwoods village I ever saw, approached it in picturesque, devil-may-care abandon." Muir did concede that despite the town's haphazard collection of houses built on swampy ground, Wrangell was a tranquil place. There were no noisy brawls in the streets and the weather was mild.

Muir himself was a bit of a curiosity. The townspeople wondered what he was up to wandering about the forest, examining plants and trees with no apparent objective. One resident observed Muir "on his knees, looking at a stump as if he expected to find gold in it."

A Presbyterian mission had been established in Wrangell, where Muir met Dr. Sheldon Jackson (a missionary who would become widely known in Southeast Alaska) and Reverend **Samuel Hall Young**, who became Muir's lifelong friend. In his book *Travels in Alaska*, Muir describes Young as an adventurous evangelist. Of course, anyone who associated with Muir had no choice but to embrace adventure.

On the first climb Young made with Muir, the young missionary dislocated both arms when he slipped near the top of Glenora Peak and found himself hanging from a crumbling precipice on the edge of a thousand-foot drop. Muir saved his new climbing companion and it was the beginning of a close friendship.

During his stay at Wrangell, Muir also met Chief Shakes of the Stikine tribe who invited Muir and the missionaries to a potlatch. Theatrical imitations of several animals were performed so convincingly that when "the door of the big house was suddenly thrown open and in bounced a bear," they were all quite startled until they realized it was a man wearing a bear skin. Gifts were handed out at the end of the potlatch and Muir, adopted by the tribe, was given the Tlingit name of Ancoutahan ('adopted chief') which would protect him in his travels.

The Stikine village visited by John Muir in 1879 was situated on a small island known as **Shakes Island** and a replica of that tribal house is now a major tourist attraction. It was built in the traditional manner, without nails but by using adzes to shape and join the posts, beams and planks. Muir was so impressed with the Tlingit workmanship he stated that "with the same tools, not one in a thousand of our skilled mechanics could do as good work." The original interior houseposts of the clan house,

A Tlingit tribal house stands on Shakes Island in Wrangell.

which were brought from a previous village, are now housed in the Wrangell Museum. Replica poles grace the inside and outside of the tribal house and the clan's bear crest frames the entrance.

Other carved poles about town include a replica of the Three Frogs Totem, designed to shame the neighboring Kiksadi clan (whose crest was the frog) into repaying a debt. Bear Up The Mountain pole tells the story of a grizzly bear (his prints shown climbing up the pole) who led the Shakes clan to safety when threatened by a great flood. Totem poles of the Kiksadi clan are displayed in a small park on Front Street where false-fronted wooden buildings preserve the town's pioneer heritage.

On Church Street is the oldest protestant church in Alaska, the First Presbyterian Church. It was founded in 1879 and, twice damaged by fire, has been extensively renovated. A large, red neon cross was erected in 1939 and serves as a navigational light for local mariners.

Outside the **public library**, located on 2nd Street, are two totem poles as well as some petroglyphs carved on rocks in the grass. Several petroglyphs can also be viewed in the **Wrangell Museum** next door and even more petroglyphs are found (after some searching) on the beach a half mile north of the **ferry terminal**. At low tide, about 40 rock engravings of prehistoric images – animals and human faces – are exposed. People are allowed to take rubbings of them and museum staff are happy to explain how this is best done.

Outside of Wrangell, opposite the south end of Sergief Island, is **Garnet Ledge**. Its red transparent mineral was mined in 1915 by Alaska Garnet & Manufacturing Company – apparently the world's first all-women corporation. The ledge is now the property of the children of Wrangell (adults need a permit to remove garnets) and youngsters here spend part of their summer holidays selling these local gems to visitors.

North of Wrangell, lies **Wrangell Narrows** – an important waterway in Southeast Alaska which is used by fishboats, tugs, small cruise ships and the Alaska State Ferry. This long, narrow channel (20 miles in length and, at places, only 300 feet in width) is squeezed between two islands and well marked with over 60 navigational aids. Wrangell Narrows has been dubbed Christmas Tree Lane for its nightly blinking of red and green lights. The narrows are very scenic, winding past log cabins and fishing lodges nestled at the foot of treed slopes.

Petersburg (pop. 3,800)

At the north end of Wrangell Narrows, on Mitkof Island, is the fishing port of Petersburg. Founded by Norwegian immigrants at the turn of the century, the town's site was chosen for its natural harbor and the dramatic backdrop of glacier-draped mountains which reminded Peter Buschmann of the fjords back home. He moved here in 1897 and began fishing for salmon and halibut.

Glacier-clad mountains provide a scenic backdrop at Petersburg.

'Peter's Burg' grew quickly as fellow Norwegians joined Buschmann and, utilizing the ample timber supply, began building a neatly planned Scandinavian community. Buschmann was manager of the Icy Straits Packing Company, which constructed a sawmill, wharf, warehouses, bunkhouses, store and cannery. Fish packing was a year-round operation with salmon caught each summer, halibut and herring in the spring, crab over the winter and shrimp throughout the year. The pack ice was supplied by nearby Le Conte Glacier.

Unlike some of the goldmining towns of this era, there was no boom and bust cycle in Petersburg. The people here were industrious, community minded and proud of their Scandinavian heritage. They decorated their neat wooden homes with traditional rosemaling (fanciful floral designs painted in bright colors) and built a Sons of Norway Hall in 1912 for Saturday night socials. Many a Petersburg fisherman met his future wife at one of these dances.

Norwegian Independence Day is celebrated annually with a Little Norway Festival held on the weekend nearest May 17th. Residents of Petersburg dress in traditional costume, prepare lavish smorgasbords and dance to Norwegian folk music. As part of the festivies, a replica Viking ship called *Valhalla* (built in 1976 for the nation's bicentennial) is launched by local fishermen dressed as fierce Norsemen.

Town maps and brochures are available at the Chamber of Commerce **Information Center**, located in the Harbor Master Office overlooking North Harbor. The *Valhalla* is on display beside the **Sons of Norway Hall** at the entrance to Hammer Slough, which is built on pilings. Hammer

Petersburg has retained its Norwegian heritage with such attractions as the historic Sons of Norway Hall and a replica Viking ship.

Slough's plank streets and brightly colored buildings are a favorite subject for local artists and their paintings are displayed in the town's shop windows.

Historic **Sing Yee Alley** is named for a local businessman, and the **Clausen Museum** provides insight into Alaska's fishing industry as well as Petersburg's past. Steamers used to deliver freight from the south, and whalers on their way north would pull into Petersburg to stock up with coal. In the Dirty Thirties, farmers from the Dakota Dustbowl came to try their hand at fishing, quickly learning how to lasso icebergs in Frederick Sound and tow them into port for crushed ice.

At **Eagle's Roost Park** along Nordic Drive, the women of Petersburg used to gather (before fishboats carried radios) and watch anxiously for their husbands and sons returning from the fishing grounds. Today this is a good vantage for watching both the marine traffic in Wrangell Narrows and the eagles roosting in the spruce trees.

Another good spot to view Wrangell Narrows is at **Papke's Landing** – located along Mitkof Highway which runs parallel with the Narrows. An old-timer named Herman Papke lived here in a cabin and would phone the Petersburg switchboard when he saw a steamer coming up the narrows so that the townspeople could be ready on the dock to greet it. Other sights along **Mitkof Highway** are the Falls Creek Fish Ladder and Blind Slough, where trumpeter swans spend the winter.

Glaciers of the Stikine Icefield drain into Frederick Sound, and nearby **Le Conte Glacier** is the southernmost active tidewater glacier in Alaska. Visible from Petersburg, it is actively calving and can be viewed on jetboat tours. Looming above Le Conte Glacier is **Devil's Thumb** peak – a majestic sight with its pyramid-like peak jutting through the ice and snow.

Hammer Slough at low tide.

JUNEAU

POPULATION: 31,000
ANNUAL RAINFALL: 55 inche[s]
DISTANCE TO KETCHIKAN: 324 mile[s]
DISTANCE TO SKAGWAY: 118 mile[s]

CRUISE ROUTES

MAIN ROUTES:
ALTERNATE ROUTES:
NATIVE SETTLEMENTS: ●

Skagway

LYNN CANAL

Glacier Bay

Favorite Channel

Juneau Icefield

Taku Inlet

Mendenhall Glacier

ICY STRAIT

Mansfield Peninsula

Douglas Is.

★ JUNEAU

CANADA
USA

Icy Strait Point

Hoonah

GASTINEAU CHANNEL

Taku Harbor

Sawyer Glaciers

CHICHAGOF ISLAND

CHATHAM STRAIT

ADMIRALTY ISLAND

STEPHENS PASSAGE

Tracy Arm

Stikine Icefield

N. Dawes Glacier

Endicott Arm

Ford's Terror

PERIL STRAIT

Angoon

Windham Bay

S. Dawes Glacier

Hobart Bay

Five Finger Is.

Sitka

Pt. Gardner

FREDERICK SOUND

Kake

PETERSBURG

BARANOF ISLAND

KUIU ISLAND

KUPREANOF ISLAND

Wrangell Narrows

GULF OF ALASKA

Bay of Pillars

KEKU STRAIT

SNOW PASSAGE

WRANGELL

N

Port Protection

Zarembo I

0   30

Miles

Cape Ommaney

SUMNER STRAIT

El Capitan Passage

Cape Decision

JUNEAU
& TRACY ARM

The mainland mountains of southeastern Alaska are dominated by two massive ice fields. Mountains poke their craggy peaks through thick layers of ice and snow, and glaciers flow down these rugged slopes. Those that reach tidewater are found at the heads of fjords and inlets, where they discharge crystalline ice chunks into the still water.

The southerly **Stikine Icefield** drains its glacial meltwater into **Frederick Sound** and **Stephens Passage**. These two bodies of water join at the top of Kupreanof Island where they form a major marine intersection with 138-mile-long **Chatham Strait** – the most extensive of Southeast Alaska's channels. Because of Chatham Strait's long fetch and exposure to the Gulf of Alaska, the seas off Point Gardner can be steep and choppy in a winter storm. This is of little concern to the cruise ships that glide past this point throughout the summer, but was of great concern to the native guides who were paddling a canoe across these waters in October 1879.

The man who had chartered their canoe was **John Muir**, the famous and fearless naturalist who was determined to see as many glaciers as possible on his first visit to Alaska. His new friend, the Presbyterian missionary **Samuel Hall Young**, had come along to spread the gospel while the irrepressible Muir preached his own 'glacial gospel' to anyone who cared to listen. The canoe's crew were, in Muir's words, "Toyatte, a grand old Stickeen nobleman, who was made captain, not only because he owned the canoe, but for his skill in woodcraft and seamanship; Kadachan, the son of a Chilcat chief; John, a Stickeen, who acted as interpreter; and Sitka Charley."

Their departure from Wrangell wasn't a happy scene. There were, as Muir said, a few domestic difficulties. Toyatte's wife wept bitterly for fear he would be killed, and Kadachan's mother accused Mr. Young of talking her son into going on a dangerous voyage among unfriendly tribes. "If my son comes not back," she said, "on you will be his blood, and you shall pay." Needless to say, no one wished them a *bon voyage*.

John Muir

(Above) A humpback whale feeds in Stephens Passage. (Below) Small-ship cruisers take a close look at an iceberg in Tracy Arm.

The crew were concerned about crossing Frederick Sound so late in the season and they spoke of it repeatedly as they headed north up Keku Strait, a winding, intricate channel used only by small craft. Toyatte was having sleepless nights in anticipation of Frederick Sound but the wind was calm when they crossed this "broad water." Their canoe "tossed like a bubble on the swells coming in from the ocean" and they rounded Point Gardner without incident.

Tracy Arm

The cruise ships traverse **Stephens Passage** on their way to or from Juneau, and a daylight voyage along this waterway is filled with natural wonders. Shimmering icefields grace the mainland mountains, floating ice sculptures drift down the wide channel, and humpback whales blow puffs of mist into the air as they feed near the water's surface. At night, when the air is still, the thunderclap sound of their tails smacking the water can be heard in distant bays.

Halfway along Stephens Passage lies a dramatic inlet containing two fjords – Endicott Arm and **Tracy Arm**. They each branch into the mainland mountains for a distance of 25 miles before reaching the retreating glaciers that carved them.

Muir explored both these arms in the summer of 1880, and his guides were worried about their canoe being crushed by the ice that clogged Endicott Arm as they carefully paddled their way to the head of the fjord. Along the way they investigated a canyon of water that flows into Endicott Arm and was later named **Ford's Terror** for a man who, in 1889, rowed through its narrow entrance at slack tide. The water was as still as a pond when he rowed in. Then the tide started running and he was trapped inside for six hours, while his boat was pushed about by swift currents and battered by chunks of ice.

Muir also explored **Tracy Arm**, tracing this fjord to **South Sawyer Glacier** at its head. It took a full day to reach the tidewater glacier, and that night Muir pitched his tent on a boulder-covered shore while his guides remained in the canoe to prevent it from being crushed by drifting ice. Whenever a large chunk of ice drops into the water, it sends waves fanning outward until they hit the steep-sided shores of the fjord and rebound. When these rebounding waves collide with the initial waves, they create erratic seas that set the ice pack into motion. Small vessels must be careful not to get too close to a glacier that is actively discharging ice in case they get caught in a churning ice pack. Harbor seals raise their pups on these icepacks, which are relatively safe from predators. When a wave surges through an icepack, seals lounging on the floes will slowly rise with the swell as if nonchalantly enjoying the ride.

Tracy Arm is less than a mile wide throughout most of its length, its cliff walls rising skyward 2,000 feet. Clinging to the schist and granite rock are moss,

(Above) A seal rests on the pack ice in front of Sawyer Glacier in Tracy Arm (below).

Anne's Alaska Journal

My first trip up Tracy Arm – and my first encounter with a tidewater glacier – was by sailboat with my husband. A few years earlier some boating friends of ours had taken a dramatic photo of their sailboat in the pack ice here for their Christmas card, and we wanted to do likewise.

The weather was fair when we dropped anchor in Holkham Bay at the mouth of Tracy Arm but we awoke the next morning to a downpour that can only be characterized as Alaskan as we embarked on a six-hour journey to the head of Tracy Arm to view the South Sawyer Glacier. The driving rain dampened our enthusiasm at the outset, but as we glided past sheer granite cliffs, tumbling waterfalls

and beautiful blue icebergs we were caught up in the wonder of this unique place.

At last we came around a final bend and, to the sound of distant rumbling, caught our first view of South Sawyer Glacier. Harbor seals swam among the icepack, poking their heads out of the water to look at us before submerging and resurfacing in a different spot, but we were transfixed by the beauty of the glacier and the shades of blue in the ice. The rumbling we heard, which sounded like thunder, was the ice cracking and calving.

It wasn't until the next day, however, that the clouds lifted and we were able to get our Christmas card photo. Icebergs of various sizes were floating around our anchorage, so we rowed to one nearby and I clambered aboard with our Scottish terrier tucked under my arm. It was then that I realized just how slippery the ice is, and the precarious position my nervous dog and I were in. I learned later that these bergs can roll without warning. Fortunately, Bill got the photo we wanted and our friends all got a chuckle when they received their cards that Christmas. Our dog, however, was not amused.

Taku Glacier is the largest of the Juneau Icefield.

scrub and spruce trees. Hanging falls plunge down these steep sides into water that is a thousand feet deep and milky green in color, due to suspended sediments carried in glacial runoff.

North of Tracy Arm, at the top of Stephens Passage, is another glacier to be reckoned with. **Taku Glacier** pushed its terminus well into Taku Inlet in the late 1800s when the glacier – fed by its substantial snow accumulation area – advanced four miles.

Taku is the principal outlet glacier of the massive **Juneau Icefield**, which occupies 700 square miles of land. All of the Juneau Icefield's outlet glaciers are retreating except for Taku, which is slowly advancing over its outwash plain. It is no longer calving, so the glacier is not losing mass to icebergs.

Less than a mile from Taku's terminus is Norris Glacier, which is retreating and thinning rapidly.

JUNEAU

Alaska's state capital, Juneau is a popular port of call for ships sailing the Inside Passage. It's a sprawling city, with most of its 31,000 residents living in the Mendenhall Valley, but the downtown area is fairly compact.

Getting Around

The **main cruise dock** is a short stroll from the main attractions and nearby shopping streets; the **A-J cruise ship dock** is a four-minute shuttle bus ride to downtown Juneau. If both cruise piers are full, ships will anchor in Gastineau Channel and tender their passengers ashore.

A visitor information building is located at the main dock and a visitor information kiosk is also situated in **Marine Park**. The Seadrome Travel Center, which sells local tours, is opposite the floatplane dock. Other local tour companies have booths near the cruise pier where **shuttle tickets to Mendenhall Glacier** can be purchased ($10 each way).

A trolley car departs regularly from the cruise ship dock on 45-minute, round-trip tours of downtown Juneau. Tickets cost $25 and riders can hop off and on along the route. Many choose to stay aboard for the entire narrated tour, then get off and on at various attractions at their leisure. Other tours are available, including one to Mendenhall Glacier.

For hiking suggestions in the Juneau area, see page 224.

Juneau's History

Cruise ships use the southern entrance to **Gastineau Channel**, which lies along a fault (a fracture in the earth's crust). When ice covered this entire area, it gradually ground away the weakened bedrock of the Gastineau fault. These sediments ended up as surface material and, in 1880, gold particles were discovered lying on the beaches of Douglas Island. A lode claim here was sold by a prospector to John Treadwell, who then built a mine. The Treadwell mining complex eventually became

(Top to bottom) Juneau's trolley car. Kiosks selling local tours are near the docks. City Hall is adorned with a Tlingit mural.

the largest in the world, extracting more than $70 million worth of gold out of the metamorphosed rock.

On the other side of the Gastineau Channel, two down-and-out prospectors named Richard Harris and Joe Juneau also found gold in 1880. They had been hired by a German mining engineer named George Pilz, who was offering a reward of 100 Hudson's Bay blankets to anyone who could show him where a substantial deposit of gold-bearing ore existed. A Tlingit named Kowee led Juneau and Harris up Gold Creek to Quartz Gulch – so named by Harris when he saw the quartz veins of this metamorphic rock. They contained more brilliant streaks of gold than he had ever before seen in one gulch.

Claims were quickly staked and within a year the number of prospectors camped in shacks along Gastineau Channel was large enough to form a small town. Prospectors, who found

An old Juneau gold mine.

nuggets as big as beans, eventually cleaned out the placer gold and mining companies took over, tunneling into mountainsides to extract underground deposits. Between 1881 and World War II, the Juneau Gold Belt yielded 6.7 million ounces of gold and 3.1 million ounces of silver. The last of three major mines in the Juneau area closed in 1944.

At the turn of the last century, Alaska's capital was moved from Sitka to Juneau. In addition to its lucrative gold mining operations, Juneau was on the steamer route to the gold-rich Klondike in Canada's Yukon territory.

Alaska was granted statehood in 1959 and Juneau has remained the capital despite complaints that the city is not accessible by road and that a location near the major population centers of Anchorage and Fairbanks would make more sense. Government jobs provide 50 percent of Juneau's employ-

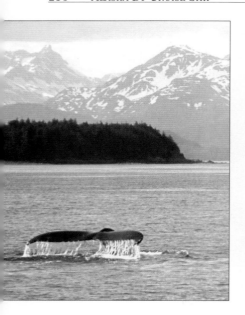

Humpback whales, sea lions and views of the Juneau Icefield are highlights of a boat excursion in Lynn Canal near Juneau.

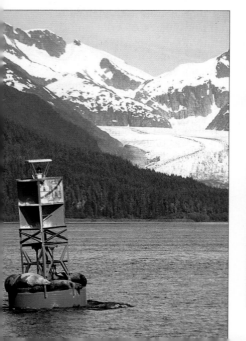

ment and many work in the S.O.B. (State Office Building). Despite Juneau's urbanization, wilderness remains right at the doorstep, with black bears often wandering into town. When an orphaned cub climbed onto the trash receptacle outside Bartlett Memorial Hospital's emergency entrance, it was quickly rescued and flown to Bear Country USA in South Dakota.

WHALEWATCHING

If seeing a humpback whale is a priority, be sure to reserve a whalewatching excursion out of Juneau, where humpback whales feed throughout the summer in nearby Stephens Passage and Lynn Canal. Wildlife Quest, operated by Allen Marine Tours and offered by most cruise lines' shore excursion departments, offers half-day excursions out of Auke Bay on board specially built vessels equipped with waterjets for speed and maneuverability. The marine life can be viewed from inside a comfortable cabin with large windows or from the upper deck, while an on-board naturalist provides commentary.

If you would prefer to join a smaller group aboard a whale-watching vessel, Alaska Whale Watching offers half-day tours at competitive rates for groups of up to six passengers. This tour operator also offers half-day and full-day sportfishing trips aboard 30' cabin cruisers. Bookings should be made in advance, either directly with the company (www.alaskatrophy-fishing.com) or through your cruise line's shore excursion department.

Shore Excursions

JUNEAU

A major port of call, Juneau offers an exciting array of shore excursions. **Mendenhall Glacier** is featured in several types of shore excursion – coach tour, flightseeing and helicopter viewing/landing. Mendenhall can also be viewed from the water while whalewatching in Lynn Canal or while paddling a canoe near the glacier's face on Mendenhall Lake. (For more information on Mendenhall Glacier, see pages 222 to 225.)

Flightseeing excursions over the **Juneau Icefield** will provide views of several glaciers (in addition to Mendenhall), and helicopter excursions will land you on a glacier for an interpretive walk. One popular helicopter excursion lands you at a **dog sled camp** where you can try your hand at mushing (see pages 223-224). Also popular is the flightseeing trip over several glaciers to historic **Taku Lodge** for a salmon bake (see page 223).

Juneau's **goldmining history** is highlighted on tours of the Gastineau-Juneau Mine or panning for nuggets in Gold Creek. Guided rainforest hikes, mountain biking, sea kayaking and river rafting are also offered. View a rainforest canopy from zip lines and suspension bridges at Alaska Canopy Expedition.

Local Attractions

Situated on the waterfront is the Naa Kahidi Theater, a clanhouse-style theater where performers dramatize traditional native legends. It is located in the **Cultural Arts Park 1** adjacent to the Alaska Native Artists Market.

Not to be missed is the **Mount Roberts Tramway 2** which whisks visitors 2,000 feet above the harbor to an observatory offering panoramic views of Juneau and the surrounding area. Well-marked trails of various lengths lead from the restaurant/theater complex to alpine meadows and the edge of the snowpack. ($33 per adult; $16 for six to 12-year-olds.)

From the cruise dock, it's a short walk to the **shops** on **Franklin** and **Front Streets**. These streets are lined with **historic buildings** such as the restored Alaskan Hotel & Bar

which first opened in 1913 and, across the street at 174 S. Franklin, the turreted Alaska Steam Laundry Building, built in 1901. At 202 Front Street you'll find the elegant Valentine Building, built in 1914 by a local jeweller and long-time mayor. In August 2004 a fire erupted in the century-old Endicott Building on the southeast corner of Front and Seward. Fire crews quickly contained the blaze, dousing the roofs of nearby wooden buildings built during the Gold Rush era.

The **Red Dog Saloon 3** is one of the first landmark buildings to your left if you're walking up South Franklin Street from the cruise ship dock. This building is not historic but is a popular tourist attraction with its honky-tonk atmosphere.

A post office is located on Seward, not far from the main

MOUNT ROBERTS ALPINE TRAILS

Father Brown's Cross (elevation 2,030')

Trail to Father Brown's Cross (.5 mile)

Observation Deck

Subalpine meadows

Alpine Loop Trail (.5 mile)

Nature Center

Upper Terminal

Observation Deck

Trail to Juneau (2 miles)

MOUNT ROBERTS

A-J cruise ship dock (4-minute shuttle ride)

FRANKLIN

i

Gastineau

1

2

3

Admiralty

FRANKLIN

Ferry

Marine Park *i*

Second

FRONT

P.O.

P.O.

Seward

Third

Fourth

Fifth

Sixth

Seventh

MARINE WAY

Seadrome

Coast Guard Dock

Gastineau Channel

To Mt. Roberts Trailhead

Nelson

East

Harris

Gold

Basin Rd

N

400

0

Yards

7

8

4

5

6

MAIN

Dixon

To Perseverance Trailhead

Gold Creek

Cope Park

Goldbelt

Calhoun Ave.

DIXON

9

Willoughby

Dixon

Village

Willoughby

WHITTIER

EGAN DRIVE

12

Capital

A - Street

B - Street

C - Street

D - Street

Eighth

Ninth

Tenth

Eleventh

Twelfth

Glacier Ave.

Glacier Ave.

11

10

EGAN DRIVE

JUNEAU

Juneau Visitor Information Center which is housed in the **Davis Log Cabin** 4, a replica of Juneau's first public school. One block up, on Fourth, is the **Alaska State Capitol** 5. It was built as the Federal & Territorial Building in 1930 and while it does not have the traditional domed roof of a capitol, it does have an impressive facade of Tokeen marble columns. The ground floor lobby, decorated in blue and gilt, houses an information desk for visitors interested in taking a guided tour. Across from the Capitol, on Main and Fourth, is the **Juneau-Douglas City Museum** 6 with displays that capture the city's gold mining era.

On Fifth and Gold, about three blocks from the State Capitol, is the **St. Nicholas Orthodox Church** 7, built in 1894 – nearly 30 years after Russia sold Alaska to the United States. Although the majority of Russian priests left Alaska at the time of the sale in 1867, they soon regrouped and began returning under the terms of the Treaty of Cession which guaranteed freedom of religion and allowed the Orthodox Church to retain its property and continue its mission in Alaska.

Gold Street leads up to Seventh Avenue where the **Wickersham House** 8 is also open to the public. James Wickersham was a pioneer judge who came to Alaska in 1900. He traveled throughout much of interior Alaska – by sternwheeler in summer and dog sled in winter – and delivered justice to gold mining set-tlements along the Yukon River.

Wickersham, a respected judge, was also a consummate politician who strove tirelessly for Alaska's territorial status, which was granted in 1912. He introduced the first statehood bill four years later and won congressional approval for the establishment of Mount McKinley (now Denali) National Park in 1917. Judge Wickersham spent his final years in Juneau and the house in which he lived is furnished with such items as his 1904 gramophone and his Chickering concert piano, previously owned by the Russian government in Sitka.

The Mount Roberts tramway provides spectacular views and a chance to hike through alpine meadows.

*(Above) The Red Dog Saloon.
(Below) The streets of downtown
Juneau are lined with gold rush
era buildings now housing shops
and local businesses.*

Outside the Wickersham House, stairs lead back down to Fifth Avenue, as does Main Street – one block over. A right-hand turn onto Fifth will take you across a pedestrian bypass on your way to the **Governor's Mansion 9** at the corner of Calhoun and Distin. Built in a colonial style and fronted with white pillars, it's the biggest house in the neighborhood and has a totem pole standing out front. The mansion is the official residence of Alaska's governor and is open for viewing only by advance special request.

If you follow Calhoun Street up the hillside and across Gold Creek, you'll come to the **Evergreen Cemetery 10**, where the prospectors Joe Juneau and Richard Harris are buried near the east end of the graveyard. At the other end, off Glacier Avenue, is a monument to their Tlingit guide Kowee. Also buried here are some of those who died in the 1918 sinking of the *Princess Sophia* in Lynn Canal.

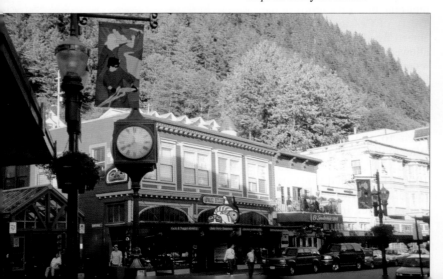

A few blocks south along Glacier Avenue, at the corner of Ninth, is the **Federal Building 11**. Outside is a bronze sculpture depicting pelicans. It was, according to local tour guides, intended for the Federal Building in Florida but a mix-up in shipping orders sent the eagle sculpture to Florida and the pelicans to Alaska. Florida decided to keep the eagle sculpture, the rationale being that eagles have been sighted there. But, as Juneau residents are fond of saying, these are the only pelicans you're going to see in Alaska.

As for eagle exhibits, you'll find a wonderful one in the **Alaska State Museum 12**, which is a 10-minute walk from the cruise docks. This popular attraction ($5 admission) features traveling collections from around the world in addition to its permanent exhibits on wildlife (the highlight of which is an eagle-nesting tree), native culture (the famous Lincoln totem pole is here) and Alaska's Russian heritage.

(Above) St. Nicholas Orthodox Church on Fifth Street.
(Below) Just a few blocks away is the Governor's Mansion.

Out of Town Attractions

Mendenhall Glacier is one of Juneau's premier attractions and can be visited by ship-organized tour or on your own by taking the shuttle bus from town ($10 each way). A visit to Mendenhall Glacier is, for many people, their first lesson in how glaciers are formed and behave. The Visitor Center, which is run by the Forestry Service and charges $3 admission, is equipped with books, pamphlets, videotapes and a model display to help explain glacial dynamics. The center's theater features a documentary on Mendenhall Glacier, and staff are there to answer any questions.

Outside, nature trails lead to various viewing points. (For information on extended hiking at Mendenhall, see page 225). Because Mendenhall Glacier has been retreating about 25 to 30 feet per year since 1750, a half mile of lake water now lies between the Visitor Center and the front of the glacier. The water of Mendenhall Lake reaches 200 feet in depth while the height of the glacier's terminus (snout) is 100 feet above

(Left) Befriending the sled dogs.

(Below) Mendenhall Glacier

lake level. One-and-a-half miles wide at its snout, Mendenhall Glacier is 12 miles in length and its measured rate of flow is two feet per day. Based on these calculations, the ice at its terminus is about 150 years old.

Another way to view the Mendenhall Glacier is by helicopter. Not only do you get a close look at its icescape of pinnacles and crevasses, you get to walk on its brittle surface. The helicopter pilot will find a safe spot to land and a guide will take you right to the edge of a deep crevasse. Other helicopter tours cover not only the Mendenhall Glacier but some of the other hanging and valley glaciers of the vast Juneau Icefield. Floatplane tours also whisk passengers over the icefield. Below the plane's wings you'll see craggy peaks all but buried in ice and snow, and valleys filled with blue seracs.

One popular flightseeing excursion takes you over the Juneau Icefield to **Taku Inlet** (see page 213) where you land in front of the historic Taku Lodge. Built of logs in 1923, this rustic lodge is known for its delicious salmon bakes and spectacular vistas, all enjoyed in a peaceful, forested setting.

Dog-sledding excursions are also popular (often selling out) and these entail a helicopter ride to a **sled camp** on Juneau Icefield where participants are briefed on the basics of the sport before an experienced musher takes you for a spin. Everyone gets to try their hand at mushing and afterwards you can spend a few minutes with the dogs, many of whom have raced in the Iditarod Trail Sled Dog Race. This tour also includes a close look at Juneau Icefield's Taku Glacier and other landmarks during the flight.

Helicopter tours to Mendenhall Glacier can include a close look at a crevasse.

(Above) A boardwalk section of the East Glacier Loop Trail near Mendenhall Lake.

Hiking Opportunities

It is possible to hike up **Mount Roberts** from the trailhead at the end of 6th Street, but this two-mile 'Lower Trail,' which ascends 1,600 feet, is uneven and often muddy. A better approach is by tram car to the mountain's nature center and from there explore the mountain trails. These are well-marked and lead to alpine meadows and the edge of the snowpack. A popular hike is to the top to Father Brown's Cross (see map page 218). Be sure to stay on the marked trails, both to preserve the vegetation and to ensure your safety. Guided group hikes of the Mount Roberts trails are available.

Perseverance Trail is a popular three-mile trail that begins at the end of Basin Road and takes three-to-four hours roundtrip to hike. Other, more strenuous trails branch off the Perseverance Trail.

The trails at **Mendenhall Glacier** are also recommended, with maps available at the Visitor Center. The East Glacier Trail is a

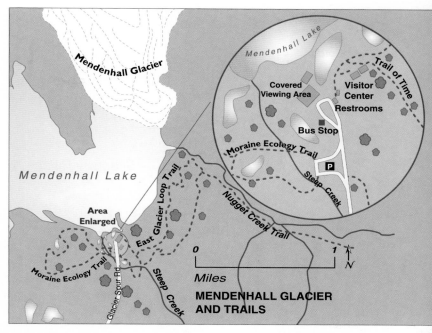

MENDENHALL GLACIER AND TRAILS

3.5-mile loop that ascends 400 feet and takes two-to-three hours roundtrip to hike. Shorter hikes can be enjoyed on several half-mile loop trails near the Shuttle Bus Stop, which is a short walk to the Visitor Center.

(Opposite) A quiet trail on Mount Roberts. (Below) The view from Mount Roberts of a cruise ship departing Juneau along the Gastineau Channel.

Bennett
Lake

Tutshi
Lake

Lindeman
Lake

*Chilkoot
Pass*

The 'Golden Stairs'

White Pass
Summit

*Summit
Lake*

DEAD HORSE
GULCH

TUNNEL
MOUNTAIN

Skagway River

Taiya River

Dyea

SKAGWAY

CANADA
USA

Klukwan

Chilkat River

*Taiya
Inlet*

Haines

*Haines is only 15 miles by water
from Skagway but 359 miles by
road via Whitehorse!*

N

0   15

Miles

GLACIER BAY

LYNN CANAL

*Berners
Bay*

Pt Bridget

Sentinel Is.

*Vanderbilt
Reef*

X

*Favorite
Channel*

Shelter Is

Pt.
Retreat

Juneau

*Funter
Bay*

Point
Couverden

ICY STRAIT

CHICHAGOF
ISLAND

SKAGWAY

POPULATION:	900
ANNUAL RAINFALL:	29 inches
DISTANCE TO JUNEAU:	120 miles
DISTANCE TO SITKA:	215 miles

CRUISE ROUTES

MAIN ROUTES:	– – – – –
ALTERNATE ROUTES:	- - - - - -
TRAIL OF '98:	••••••••••

SKAGWAY
& THE YUKON

Alaska's colorful gold rush history is showcased in Skagway – Gateway to the Klondike. Scenically situated at the head of a stunning fjord, the small town of Skagway springs to life each summer with the arrival of the cruise ships. Compact and easy to explore on foot, Skagway came into being when gold fever swept across North America in the summer of 1897 with news that prospectors had struck it rich in the Klondike, touching off the largest gold rush in history.

Skagway was a single homestead when the first steamship filled with prospectors heading to Canada's Yukon pulled up to the dock. Saloons and brothels were quickly constructed and a boom town was born. Soapy Smith and his gang of con men soon controlled the town's activities and Superintendent Sam Steele of the Northwest Mounted Police called Skagway "the roughest place in the world . . . little better than hell on earth."

Today the streets of Skagway are strolled by law-abiding cruise passengers reliving the town's gold rush days. Many of the original buildings still stand and several of these have been painstakingly restored by the National Park Service.

Skagway's gold rush buildings

An Alaska Steamship heads up Lynn Canal to Skagway.

The Klondike Gold Rush

Captain Vancouver must have been particularly homesick while surveying **Lynn Canal**. Not only did he name Point Couverden at its western entrance for his ancestral home in the Netherlands, he also named Berners Bay and Point Bridget for his mother – Bridget Berners. The inlet itself is named for Vancouver's birthplace of King's Lynn in Norfolk, England. This nostalgic naming of landmarks took place in the summer of 1794, during Vancouver's third and final season on this coast.

Homesick as Vancouver and his men no doubt were by this point in their lengthy voyage, the Tlingits who lived here were quite at home. Their main village of Klukwan was located near the mouth of the **Chilkat River** at

the head of Lynn Canal. Not only was the Chilkat River a fine salmon stream, its valley was a trade route to the interior, where the vast Athabascan region extended across much of the continent to Hudson Bay in northern Canada.

When explorers of Britain's Hudson's Bay Company (HBC) began building forts on the western edges of Athabascan territory, they came face to face with Tlingit tribes. Traveling upriver from their coastal villages, the Tlingits were not pleased to encounter white men taking possession of their fur trade territory and would attack their forts.

As the fur trade began running out of steam, gold prospectors started trickling into the Yukon area. **Forty Mile** became the largest settlement in the Yukon when gold was discovered in nearby tributaries in 1886. The miners' law of those times is reflected in a notice that was posted downriver at Circle City, Alaska : TO WHOM IT MAY CONCERN: At a general meeting of miners held in Circle City it was the unanimous verdict that all thieving and stealing shall be punished by whipping at the post and banishment from the country, the severity of the whipping and the guilt of the accused to be determined by the jury.

Frontier justice worked well and peace generally prevailed. Cabins were left unlocked and stocked with firewood. Failure to replace this fuel was a major offense, for the next visitor might arrive so cold and exhausted that only an instant fire could save his life. Miners' meetings were usually held in saloons and if a jail was needed at the conclusion of a hearing, one was quickly constructed. At Circle City, a notice on the jail's door stated that "All prisoners must report by 9 o'clock p.m., or they will be locked out for the night." When Judge James Wickersham arrived in the American part of the Yukon River valley and introduced himself to one old sourdough as "the district judge of the Territory of Alaska" the response was "Oh, the hell you are!"

While the boom towns of Forty Mile and Circle City attracted men and women in search of gold, a different sort of white man was roaming the Yukon River area. His name was George Washington Carmack and he arrived from California as a dishwasher on a Juneau-bound steamer. However, rather than pursuing the riches of gold, he instead adopted the native way of life.

The Yukon prospectors called him Siwash George. He married a native woman and lived off the land with her people. His closest companions were his brother-in-law, Skookum Jim, and another native called Tagish Charlie.

In July of 1896, Carmack headed upstream from Forty Mile to the **Klondike River** to do some salmon fishing. There he was joined by Jim, Charlie and his wife Kate. The salmon run was poor, so the men decided to cut timber and sell it to the sawmill at Forty Mile. On their return trip, they ran out of dried salmon and stopped to hunt. Jim set off with his .44 Winchester and shot a moose which he butchered and cooked beside **Rabbit Creek** while awaiting the other two men. At one point he knelt beside the creek to take a drink of water and

William Moore built Skagway's first cabin.

The future site of Skagway, before the Klondike Gold Rush.

there, glistening in the creek bed's gravel, was more raw gold than he had ever before seen.

When the other two arrived and Jim told them about his find, their reaction was in keeping with the occasion. Carmack, staring into the water, first rubbed his eyes then reached down and picked up a dime-sized nugget which he put between his teeth and bit on. Charlie grabbed a pan and shovel and almost fell into the creek in his excitement. Carmack grabbed the shovel from Charlie and dug into the loose bedrock. He later described the raw gold as "laying thick between the flaky slabs, like cheese sandwiches." With a full pan of gold and gravel, Carmack set it on the ground and the three men danced around it, performing a combination of "Scottish hornpipe, Indian fox trot, syncopated Irish jig and a sort of a Siwash Hula-Hula."

The next morning Carmack blazed with an axe this message on a spruce tree: *TO WHOM IT MAY CONCERN: I do, this day, locate and claim, by right of discovery, five hundred feet, running up stream from this notice. Located this 17th day of August, 1896.   G. W. Carmack*

Under Canadian mining law, a prospector was allowed only one 500-foot claim per creek, except for the man recording the discovery who could stake two claims. All subsequent claims were then numbered in relation to the discovery claim. At Rabbit Creek – promptly renamed **Bonanza Creek** by Carmack – the discovery claim was shared by Carmack and Jim, but registered in the former's name. Carmack also claimed Number One Below (downstream) while Jim claimed Number One Above (upstream) and Charlie claimed Number Two Below.

When Carmack returned to Forty Mile to register his claim at the mining recorder's office, he decided to stop first at Bill McPhee's saloon. He ordered a couple of drinks at the bar – to calm himself down – then turned to face the crowded, smoky room full of miners. "Boys," he said, "I've got some good news to tell you. There's a big strike up the river." This announcement fell on skeptical ears, for Carmack had a reputation for telling tall tales. But when he held up the gold he had just scooped from Bonanza Creek, everyone believed him. Within a month of Carmack's discovery, 200 claims were staked on the Bonanza and its tributaries. But no one knew which claims would produce gold and which ones were 'skunks'. Luck determined whether a man struck it rich. A cheechako (newcomer) was as likely to hit pay dirt as a sourdough (seasoned miner). All each man could do was start working his claim and hope for the best.

Throughout the winter of 1896-97, men of varied backgrounds and nationalities dug into the

Skagway as it looks today, a full century after its boomtown days.

Klondike's creek beds with picks and shovels. Malnourished and dirty, many suffered from scurvy. They slept in ramshackle huts where lice thrived in their unwashed bedding. But all were driven by gold fever as they scraped away the surface muck and burned fires to thaw the frozen ground to remove gravel covering the bedrock. Upon hitting bedrock, the pay gravel was removed by tunneling into the side of the creek bank (drifting) and hauling the gravel out with a hand-turned windlass. This was done in winter, when permafrost eliminated the need to shore the shafts and drifts with timbers. This backbreaking work continued until spring, when meltwater was used for sluicing the piles of bedrock gravel, to separate the gold from the gravel.

When the prospectors on Bonanza Creek and its tributaries finished sluicing their claims in

A cairn marks the spot on Bonanza Creek where gold was found in 1896, triggering the Klondike Gold Rush.

DISCOVERY CLAIM
CONCESSION DE LA DÉCOUVERTE

Circle City

Fairbanks

Arctic Circle

Alaska (USA)
Yukon (CAN)

DEMPSTER
HWY.

Eagle

Tombstone
Territorial
Park

Blackstone R.

GOLDRUSH
COUNTRY

Tok

**Dawson
City**

N. Klondike

Klondike R.

*Bonanza
Creek*

x Discovery Claim

*Eldorado
Creek*

KLONDIKE
HWY.

A
L
A
S
K
A

Y
U
K
O
N

Yukon River

Fort Selkirk

ALASKA HWY.

Carmacks

| Dyea to Chilkoot Pass   – 16 miles |
| Dyea to Yukon R. Headwaters – 33 mi |
| Skagway to Whitehorse   – 112 miles |
| Trail of '98: ●●●●●●●●●●●●●●●●● |

Burwash
Landing

Kluane Lake

MT. LOGAN

∧

Kluane
National
Park

Haines
Junction

T
E
R
R
I
T
O
R
Y

Whitehorse ★

Trail of '98 ● **Carcross**

*Bennett
Lake*

S
T
.

E
L
I
A
S

M
O
U
N
T
A
I
N
S

*Chilkoot
Pass*

*White
Pass*

Watson
Lake

Dyea ● **Skagway**

B
R
I
T
I
S
H

C
O
L
U
M
B
I
A

N

0   150

Miles

Juneau ★

the early summer of 1897, many were rich men. With their moose-hide pokes and pickle jars filled with gold, they boarded two stern-wheelers in Dawson and headed down the Yukon River to the old Russian port of St. Michael. There they transferred onto two steam-ships – the *Excelsior* bound for San Francisco and the *Portland* bound for Seattle.

Gold fever swept the continent and the world. Men and women rushed to the Klondike, stopping at San Francisco, Seattle, Victoria or Vancouver to outfit themselves before heading north. Those who could afford the passage took a steamer to St. Michael, then a paddlewheeler up the Yukon River. Others ascended the Stikine River and Alsek River or hiked from Edmonton, Alberta through boggy, mosquito-infest-ed wilderness. The majority, however, headed up Lynn Canal to Skagway.

In the early summer of 1897, only one family lived in Skagway. William Moore, a former riverboat captain and prospector, had antici-pated a gold rush to the Yukon and constructed a cabin and wharf here. But when the first shipload of pros-pectors arrived at the 'Mooresville' wharf on July 26, 1897, the survey-ors who spilled off the steamer ignored Moore's homesteading claim and quickly laid out a new town which they called Skaguay. The spelling of this Tlingit name (its meaning open to interpretation) was changed to Skagway when a post office was established. Moore, who owned a sawmill and ware-house in addition to the wharf, prospered.

During the winter of 1897-1898, thousands of stampeders ascended the Chilkoot Trail's Golden Stairs on their way to the Klondike.

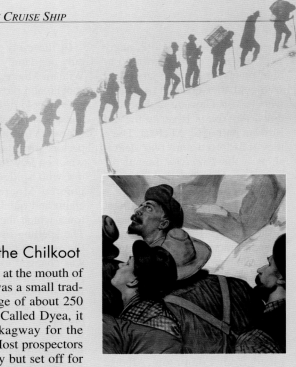

Facing Up to the Chilkoot

Three miles away, at the mouth of the Taiya River, was a small trading post and village of about 250 Chilkoot natives. Called Dyea, it competed with Skagway for the gold rush trade. Most prospectors landed at Skagway but set off for the goldfields from Dyea via the 33-mile **Chilkoot Trail** – the 'poor man's route' which included a quarter-mile vertical ascent of 1,000 feet up the 'Golden Stairs' cut into the ice. The **White Pass**, which starts at Skagway, was used by those who had could afford pack horses. This route was 10 miles longer than the Chilkoot but not as steep. Nonetheless, the route's boulders, rocks and muskeg earned it the name Dead Horse Trail during the winter of 1897-98. One stampeder who traveled both trails would later say it didn't matter which one you took, "you'd wished you had taken the other."

Overnight stops (tent cities) dotted the Chilkoot Trail, with stampeders moving their goods in five-mile relays between caches. It could take 20 trips back and forth

to cover each leg of the journey. In winter, sledges made hauling supplies a bit easier. It's estimated that 30,000 stampeders crossed the Chilkoot by these two routes, now called the Trail of '98.

The White Pass trail links up with the Chilkoot Trail at the foot of Lake Lindeman which flows via a narrow rocky stream into Lake Bennett, headwaters of the Yukon River. At the Summit, the stampeders crossed into Canadian territory. Those without a year's supply of food were turned back by the Mounties.

The majority of stampeders reached lakes Lindeman and Bennett in the spring of 1898 where they whipsawed trees into planks to build boats and rafts while waiting for the ice to melt. When the ice on Lake Bennett broke up on May 29, a flotilla of

Shore Excursions

SKAGWAY

The array of guided shore excursions offered in Skagway is extensive and includes zip lining, kayaking, canoeing, mountain biking, horseback riding and dog sledding. An enduring favorite is the train ride aboard vintage cars of the **White Pass & Yukon Route** (WP&YR) rail line for a spectacular trip along the Trail of '98 (see pages 239-240 for more detail).

Rock climbing is popular in Skagway, where participants climb and rappel off smooth granite cliffs along White Pass. This excursion is closely supervised by professional mountain guides and appeals to climbers of all abilities.

Another popular excursion is the short boat ride down Lynn Canal to Glacier Point for a safari ride and nature walk to Davidson Glacier and canoeing on the adjacent lake. The **Chilkat Bald Eagle Preserve** (near Haines) can be visited by jet boat or river raft, as can the famous **Chilkoot Trail**. It takes three to five days to hike the Chilkoot (see facing page), but cruise passengers can hike the first two miles on an organized shore excursion that

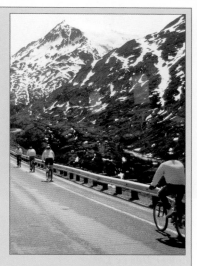

Cycling the Klondike Highway.

includes a raft ride back to the trailhead in Dyea. Another way to view the Chilkoot Trail and surrounding glacier-covered mountains is by helicopter on a flightseeing excursion. Dog sledding on a glacier is also offered, as is a visit to a back-country musher's camp where dogs train with wheeled sleds in summer. Tours of a gold dredge and miners' camp are also offered, as is a visit to Jewell Gardens, its colorful flowers and miniature garden railroad beautifully displayed at a historic homestead.

stampeders set sail down the hazardous Yukon River in their makeshift vessels. A number of these unseaworthy craft capsized and stampeders drowned in the cold churning waters of White Horse Rapids. The flotilla pressed on, traversing 500 miles of swift-flowing river to arrive, in mid-June, at Dawson City. They had reached the Klondike.

Getting Around

Skagway is compact and easy to explore on foot, with its historic buildings (housing visitor information centers) clustered at the south end of town close to the cruise piers. A municipal (S.M.A.R.T.) bus runs regularly between the cruise docks and a bus stop on Broadway Street

(Above) Rock climbing in White Pass. (Below) Good hiking near Lower Dewey Lake.

where the shops and historic buildings are concentrated (the fare is $2 or $5 for an all-day pass).

Bicycles can be rented near the docks and several car rental agencies are located in town for those who would rather drive the Klondike Highway than take the rail and/or motorcoach tour to the White Pass Summit.

Hiking Opportunities

Several good hiking trails are accessible from the cruise docks. These vary in length and include an easy, one- to two-hour roundtrip hike to the park at Yakutania Point on the waterfront. Another pleasant hike (two to three hours round-trip) is the one to **Lower Dewey Lake**. The trail is steep at the beginning, then levels off for the hike around the lake.

The mile-and-a-half walk to the **Gold Rush Cemetery** outside town takes about half an hour and can be a little dusty for the last stretch. However, the walk beyond the cemetery to beautiful **Reid Falls** is a rewarding sight. There are several other hiking trails in the Skagway area, and a detailed trail map is available at the National Park Service office.

Local Attractions

A visitor to Skagway will have no trouble reliving the excitement of the Klondike Gold Rush. Each summer, more than 300,000 people visit this town, which has a year-round population of about

900. Some days, four or five cruise ships are in port at the same time. A short walking tour is a must in Skagway and, with an average annual precipitation of less than 29 inches, a typical summer day here is warm and sunny – perfect for strolling the town's historic streets.

Near the cruise ship docks, at the foot of Broadway, is the **National Historical Park Visitor Center 1** housed inside the old White Pass and Yukon Route Railroad Depot, built in 1898 and restored by the National Park Service. Here you'll find exhibits, presentations and written information on the town's historic buildings. Ranger-led walking tours of Skagway Historic District are held throughout the day.

One block up from the Visitor Center is the **Mascot Saloon 2**, built in 1905 and restored for viewing by the National Park Service which has recreated a lifelike bar scene with mannequins dressed as locals from the gold rush era.

Historic buildings line Broadway, many of them housing private businesses. Across the street from the Mascot Saloon is the **Golden North Hotel**. Built in 1898, its lobby is decorated with antique fixtures and photographs. Two doors down is the **Arctic Brotherhood Hall 3**, its facade covered with 20,000 driftwood sticks collected and nailed to the front of this 1899 building by an early lodge member. This restored building now houses a **Visitor Information Center**. Ask for a copy of their Walking Tour map. A few doors down from the Visitor Information Center, at the corner of Second and Broadway, is the **Red Onion Saloon**. One of Skagway's best-known watering holes, it was a dining spot for Robin Williams and fellow cast members when *The Big White* was filmed in Skagway in May 2004.

On the south side of Second Avenue is **Jeff Smith's Parlor, 4** the saloon owned by Skagway's

(Below) National Park's Visitor Center and interior of its refurbished Mascot Saloon (right).

TO GOLD RUSH
CEMETERY
(1.5 m. from 1st Ave.)

KLONDIKE HWY.

Icy Lake

Jefferson R. Smith
Died July 8 1898
Aged 38 Years

*Grave of Soapy
Smith at Gold Rush
Cemetery*

15th Ave.

14th Ave.

SKAGWAY

*Observation
Platform*

10th Ave.
9th Ave.
8th Ave.
7th Ave.
6th Ave.
5th Ave.
4th Ave.
3rd Ave.
2nd Ave.
1st Ave.

Alaska St.
State St.
Broadway St.
Main St.
Spring St.

P.O.

7
6
i **3** **2**
4 **1**
5

S
K
A
G
W
A
Y

R
I
V
E
R

DYEA ROAD

0   500
Yards

N

Park Trails - - - - -

*Lower Dewey
Lake*

AIRSTRIP/
HELIPORT

Point St.

*Footbridge
to park*

*Pullen
Creek Park*

SMALL BOAT
HARBOR

*Ships registry a
Railroad Dock*

Terminal Way
Ore Dock Rd.
Congress Way

*Smugglers
Cove*

**BROADWAY
DOCK**

S.S.PRINCESS CHARLO
CAPT. W.O. PALMER
1929

*Yakutania
Point*

**ORE
DOCK**

**FERRY
DOCK**

**RAILROAD
DOCK**

Taiya Inlet

White Pass & Yukon Rail operates vintage rail cars.

infamous Jefferson Randolph 'Soapy' Smith, who led a gang of criminals that controlled the town. Smith was killed in a shoot-out with surveyor Frank Reid, who later died of his gunshot wounds. A cairn at the foot of State Street (where it crosses 1st Avenue) marks the spot where Reid gunned down Soapy Smith on the evening of July 8, 1898. Reid and others were guarding the entrance to the Juneau Co. wharf where a mass meeting was being held to organize the towns-people against Soapy Smith and his gang.

Back on Broadway, opposite the National Park Headquarters, is the former residence of **Martin Itjen** **5**, which now houses a summer office of Parks Canada. A prominent local businessman, Itjen established the **Skagway Street Car Company** in 1923 when U.S. President Harding came for a visit and was charged 25 cents for a tour in Itjen's car. Soon Itjen was offering tours to All Points of Interest, and these entertaining excursions in vintage streetcars are still a popular attraction. Other buildings of note include the **Moore Cabin** **6** built by William Moore in 1887 (see photo, page 229); and **Skagway City Hall** **7**, built of stone in 1899 by the Methodist Church and now housing the Trail of '98 Museum.

The **White Pass & Yukon Route** (WP&YR) railroad is one of Skagway's most popular attractions but its construction was a massive challenge. Workers, suspended by ropes, had to chip and blast their way through barriers of rock to build this mountain-pass rail line. Accidents claimed lives and gold fever regularly swept through the work gangs, depleting their numbers. Against tough odds, the narrow-gauge railroad was completed in the summer of 1900 – after the big rush to the Klondike was over. The rail line transformed Skagway into a shipping port and during construction of the Alaska Highway, thousands of army troops landed here. Shortly after the Klondike Highway from Skagway to Whitehorse was completed in 1978, the railroad was closed. However it was reopened in 1988 to provide summer passenger service.

The rail trip is a fascinating blend of dramatic scenery and history. As the train rolls out of Skagway, it passes the Gold Rush Cemetery – resting place of Soapy Smith and Frank Reid – then follows the river valley past glacier-fed waterfalls and overhanging rock ledges. The train slowly climbs from sea level to 2,865 feet at the Summit. Along the way, passengers get a close look at the Glacier Gorge chasm as the train steams across the abyss and into Tunnel Mountain. The ascent continues past Inspiration Point (with its mountaintop view of Lynn Canal) and Dead Horse Gulch (where 3,000 pack animals died of exhaustion from carrying heavy loads up the steep climb).

Another tunnel – Steel Bridge – is followed by a cliffside glimpse of the famous Trail of '98. Then it's over the **White Pass Summit**, where only those stampeders with a ton of supplies (enough for one winter) were waved on by the Mounties into Canada. This is the turn-around point for passengers taking the three-and-a-half hour rail trip, but the rail line continues to Whitehorse, Yukon Territory. Stops along the way include **Fraser Station** in British Columbia, where Canadian customs is cleared, and **Carcross** – originally called Caribou Crossing – at the top of Lake Bennett where it flows into the Yukon River. The three natives with George Carmack when they discovered gold on Bonanza Creek – Skookum Jim, Tagish Charlie and George's wife Kate – are buried in the Carcross cemetery. Full-day shore excursions out of Skagway go as far as Carcross via motorcoach before returning to the ship.

The Skagway Street Car company has been offering local tours since 1923.

The Yukon

The White Pass and Yukon Railroad takes passengers right to Summit Lake in British Columbia.

Whitehorse, the capital of Canada's Yukon Territory, is where Skagway residents do most of their shopping, while Whitehorse residents keep their recreational boats moored at the marina in Skagway. Whitehorse takes its name from the nearby Whitehorse Falls. When stampeders traveled this treacherous section of the Yukon River, they said the frothy white water looked like a horse's mane. To avoid the rapids spilling from **Miles Canyon**, stampeders hauled their goods on horse-drawn trams past this section of river. The rapids were eliminated in 1958 with construction of a hydroelectric dam, followed a year later with a fish ladder – billed as the world's longest wooden one – which allows migrating salmon to bypass the dam. Visitors can enjoy the riverside foot trails and suspension bridge now spanning Miles Canyon.

Attractions in Whitehorse include the S.S. *Klondike*, largest sternwheeler to ply the Yukon River, and the MacBride Museum, a complex of log buildings which includes the first cabin built by Sam McGee – a prospector and friend of **Robert Service** who was immortalized in Service's famous poem *The Cremation of Sam McGee*. McGee had given permission to Service to use his name, but when he realized people were laughing at his name-sake, he got even with Service by taking him on a fishing trip near the worst part of Whitehorse Falls before finally putting his terrified passenger ashore.

Whitehorse, home to more than two-thirds of the Yukon's total population of 30,000, is a major stop along the **Alaska Highway**. This famous stretch of highway was built by the U.S. Army Corps of Engineers during World War II, in a race against time and sub-arctic conditions, after Japan bombed Pearl Harbor. With America's west coast shipping lanes vulnerable to Japanese attack, the highway was deemed crucial for securing Alaska and providing a vital supply link. The situation became crucial when Japanese troops invaded the Aleutian Islands in June 1942. American soldiers battled freezing temperatures and rugged terrain to lay a highway across 1,520 miles of mountains and muskeg between Dawson Creek (Mile 0) in northern British Columbia, and Fairbanks, Alaska. Construction began on

A sightseeing boat tours Miles Canyon, near Whitehorse.

March 9, 1942, with work crews bulldozing from either end. They met at Soldiers' Summit, near Kluane Lake in the Yukon. A pilot road was opened on November 20 and the following year a permanent road was completed and named the Alcan Military Highway. After the war, the highway was turned over to civilian contractors, regraded, widened and opened to unrestricted travel. Today most of the highway is asphalt-surfaced, but improvements and repairs are ongoing.

Points of interest long the Alaska Highway, east of Whitehorse, include **Liard Hotsprings**, where army workers soaked their tired muscles in 1942, and nearby **Watson Lake** with its famous wall of sign boards. The first signpost was carved by a homesick G.I. in 1942, and hundreds of signs, license plates and other paraphernalia now line the roadside. The Alaska Highway also traces the eastern boundary of **Kluane National Park**.

Kluane is a native name for 'place of many fish' and this remote wilderness park is also a place of many mountains, containing the most extensive non-polar icefields in the world. The Saint Elias Mountains run through the park where **Mount Logan**, Canada's highest peak at 19,850 feet, stands in ice that's a mile deep. Winter storms off the Gulf of Alaska bring snowfall so heavy that up to 10 feet can fall in 24 hours. When this happens, "You have to shovel all day long," according to one park warden, "or else you simply get buried."

The Visitor Centre at **Haines Junction** features exhibits on the park's spectacular scenery, much of it hidden behind a front range of mountains. The **Kluane Range** is visible from the Alaska Highway, its peaks including **Mount Kennedy** – named for President John F. Kennedy. In March 1965, his brother Robert, accompanied by seven experienced mountaineers, was the first to ascend this peak. The more distant Icefield Range lies west of the Kluane Range and contains **Mount Logan**, a massif measuring 100 miles around its base and nearly 10 square miles at its triple-peaked summit, making it one of the largest physical landforms on Earth. It was first climbed by a party of mountaineers in 1925 but remained unchallenged again until 1950. Mount Logan, which takes about 30 days to climb, is a daunting challenge for serious climbers because of its harsh weather.

For most visitors, a flightseeing tour is the best way to view Kluane's magnificent icefields. At the base of these ice-covered slopes, the glaciers are slowly retreating, their melting ice revealing a host of ancient artifacts. Recent finds include a hunting dart dating back 9,000 years, when herds of caribou – hunted by humans with bows and arrows – would gather on the snouts of glaciers to escape swarms of summer mosquitoes. Glacial ice preserves organic material, such as wood, antler, bone, leather and sinew, and the items being surrendered by the retreating glaciers are providing archeologists with direct radiocarbon dating. The ice also preserves caribou dung, massive

The Klondike River and Yukon River meet at Dawson City.

piles of which have been exposed during the summertime melt.

North of Kluane is the Yukon's **Klondike** region where **Dawson City** was once the most famous boomtown in North America. The North Klondike Highway, a detour off the Alaska Highway near Whitehorse, traces the Yukon River valley to Dawson City, which sprang to life in the summer of 1897. The **Northwest Mounted Police**, anticipating an onslaught of stampeders, built a fort here that summer but in their haste they did a few things wrong. When clearing the land, they scraped away the moss covering the permafrost. This allowed the sun to melt the topsoil and the fort's foundations soon settled into a knee-deep morass. Also, green logs were used in construction and they began to shrink and warp. As buildings fell apart, the Mounties were kept busy reconstructing their fort when they weren't enforcing law and order among Dawson's 30,000 new residents.

Among these new arrivals was a young American prospector named **Jack London**. He lived only briefly in the Yukon but turned his experiences into masterful stories, including his famous novels *The Call of the Wild* (a bestseller in 1903) and *White Fang* (published in 1906). His cabin, built on Henderson Creek in 1899, has been moved to Dawson City and reconstructed to house the **Jack London Interpretation Centre**. It stands on Author's Avenue, as does the childhood home of **Pierre Berton**, Canada's popular historian who wrote several bestselling books about the Klondike Gold Rush. The Yukon's most famous poet was the British-born **Robert Service** who immigrated to Canada in 1894. He worked for a bank in Victoria and other locations before being stationed at Dawson City. Service published his first collection of poems in 1907. Called *Songs of a Sourdough* (republished in 1916 as *The Spell of the Yukon*), this first volume included *The Shooting of Dan McGrew*. Service, profoundly influenced by Rudyard Kipling, became known as 'The Canadian Kipling' and his restored cabin on Author's Avenue is a major visitor attraction run by Parks Canada, where his poetry is recited twice daily throughout the summer. Two dozen heritage buildings in Dawson City are maintained by Parks Canada as visitor attractions, including a reconstruction of the 1899 **Palace Grand Theatre**. Another local attraction is **Diamond Tooth Gerties Gambling Hall**, operated by the Klondike Visitors Association, where the roulette wheels spin and blackjack is played in a gold rush atmosphere of honky-tonk music and can-can dancing.

The **Dempster Highway** stretches north of Dawson City across the Arctic Circle to Inuvik in the Northwest Territories. Completed in 1978, this unpaved two-lane highway sits atop a gravel berm four to eight feet thick, designed to insulate the permafrost and prevent it from melting, which would cause the ground to soften and the road to sink. The Porcupine herd of **caribou** roam this vast territory and about half of the herd (which numbers 120,000 in total) crosses the Dempster Highway during spring and fall migrations. By August, the green tundra vegetation becomes an explosion of reds and golds, blanketing entire valleys before yielding to winter frosts. At its south end, the highway runs through **Tombstone Territorial Park**, where ridgetop trails provide sweeping views of broad valley floors and black granite peaks.

Tombstone Park, established in 1999, protects 1,400 square miles of sub-arctic landscapes in the south Ogilvie Mountains. Tombstone Mountain is the best-known landform in the park, which contains a variety of seldom-seen permafrost landforms such as pingos (small hills) and patterned ground. The Tr'ondek Hwech'in peoples have inhabited this area for at least 8,000 years. The boreal forests provided wood, and chert (a rock used to make stone tools) was available at Tombstone Mountain. Fishing was good in the Blackstone River, while the open tundra provided good visibility for hunting the region's large mammals – bear, moose, caribou and Dall sheep. Many species of birds – both boreal and arctic tundra – nest within the park.

Beautiful landforms are found in Tombstone Territorial Park.

Haines (pop. 2,500)

While the Klondike gold rush was creating the boom towns of Dawson City and Skagway, another entrepreneur named **Jack Dalton** was trying to get a piece of the stampede action in Haines – 15 miles south of Skagway on the west side of Lynn Canal.

Haines had been founded by the Presbyterian missionary **Samuel Hall Young** in 1880. He was given land for building a mission by the Chilkat natives whom he visited with **John Muir** in 1879. So impressed were the Chilkat chiefs with Muir's brilliant oratory, they wanted him to

THE SOPHIA TRAGEDY

When the great gold rush died down in the Klondike, the prospectors gradually sold their claims to mining companies which continued mining the area's pay gravels with machinery. Each fall most of the miners, riverboat crew and others who worked in the Yukon would head south for the winter. On October 23, 1918, a full boatload of people coming out of the Klondike for the winter boarded the ill-fated *Princess Sophia* (a CPR steamship) in Skagway.

Carrying 343 passengers and crew, the *Sophia* was heading down Lynn Canal in a snowstorm when, two hours past midnight, she grounded on Vanderbilt Reef. Her distress calls were answered by a variety of smaller vessels which stood by at dawn in choppy seas, waiting for the *Sophia* to transfer her passengers to the waiting vessels. But the seas were too rough to safely launch the small boats and the *Sophia*'s captain decided the passengers would be safer on board the stranded ship. The next night, shrieking winds pushed the *Sophia* off Vanderbilt Reef and she plunged into the icy water. All 343 people on board drowned in the stormy seas, including Walter Harper – the first man to set foot on Mt. McKinley's summit.

A few years before Princess Sophia's sinking, Princess May grounded on Sentinel Island but refloated with little damage.

run the mission but had to settle for Mr. Young, who named it after Mrs. F. E. Haines – chief fund-raiser for the mission.

When Jack Dalton arrived at Haines, several canneries had been built and a wagon road wound its way from nearby Pyramid Harbor to the Yukon River, following roughly the route of today's Haines highway. He built a few posts along this trail, called it the **Dalton Trail**, and charged stampeders $2 per head of cattle and $2.50 per horse. Historic stops on the Dalton Trail include Glacier Camp – from which 26 glaciers can be seen – and the abandoned native village of Nasketahin, where traditional spirit houses stand in the local graveyard.

The Chilkat tribe of Tlingits display their famous Chilkat blankets and other craftsmanship at the **Center for the Arts** on the Fort Seward grounds. **Fort Seward** was built in 1903 during a border dispute with Canada. This U.S. army post was closed in 1946, then bought by a group of World War II vets who turned the white frame buildings and lawn-covered grounds into private residences and commercial enterprises.

The **Sheldon Museum and Cultural Center**, housed in the original Presbyterian mission, is located at the corner of Main and Front streets.

Northwest of Haines, several thousand bald eagles gather each fall along a five-mile stretch of the Chilkat River to feed on chum salmon. The **Alaska Chilkat Bald Eagle Preserve** protects a 48,000-acre section of this river valley. The eagles can be seen from the Haines Highway, which runs parallel to the river, and the highest concentration of eagles occurs between Mileposts 17 and 22 from Haines. This preserve can be visited by shore excursions from Haines and Skagway (see page 235). Passenger ferries operated by Chilkat Cruises make regular 35-minute trips between Haines and Skagway.

The Alaska Chilkat Bald Eagle Preserve near Haines supports a thriving population of bald eagles, especially in autumn.

GLACIER BAY

CRUISE ROUTES

MAIN ROUTES:
ALTERNATE ROUTES:
NATIVE SETTLEMENTS: •
WHALE GROUNDS:

BRITISH COLUMBIA
ALASKA

SKAGWAY

HAINES

Takhinsha Mtns

LYNN CANAL

Grand Pacific Glacier

Muir Glacier

Marjerie Glacier

GLACIER BAY

BERNERS BAY

Johns Hopkins Inlet

Mt. Fairweather

Fairweather Range

Glacier Bay

Saginaw Channel

Favorite Channel

Lituya Bay

NATIONAL PARK PRESERVE

Beardslee Islands

Bartlett Cove

JUNE

La Perouse Glacier

Brady Glacier

• Gustavus

Taylor Bay

Pt. Aldophus

ICY STRAIT

Cape Spencer

Elfin Cove

Icy Strait Point

• Hoonah

To Hubbard Glacier

CROSS SOUND

Pelican

CHICHAGOF ISLAND

ADMIRA

ISLAN

CHATHAM STRAIT

YAKOBI ISLAND

N

To Sitka

ALEXANDER

0   30

ARCHIPELAGO

Peril Strait

Miles

GLACIER BAY
& ICY STRAIT POINT

When John Muir discovered Glacier Bay in 1879, it was – and still is – in the process of creation. Glaciers that had filled the entire bay a mere century before Muir's first visit were now staging a drastic retreat, leaving behind a freshly exposed landscape of newborn islands and inlets.

Neither Muir nor his traveling companions fully believed Sitka Charley when he first described Glacier Bay – at least not the part about the absence of trees. After all, Charley hadn't visited this bay of 'ice mountains' since he was a boy on a seal hunt with his father, and none of them had ever seen a woodless shoreline in this land of rainforests. Nonetheless, they turned up Icy Strait, as directed by young Charley, to see this mysterious bay for themselves. It was the fall of 1879 and

John Muir, with the help of Presbyterian missionary **Samuel Hall Young,** had convinced four native men at Fort Wrangell to take him north to see the glaciers. Despite the imminent onset of winter, this brave party piled into a canoe and headed north.

In his book *Travels in Alaska*, John Muir describes how, upon arriving at the entrance to Glacier Bay, he could see little because of thick weather. Captain Vancouver's chart, "hitherto a faithful guide," was of no use because Glacier Bay had been completely clogged with ice when Vancouver sailed past less than a hundred years earlier.

GLACIER BAY AT A GLANCE
Icy Strait Point: page 259
Anne's Alaska Journal: pg 263

Glacier Bay is a stunning sight.

That wall of ice had now retreated more than 40 miles and this newly landscaped bay awaited discovery by Muir, a man fascinated with glaciers and the way they sculpted the earth. At Glacier Bay he could see the glaciers in action and he no longer had to speculate about their movements as he had done in the Sierra Mountains of California. Here was a living science experiment, proof at last "that this is still the morning of creation." But first he had to convince his traveling companions of the wondrous opportunity before them.

Near the entrance to Glacier Bay they had come across a camp of Huna seal hunters, who were curious about this motley crew "coming to such a place, especially so late in the year." They had heard of Reverend Young but wondered what a missionary was doing in this lonely, desolate bay.

"Was he going to preach to the seals and gulls, they asked, or to the ice mountains?"

Muir's native guides explained everything to the Huna hunters and one of them agreed to join the expedition as a guide. Next morning they sailed up the bay in cold, pelting rain and made camp just beyond **Geikie Inlet**. The next day, while the party stayed put due to bad weather, Muir climbed the mountain slopes above their camp for a cloud-fringed view of the bay. It was filled with icebergs and fed by many glaciers.

When Muir returned to camp, Young took him aside and told him their guides were discouraged, fearing this expedition would end in disaster. They questioned Muir's desire to go mountain climbing in a storm and figured he "must be a witch to seek knowledge in such a place as this and in such miserable weather." Rising to his reputation as an eloquent speaker, Muir addressed his demoralized crew. He reassured them that luck always followed him and told them to put away their childish fears. This pep talk worked wonders and, although it was still sleeting rain the next morning, they pushed on towards the head of the bay.

They spent five days in Glacier Bay while Muir sketched, made notes and observed glaciers calving chunks of into the water, described by Muir as a "crystal wall . . . thundering gloriously."

A wall of ice blocked Glacier Bay's entrance when Captain Vancouver sailed past in 1794.

Inside Glacier Bay

Glacier Bay National Monument was established in 1924 and renamed Glacier Bay National Park & Preserve in 1980. Glacier Bay lies in the middle of this huge preserve, which encompasses 3.2 million acres and contains 11 glaciers that reach the sea. Eight of these tidewater glaciers are within Glacier Bay. Park headquarters are located at **Bartlett Cove**, just inside the entrance to Glacier Bay on the eastern shore. A ranger station, lodge and campground are located in Bartlett Cove and cruise ships entering Glacier Bay will pause outside the cove to await the embarkation of two park rangers who explain the sights and wonders to the ship's passengers.

Vessel traffic within Glacier Bay is tightly regulated. There are strict limits placed on the number of cruise ships, sightseeing boats and private pleasurecraft allowed into the bay at any one time, and permits must be obtained beforehand. Commercial fishermen are not allowed to trawl in these waters or catch certain marine life, such as herring, shrimp and pollock. The reason for these restrictions is to protect the **humpback whales** that feed in Glacier Bay.

A sudden decline in the number of humpback whales feeding in the bay was recorded in July of 1978 and 1979. More recent studies indicate this may have been a normal seasonal decline, with the whales using Glacier Bay as their early summer feeding grounds before traveling elsewhere in late summer. However, to be on the safe side, measures were taken to protect the whales from excessive disturbance to their feeding grounds.

Today the annual number of humpback whales sighted in Glacier Bay is increasing, with about 150 currently counted each summer inside the bay (and that many or more outside the bay's entrance, in Icy Strait.) During the whale season in Glacier Bay – June 1 to August 31 – no vessel

A ship's tender brings park rangers aboard at the entrance to Glacier Bay.

A ship glides close to Marjerie Glacier at the head of Tarr Inlet.

is allowed to come closer than a quarter of a mile to a feeding whale or to follow a whale without maintaining a distance of at least one-half mile. Park hydrophones measure vessel noise and its effect on the whales.

Harbor seals are a common sight on the ice floes of Glacier Bay, while overhead you'll see gulls (both glaucous-winged and mew), black-legged kittiwakes and Arctic terns. On shore you may spot a brown bear or mountain goat.

As your ship proceeds up Glacier Bay, you will see a raw landscape of freshly exposed rock and soil. Lichens and mosses are the first forms of vegetation to reclaim deglaciated land. They break down the rock and enrich the soil so that small flowering plants and low bushes can grow. Thickets of alder and willow are the next to take hold. They build up the soil and are eventually replaced by spruce trees.

Forests at the entrance to Glacier Bay gradually give way to more recent stages of growth until, near the snout of each glacier, the immediate landscape is one of silt, sand and gravel. In Tarr Inlet, at the very head of Glacier Bay, the exposed rock on the northeast side of the fjord is over 200 million years old, while that on the southwest side is about 90 million years old. They belong to separate terranes (fragments of the earth's crust) which nudged their way up the west coast and are now wedged between the Pacific Plate and the North American Plate.

At the head of Tarr Inlet is the **Grand Pacific Glacier**, which retreated another 15 miles after Muir first sketched it in 1879, leaving **Russell Island** in its wake as it retreated up Tarr Inlet. The glacier crossed the border into Canada between 1913 and 1916, then stopped retreating in 1925. It readvanced and was on the verge of rejoining the **Margerie Glacier**, from which it separated in 1912, when it began receding again. Kittiwakes nest in rocky cliffs between the two glaciers. Here they wait for the glaciers to drop their ice into the sea; this churns up the water and brings baitfish – on which they feed – to the surface.

Grand Pacific Glacier

Takhinsha Mountains

Marjerie Glacier

1907

TARR INLET

Rendu Glacier

Johns Hopkins Glacier

Johns Hopkins Inlet

RUSSELL ISLAND

1880

Carroll Glacier

Muir Glacier

Lamplugh Glacier

Reid Glacier

Queen Inlet

Burroughs Glacier

Hugh Miller Inlet

1907

MUIR INLET

Brady Icefield

Geikie Inlet

1860

1860

Adams Inlet

DRAKE ISLAND

Brady Glacier

GLACIER BAY

MARBLE ISLANDS

CRUISE SHIP ROUTE – – – – –

WILLOUGHBY ISLAND

Beartrack Cove

N

BEARDSLEE ISLANDS

0   10

Miles

Historic extent of glaciation

1794

PARK BOUNDARY

1750–1780

Barlett Cove

● Visitor Center

PARK RANGER STATION

LEMESURIER ISLAND

● **Gustavus**

PLEASANT ISLAND

(Above) First surveyed by John Muir in 1879, Johns Hopkins Inlet, with nine glaciers, is one of Glacier Bay's most dramatic inlets. (Below) John Muir (on the right) and John Burroughs were members of the Harriman Expedition which visited Glacier Bay in 1899. (Opposite page) View into Johns Hopkins Inlet.

A tidewater glacier's dimensions are constantly changing but the Grand Pacific Glacier is about 35 miles long and two miles wide, with a terminus measuring 60 feet high (above the waterline). The 20-mile-long Margerie Glacier is one mile wide with an ice face (terminus) rising 250 feet above the waterline, with about 100 feet below the water.

The adjacent inlet – **Johns Hopkins** – is 10 miles long and contains nine separate glaciers.

Toyatte, Kadachan, John and Charley Glaciers are all named for Muir's guides on his first trip to Glacier Bay in 1879. The advancing **Johns Hopkins Glacier** is about 12 miles long and one mile wide, with a terminus that is 250 feet above the waterline and 200 feet below. The stable but thinning **Lamplugh Glacier** is 16 miles in length with a terminus that's 180 feet above water but only 10 to 40 feet below.

Nearby **Reid Glacier** calves very few icebergs and is retreating entirely through melting and evaporation.

Muir Glacier, one of the retreating glaciers that carved Muir Inlet, was a big producer of icebergs when John Muir studied it in the late 1800s. He camped on shore, living in a hut near the face of the glacier that bears his name.

Muir made himself a sled so he could travel across Muir Glacier and study its tributaries. He camped at night on the glacier and awoke on the seventh day of this expedition to discover he was nearly blind from the glare of the ice. Everything he looked at had a double image. He kept a snow poultice bound over his eyes and dryly commented in his notes that this was the first time in Alaska he had gotten too much sun.

His eyes recovered and a few days later, back at his hut, he stayed up all night watching an aurora borealis light the sky above his glorious world of ice mountains.

Muir Glacier is fed by the snow-covered slopes of the **Takhinsha Mountains** and, like other glaciers on the east side of Glacier Bay, has retreated since Muir's visit. A few glaciers on the west side of Glacier Bay are, however, advancing – due to abundant snowfall in the **Fairweather Range**, which separates Glacier Bay from the Gulf of Alaska. **Mount Fairweather** – the tallest peak in the range at 15,300 feet – was named by Captain Cook in 1778.

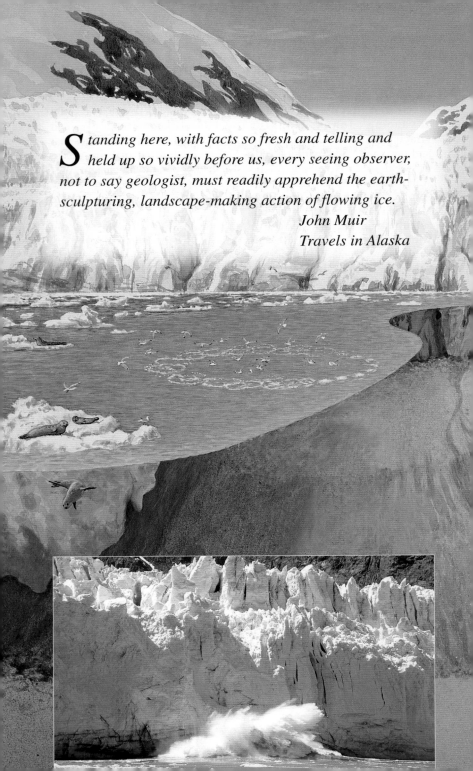

S tanding here, with facts so fresh and telling and
held up so vividly before us, every seeing observer,
not to say geologist, must readily apprehend the earth-
sculpturing, landscape-making action of flowing ice.

John Muir
Travels in Alaska

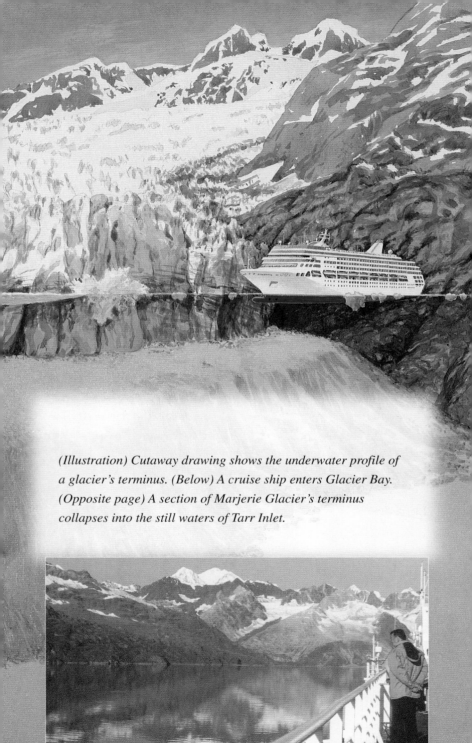

(Illustration) Cutaway drawing shows the underwater profile of a glacier's terminus. (Below) A cruise ship enters Glacier Bay. (Opposite page) A section of Marjerie Glacier's terminus collapses into the still waters of Tarr Inlet.

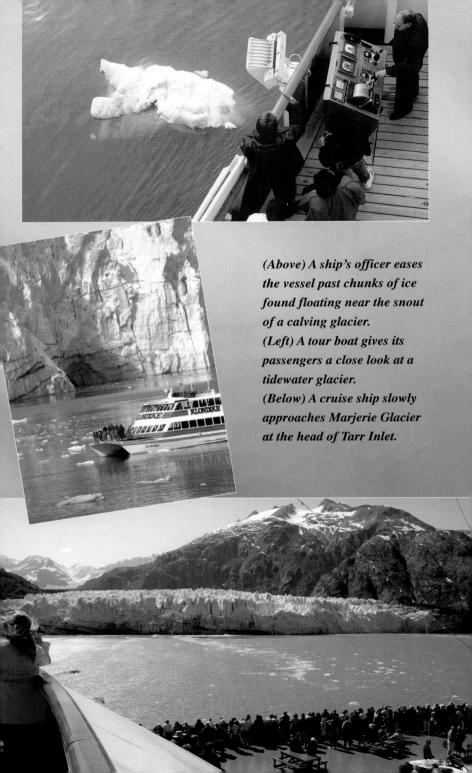

(Above) A ship's officer eases the vessel past chunks of ice found floating near the snout of a calving glacier.

(Left) A tour boat gives its passengers a close look at a tidewater glacier.

(Below) A cruise ship slowly approaches Marjerie Glacier at the head of Tarr Inlet.

Icy Strait Point

Hoonah is a Tlingit community situated in a sheltered inlet off Icy Strait – so named for the ice floes that drift out of Glacier Bay throughout the winter. Seal hunters by tradition, the Hoonah Tlingit once lived in Glacier Bay until advancing ice forced them to abandon their homes. They originally named their new village Huna, which means Protected From the North Wind, but this was later changed to Hoonah, meaning Village by the Cliff.

Many of Hoonah's residents, who today number about 900, were once employed at the large cannery built north of their village in 1912. In the 1990s the local native corporation, Huna Totem, hired logging contractors to clear-cut most of the marketable timber standing on native-owned land. When the logging ended, so did employment opportunities for many of Hoonah's residents, so a new local industry

The view of the Fairweather Range from a ship in Icy Strait.

was created with the conversion of the now-derelict cannery into a museum and retail shopping complex for the benefit of visiting cruise passengers. Named **Icy Strait Point** and located just down the road from Hoonah, this new port of call received its first cruise ship in May 2004 when Celebrity Cruises' *Mercury* dropped anchor in the harbor and tendered its passengers ashore, where they were greeted by Tlingit dancers and singers.

Attractions at Icy Strait Point include the beautifully restored cannery with is cannery tours and shops selling locally made crafts. At the adjacent **Native Heritage Center**, Tlingit artifacts are on display and Tlingit culture is showcased in live performances of song, dance and storytelling presented at Journey through Time. A public beach trail traces

(Above) The refurbished can-nery at Icy Strait Point. (Below) Elfin Cove is a friendly fishing port located off Icy Strait.

the shoreline and connects with a nature trail that meanders for about a quarter of a mile through a second-growth rainforest.

Shore excursions at Icy Strait Point capitalize on the remote wilderness setting and include mountain biking and ATV expeditions. Brown bears can be watched from viewing platforms, or you can strap yourself into a harness seat for a thrilling ride on the ZipRider, which descends 1,300 feet from mountaintop to beach. Sea kayaking and fishing trips to catch halibut or salmon are also offered, as are boat excursions to view the humpback whales that frequent the waters off Point Adolphus in Icy Strait, which is one of their prime summer feeding grounds.

The Fairweather Coast

Cruise ships proceeding through Cross Sound provide passengers with a fleeting view of **Brady Glacier**, which flows into Taylor Bay. Less easy to spot is the tiny community of **Elfin Cove** opposite Brady Glacier on the northern tip of Chichagof Island. Elfin Cove is a boardwalk community of about 50 year-round residents. In summer the population swells to 200 with fishboats coming and going to take on fuel, water and provisions before heading out into the Gulf of Alaska to fish the famous Fairweather Bank. Gentle ocean swells wash into Cross Sound and brown **sea otters**, floating on their backs, are often seen in these waters.

Cape Spencer marks the northern end of the Inside Passage and the beginning of the Gulf's mainland coast. A light is housed here in a white, square concrete tower atop a rocky islet, and is a welcome sight for fishermen returning from the Gulf to inside waters. Captain Vancouver named this cape in 1794 for a British earl whose descendants would include Lady Diana Spencer.

Cruise ships proceeding north, toward Hubbard Glacier or Prince William Sound, sail past the seaward portion of Glacier Bay National Park & Preserve, where an unobstructed view of the **Fairweather Range** is one of Alaska's most spectacular sights. Some of the highest coastal mountains in the world ring the Gulf of Alaska. Their upper slopes covered with ice and snow, they rise abruptly from the edge of the sea, their steep summits towering within 15 miles of the shoreline. Fishboats are dwarfed as they pass beneath the magnificent peaks of the Fairweather Range. The sprawling **La Perouse Glacier** – at the base of Mount La Perouse – is the only tidewater glacier in Alaska that calves icebergs straight into the open Pacific.

About 20 miles northwest of La Perouse Glacier is famous **Lituya Bay**, site of the largest wave ever recorded in Alaska. It was witnessed one July evening in 1958, when an Alaska fisherman was jarred awake by the sudden pitching and rolling of his boat at anchor in Lituya Bay. He rushed to the wheelhouse and looked out at a scene that drove all thought from his mind: the mountains at the head of the bay were moving.

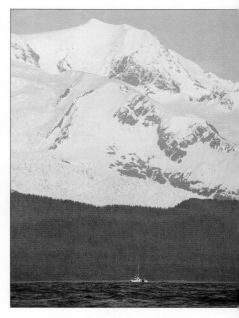

Fairweather Range is among the world's tallest coastal mountains.

Mesmerized by this impossible sight, he watched the massive mountains twist and shake, then heave an avalanche of snow and rock into the water. Up rose a 1,700-foot wall of water that lashed against one mountainous shore and then another before roaring down the bay toward him at 100 mph. The fisherman and his battered boat somehow survived, but two other fishboats were swept from the bay, one of them vanishing.

This was not the first giant wave to strike Lituya Bay, nor will it be the last. An active fault runs through the Fairweather Mountains at the head of Lituya Bay and another earthquake could hit at any time. Called everything from "bewitcher" to "death trap,"

La Perouse Glacier

Lituya Bay is breathtakingly beautiful. Mountains stand like snowy sentinels at the head of the bay, their rugged crowns and shoulders draped with glaciers, their lower portions consisting of exposed rock and stands of spruce timber. A line of demarcation between the light green of young trees and the darker green of old growth shows how high the 1958 wave surged up the sides of the bay, denuding the lower slopes.

The Tlingits believed the bay's recurring giant waves were caused by an underwater sea monster who disliked people and occasionally threw a temper tantrum. They established summer villages near the bay's entrance and hoped for the best. Unfortunately, Tlingit legends recall giant waves wiping out entire villages and canoe-paddling men drowning in churning seas at the entrance. This pincer-like entrance is guarded by a submerged bar – the end moraine of the glacier that carved Lituya Bay. The tide rushes in and out of this deep bay with hardly a pause, and the tightly squeezed currents at its entrance can be treacherous.

When the French explorer **La Perouse** sailed his two frigates through this narrow entrance in 1786, the wind shifted in mid-passage and he noted afterwards in his log that "during thirty years experience at sea, I never saw two ships so near destruction." Ten days later he sent three boats to survey the entrance. One was swept through roaring breakers out to sea and the other two were wrecked at the entrance, with 21 men perishing, their bodies lost.

No one lives permanently in Lituya Bay, although for years a man named Jim Huscroft lived in a cabin on Cenotaph Island in the middle of the bay where he raised foxes. The only boats to pull in now are fishboats and the occasional pleasure boat. Floatplanes sometimes drop off or pick up mountaineering expeditions. A Canadian team of climbers that had ascended Mount Fairweather was picked up at the head of Lituya Bay just hours before the 1958 earthquake struck.

Anne's Alaska Journal

The first time Bill and I ventured past Cape Spencer into the Gulf of Alaska in our 35-foot sloop, the weather couldn't have been finer. Fishermen on the VHF radio said they'd rarely seen the Gulf so calm. Apart from some high feathery cloud, the sky was a blue backdrop for the snowy white mountains passing to starboard. We were on our way to Lituya Bay and were timing our arrival at its entrance to coincide with highwater slack. Despite four knots of current pulling our boat sideways off the range markers and the nearby breakers shattering into spray, Bill eased our boat through the tricky entrance channel with unquestioning faith in our small diesel engine. Inside, the bay opened up to reveal its stunning setting. As we rounded the cliff-side gull rookeries of Cenotaph Island, we came upon a dozen anchored fishboats. They were waiting for the one-day halibut opening in the Gulf. Moored among these fishboats was a classic wooden ketch named *Gipsy* from Juneau. Her owners, Bill and Toni, promptly motored over in their skiff to say hello. We spent the next three days' in their company, sharing pot luck dinners and heading ashore together to explore one of the glaciers at the head of the bay where we beached their skiff on an outwash plain and tied the painter around a big boulder of ice lying there. It was both easy and difficult to leave Lituya Bay. The bay's beauty is mesmerizing but there's always the possibility that an earthquake could strike without warning and trigger a massive avalanche at the head of the bay. Every distant rumble is listened to with dreadful eagerness. After spending four days here, we figured we'd better not press our luck. We were up at sunrise the next morning and steaming through the entrance an hour later, with *Gipsy* right behind us. The dawn light cast a ghostly glow onto the white-peaked mountains as we drew away from Lituya Bay.

Lituya Bay

Skagway

LYNN CANAL

GLACIER BAY

GLACIER
BAY
NATIONAL
PARK
PRESERVE

Juneau
Icefield

Bartlett
Cove

Gustavus

Mendenhall
Glacier

JUNEAU

ICY STRAIT

Cape
Spencer

CROSS SOUND

Elfin
Cove

Icy Strait Point

Hoonah

TO HUBBARD
GLACIER

YAKOBI
ISLAND

Pelican

CHICHAGOF
ISLAND

Tenakee
Springs

ADMIRALTY
ISLAND

ALEXANDER

White Sulphur
Spring

GULF OF ALASKA

ARCHIPELAGO

Rum
Runner
Passage

Peril
Strait

Sergius Narrows

BARANOF

Angoon

CHATHAM STRAIT

N

Kruzof
Island

ISLAND

Mount
Edgecumbe

SITKA

FREDERICK SOUND

Warm
Spring
Bay

Kake

0   30

SITKA
SOUND

Miles

Goddard
Hotsprings

SUMNER STRA

SITKA

POPULATION:	9,000
ANNUAL RAINFALL:	97 inches
DISTANCE TO JUNEAU:	186 miles
DISTANCE TO KETCHIKAN:	258 miles

CRUISE ROUTES

MAIN ROUTES: - - - - - - -
ALTERNATE ROUTES: · · · · · · ·
NATIVE SETTLEMENTS: ●

Cape Ommaney

Cape Decision

SITKA

Sitka, a former outpost of Imperial Russia, is one of Alaska's most scenic ports. A town of 9,000 residents, Sitka enjoys a beautiful setting on the edge of Sitka Sound where Mount Edgecumbe rises above the fish-boat harbor, looking its most impressive in winter when dusted with snow. In summer the town's flower-fringed parks make strolling the winding waterfront streets a pleasant pastime for visitors – who number about 200,000 annually and arrive mostly by cruise ship. The plentiful sea otters that once attracted Russian fur traders to Sitka can be viewed in local waters.

SITKA AT A GLANCE

Russian America

The Russians gained their first toehold in North America on the outer islands of the Aleutian chain. Arriving in rickety ships from Siberia's Kamchatka Peninsula, Russian frontiersmen (called *promyshlenniki*) forced the Aleuts to hunt sea otters on a scale that quickly depleted their numbers.

Moving east along the stepping stones of the Aleutian Islands, these Russian fur traders – accompanied by their Aleut hunters – eventually arrived at Kodiak Island and, in 1784, established their first sparse settlement at Three Saints Bay. Alexander Baranof was hired by the Russian-American Company to manage

Cruise ships anchor in Sitka Sound, overlooked by Castle Hill.

this new settlement and in 1791, at the age of 44, he embarked on his first sea voyage to Russian America. The son of a storekeeper, Baranof couldn't resist the opportunity to escape both an unhappy marriage and his country's rigid class system. He was heading for a new land where social rank was secondary to ambition and hard work.

When Baranof arrived by open boat at Three Saints Bay, he was sick with pneumonia after enduring seasickness, a diet of raw fish and nights spent sleeping on wet beaches. But he was a tough, wiry man who soon regained his energy, setting off with 900 natives in 450 *baidarkas* (kayaks) on a tour of the Kodiak coastline to visit the local villages, meet the chiefs and bargain for sea otter pelts.

After a tsunami all but wiped out the Russian settlement at Three Saints Bay, Baranof took this opportunity to move everyone to a new site at the present-day city of Kodiak. From there he

Baranof's Castle was built by the Russian navy atop Castle Hill.

continued his explorations, setting off with a fleet of 90 *baidarkas* to visit the mainland. While visiting a tribe of Alutiiq in Prince William Sound, Baranof married the chief's daughter, calling her by the Russian name of Anna.

In the summer of 1795, Baranof sailed to **Sitka Sound**. He had heard much about the beauty of this natural harbor. It was inhabited by a powerful **Tlingit** clan – the Kiksadi – who lived in a village called **Shee Atika**, atop a hill overlooking Sitka Sound. Backed by mountains and fronted by sea, this Tlingit stronghold was a popular port of call for British and American merchant ships engaged in the lucrative sea otter trade.

When Baranof returned to Sitka Sound four years later with 1,100 men, he bargained with the local chief for a piece of land six miles north of the village. There, using timbers two feet thick, he built a Russian fortress protected by high watch towers. A stockade encircled its outbuildings and the new settlement was placed under the patronage of **Saint Michael Archangel**.

Baranof returned to Kodiak and an uneasy co-existence pervaded Sitka Sound, for the Kiksadi were having second thoughts about letting the Russians settle on their doorstep. Antagonism erupted into violence in 1802 when the Tlingits attacked the Russian fort and massacred most of the inhabitants. A handful escaped through the woods and were rescued by merchant ships lying at anchor in Sitka Sound.

A British merchant ship took the survivors back to Kodiak where Baranof was informed of the tragedy. Determined to retake Sitka and make it the headquarters for his company, Baranof returned two years later with a fleet of two sloops, two schooners, 300 *baidarkas* and a Russian frigate, the *Neva*.

A bloody battle ensued in which the Tlingits, led by their fearless warrior Katlian, withdrew from their hill-top village to a fort on the far side of the harbor. Under a steady bombardment of cannon fire from the *Neva*'s guns, the Tlingit depleted their ammunition and abandoned their fort in the middle of the night.

Baranof and his men burned the deserted village to the ground and in its place, on the hill overlooking the harbor, a fortified town was built. It was called New Archangel and, by 1809, close to 50 ships a year were pulling into port to trade for furs, their commanders invited to lavish dinners hosted by Baranof.

By the end of his tenure as manager of the Russian-American Company, Baranof was known far and wide as the Lord of

Alexander Baranof

Alaska. He was not without enemies, however. Many considered him a tyrant. The Orthodox clergy did not approve of Baranof's common-law marriage to Anna and their two illegitimate children, and the Russian fur traders under his employ objected to his crude management skills. When a plot to murder him and his family was uncovered, Baranof sent his wife and children to Kodiak, wrote out his will, then drank his way through the long, dark winter.

A man predisposed to black moods, he was now thoroughly demoralized and resigned his position. But when two of his replacements died en route to New Archangel, he read this as a sign that he was destined to carry on as Lord of Alaska. He became pious and sent for his wife and children. His son and daughter returned but Anna remained in Kodiak.

By 1818, the 70-year-old Baranof was no longer needed by

St. Michael's Cathedral is a Sitka landmark.

the Russian-American Company. Officials had decided the navy should run the company and two frigates were sent to New Archangel to relieve Baranof of his duties. After running the colony for 27 years, Baranof was ordered to hand over his books. It was rumored that he had embezzled company funds, but an audit revealed the books were in perfect order. Baranof, far from having accumulated great personal wealth, was almost penniless. He had, over the years, paid for improvements to the colony – such as schools – out of his own pocket while making the Russian-American Company the most profitable fur dealer in the world.

It was an emotional farewell for Baranof when the time came to board a ship bound for Russia. His daughter had fallen in love with a Russian naval officer stationed in New Archangel and would remain there. Longtime friends bid Baranof farewell, including his Aleut hunters, many of whom were devoted to the hard-drinking old Russian.

Baranof never made it back to his homeland. He caught a fever during a stopover in Indonesia and died at sea. While his body was committed to the Indian Ocean, a smooth transition to naval rule was taking place back at New Archangel, which continued to thrive. The wives of naval officers accompanied their husbands to Russian America and brought with them the culture and fashions of St. Petersburg, which earned New Archangel the epithet Paris of the Pacific.

The Tlingits were invited to return to Sitka and they settled at the foot of Castle Hill. The Russian clergy, led by such missionaries as Bishop Innocent, built a cultural bridge with the natives. Eventually a dwindling fur trade prompted Russia to sell its North American colony to the United States in 1867. New Archangel's name was changed back to Sitka, and a period of decline and lawlessness followed as Russian residents returned to their homeland.

America's purchase of Russian America attracted Protestant missionaries to Alaska, but the influence of the Orthodox church remains to this day a strong force among the native population. Russian place names have also

MOUNT EDGECUMBE

Mount Edgecumbe, seen across the water from Sitka, has been inactive for the last 200 years, although on April 1, 1974, the residents of Sitka wondered if another eruption was imminent when black smoke was seen rising from the volcano's caldera. The smoke, however, was coming from a pile of burning tires placed there by an April Fool's Day prankster.

endured. When the United States conducted a survey of its newly acquired territory, many of the Russian names were retained. Thus, the islands of Chichagof, Mitkof, Kupreanof, Wrangell and Zarembo all bear the names of naval officers who served in Russian America, and the Alexander Archipelago is named for Czar Alexander II. The island on which Sitka stands is, fittingly, named Baranof.

Getting Around

Large ships drop anchor in Sitka Sound and tender their passengers ashore to one of two small docks. One is located in Crescent Harbor beside Centennial Hall (which houses the Sitka Convention & Visitors Bureau). The other tender dock is at the base of Castle Hill, near the south end of Lincoln Street – Sitka's main shopping street. Both tender docks are within walking distance of Sitka's major attractions. Small ships dock at the Petro Marine dock or other harbor docks.

Many of Sitka's attractions are a short stroll away while others are farther afield, such as the Alaska Raptor Center which is a 20-minute walk from downtown.

A trolley bus provides a hop-on/hop-off shuttle service when large ships are in port, stopping at Sitka's main attractions, including Sheldon Jackson Museum, Sitka National Historical Park and Alaska Raptor Center.

Sitka's public blue buses follow three routes, with the Green Line running a loop through town and over the bridge.

To hire a taxi, contact Sitka Cabs (907-747-5001) or Nina's Taxi at 907-738-1931.

Bicycles can be rented at Yellow Jersey Cycle Shop on Harbor Drive across from Centennial Hall (907-747-6317; www.yellowjerseycycles.com). For suggestions about touring the area by bicycle, see the Hiking & Cycling section on page 278.

Various land and sea excursions can be booked right off the tender dock area. Flightseeing tours are also available.

Sea kayaking in Sitka Sound

A good place to have **lunch** while ashore is The Raven Dining Room restaurant at the Westmark Sitka, a popular place with locals for its fresh Alaskan halibut, salmon, crab and shrimp. King crab is especially recommended for those wishing a real, and fresh, Alaska treat.

Shopping

Sitka is a good place to shop for quality **Russian-made crafts** and artwork. The Russian American Company (407 Lincoln Street) carries an exceptional selection of Russian lacquer boxes, matryoshka nesting dolls and Faberge fine jewelry. Many gift and souvenir shops line Lincoln Street.

Shore Excursions
SITKA

With the Pacific Ocean at its doorstep, the waters off Sitka offer some of Southeast Alaska's best wildlife viewing. Sea otters are especially abundant, and humpback whales are frequently sighted. Boat cruises out of Sitka offer good opportunities to see marine mammals up close, as well as such seabirds as the colorful puffin. Very popular is the Sea Otter Quest tour operated by Allen Marine Tours aboard specially built observation vessels.

Nearby Silver Bay is a favorite fjord for sightseeing cruises. Here you can view not only the area's wildlife but also an old gold mine, a modern pulp mill and a salmon hatchery.

Sitka's historic Russian sites and a visit to the Raptor Center are covered in excursions that combine a motorcoach ride with a walking tour.

Rainforest hikes, biking tours and 4X4 off-road adventures are available, as are sea kayaking, dry suit snorkeling, underwater viewing from a semi-submersible and sportfishing excursions.

For original and replica **native artwork**, the gift shop at the Sitka Historical Museum (housed in Centennial Hall) carries hand-carved bentwood boxes, silver jewelry, spruce root baskets, potlatch bowls and satin scarves printed with totemic motifs.

Lincoln Street, the main shopping street in Sitka, is lined with inviting shops and galleries, including Old Harbor Books where you will find a good selection of Alaskana and natural history books.

Local Attractions

Harrigan Centennial Hall, which houses the **Sitka Convention & Visitors Bureau**, was built on the waterfront in 1967 to commemorate Alaska's statehood centennial. It also contains the **Sitka Historical Museum** (formerly called the Isabel Miller Museum). Exhibits here include a scale model of Sitka as it looked in 1867 (the year Alaska was transferred from Russia to the United States) and items from Vitus Bering's historic voyage of 1741, when Russians first set foot on Alaskan soil. Beautiful replicas of the museum's native artifacts can be purchased in the gift shop.

The stage of the Centennial Building's auditorium is backed by windows overlooking Sitka

(Top to bottom) Lincoln Street is lined with shops and galleries. Russian folk art sold in Sitka includes handcrafted dishware and matryoshka nesting dolls.

Sound. This waterfront view of passing fishboats and gliding eagles so impressed the violinist Paul Rosenthal when he performed here in the late 1970s with the Arctic Chamber Orchestra, he founded Sitka's Summer Music Festival. Held each year in the first three weeks of June, these classical concerts attract distinguished artists from around the world. Sitka's **New Archangel Dancers** also perform their Russian folk dances in the Centennial Building. An all-women dance troupe which was formed in 1969, they wear authentic costumes for their crowd-pleasing show.

Aspiring musicians can listen to international artists perform at Sitka's Summer Music Festival.

Between the Centennial Building and the local library is displayed a 50-foot ceremonial canoe carved by local artist George Benson in 1940. This canoe was carved from a 70-foot cedar log towed to Sitka by a fishboat from Port Renfrew at the southern tip of Vancouver Island.

From here, Harbor Drive winds in a southwesterly direction toward **Castle Hill** **1** which can be reached by a spiral path leading from a parking lot off Harbor Drive. (Stairs off Lincoln Street beside the old post office also provide access.) The sweeping view from this hilltop takes in **Mount Edgecumbe** – a dormant volcano visible across Sitka Sound on Kruzof Island. This mountain was named in 1778 by Britain's Captain James Cook.

The hilltop was originally occupied by Tlingit natives until they were driven out in 1804 by the Russians, led by Alexander Baranof, who lived here in a

wood house filled with fine furnishings, paintings and books until he was asked to retire in 1818. This house was eventually replaced with an enormous two-story log mansion called **Baranof's Castle**. Company officials held gala balls in Baranof's Castle until 1867, when Russia sold its North American colony to the United States. Prince and Princess Maksoutoff were the last occupants of the castle, which later burned to the ground. Its encircling stone walls and mounted Russian cannons are reminders of the past dramas which unfolded on this hilltop.

Stairs lead from Castle Hill down to Lincoln Street where, directly opposite, is the **Sitka Pioneers Home** **2**. It was built in 1934 – the first such facility for elderly

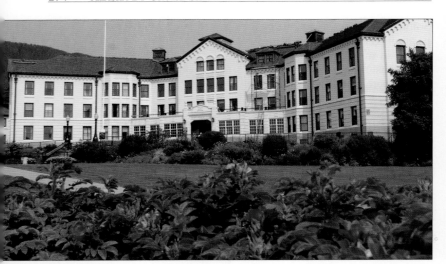

Sitka roses border the grounds of the Pioneers Home.

Alaskans – and visitors are welcome to stroll the lawned grounds where flower gardens contain native Alaskan plants. A shop in the basement sells handicrafts.

Across the street from the Pioneers Home, on the waterfront, is **Totem Square**. The totem pole displayed here was carved by George Benson. One of the pole's crests is the doubled-headed eagle of Imperial Russia. Traditionally, a clan would symbolize an enemy's defeat by borrowing its emblem. Also on display at Totem Square are a Russian cannon and some salvaged anchors from British and American fur trading ships. Opposite the square is the Sheet'ka Tribal Community House which serves as a cultural center. Nearby is a replica of the Russian Blockhouse that once separated the Russian and Tlingit sections of Sitka.

Standing prominently in the middle of Lincoln Street like a mid-channel island is **St.**

Michael's Cathedral 3. This is a splendid replica of the original church which was built from 1844 to 1848, shortly after Sitka (then called New Archangel) became the diocesan seat of the Russian Orthodox Church in Alaska (then called Russian America). A fire destroyed the cathedral in 1966, but Sitka residents managed to save most of its valuable icons, these religious works of art dating as far back as the 17th century. Many were painted on boards gilded with gold and other precious metals, and embellished with jewels. These magnificent icons, and the beautiful domed and spired architecture of the church itself – which took 10 years to rebuild from blueprints – draw thousands of visitors each summer.

Proceeding east from St. Michael's Cathedral on Lincoln Street, you'll pass the Westmark

Sitka (formerly the Shee Atika Lodge) – which is a good place to have lunch – before reaching the **Russian Bishop's House** . Built in 1842, this heritage building served as a hospital, school, rectory and place of worship. The first bishop to live here was **Father Innocent**, who had spent 10 years as a missionary in the Aleutians before arriving at New Archangel (Sitka) in 1834. An accomplished linguist, he quickly learned the Tlingit language and produced written instructional material in both Russian and Tlingit so the native children could be taught to read and write. When his wife died in 1840 he took monastic vows and was consecrated a bishop.

The navy built an imposing residence for Bishop Innocent which housed a chapel and seminary for native children. He resided here until moving to a new diocese in Siberia. In 1868 he became Metropolitan of Moscow – the highest rank in the Russian Orthodox Church – and in 1977 he was canonized a saint.

When the **Park Service** acquired the Bishop's House, a 15-year restoration project was undertaken to fix its sagging structure and restore the interior furnishings. Hundreds of experts were consulted as the painstaking work was carried out. Blackened icons were sent to an iconologist for cleaning, and teams of specialists at the Park Service's Harper's Ferry Center in West Virginia restored the house's furnishings. The first floor now contains historical and architectural exhibits. In 'The Room Revealed' a cut-

(Above) St. Michael's Cathedral
(Below) Russian Bishop's House

(Above) Sheldon Jackson College campus. (Below) Wooded trails and totem poles at Sitka National Historical Park.

away section of the building shows the sturdy scarf joints and other shipbuilding techniques used by Finnish shipwrights during construction. Upstairs is the beautiful chapel where Bishop Innocent and his fellow missionaries spent time in prayer each morning.

From the Bishop's House, the walk heading east on Lincoln Street couldn't be more pleasant. Along the waterfront are lawns, walkways and benches which overlook Crescent Harbor. Across the street, a sidewalk leads past **St. Peter's By-the-Sea** (a pretty stone church with a gift shop out back), followed by the campus of **Sheldon Jackson College** 5, which hosts summer workshops, conferences and events such as the **Sitka Summer Music Festival** and the Writer's Symposium. In 1983 the college's president, Dr. Michael Kaelke, read that **James Michener** was interested in writing a book on Alaska but was reluctant to spend time in a cold climate at his age. Dr. Kaelke promptly wrote the famous author, explaining that winter in southeastern Alaska is quite mild with temperatures often above freezing. Michener accepted the college's invitation to use it as a base from which to research and write his book *Alaska*.

The **Sheldon Jackson Museum** is an octagonal-shaped concrete building located on the college campus. It contains a fine collection of Eskimo, Aleut and Indian artifacts collected by Dr. Sheldon Jackson, a presbyterian missionary and General Agent for Education who traveled Alaska by boat, dog sled and on foot in the late 1800s. Sleds, *umiaks* and other watercraft hang from the museum's ceiling. Haida argillite carvings, a Chilkat blanket and the Raven's Head Helmet worn by Sitka Chief Katlian during the 1804 battle with the Russians, are just a few of the items on display.

At the end of Lincoln Street is the **Sitka National Historical Park**. A visitor center, located at the park's entrance, displays Tlingit exhibits and presents a recorded slide presentation on Sitka's history. Available at the **Visitor Center** is a booklet which describes each of the totem poles standing along a quarter-mile section of the Park's two miles of trails. Many are replicas of poles collected from various villages throughout southeastern Alaska for the 1904 Louisiana Purchase Exposition. They were brought to Sitka the following year and the deteriorating originals are now being preserved in storage.

Just beyond the totem poles is the site of the 1804 battle between the local Tlingits and the conquering Russians. Nearby is the site of the Tlingits' fort to which they retreated under steady Russian bombardment and from which they fled in the middle of the night when their ammunition ran out. From there the trail follows the shores of the salmon-spawning **Indian River** to a footbridge. Across it are more trails which lead to a Russian memorial for the men who died in the 1804 battle. The park trails are well maintained and provide excellent views of the harbour.

(Above) Russian Memorial in Sitka National Historical Park. (Below) A bald eagle receives rehabilitative care at the Alaska Raptor Center.

Heart Lake can be viewed on an independent cycling trip.

Located at 1101 Sawmill Creek Road, is the **Alaska Raptor Center 6**. Sick or injured birds of prey are brought here for treatment and rehabilitation before they are returned to the wild. Open houses, demonstration tours and eagle exercise sessions in a nearby muskeg field are held regularly.

Hiking & Cycling

There are plenty of scenic trails in the Sitka area, including those at Sitka National Historical Park (see previous section). Another easy hike can be taken along the Sheldon Jackson College Forest Trail which follows the Indian River through the college grounds. A bit more strenuous is the three-mile hike up the Gavan

HIKING & CYCLING TRAILS

Gavan Hill Trail

Indian River Trail (4.1 m.)

Indian River

Mt. Verstovia

SITKA

Jeff Davis

Lincoln

Tender Dock

Sawmill Creek Road

Crescent Bay

Sitka National Historical Park

Jamestown Bay

Thimbleberry Lake

To Blue Lake

Heart Lake

Fortress of the Bear

0   1
Miles   N

Sitka Sound

Thimbleberry Bay

Whale Park

Hill Trail (rated moderate, with a steep stair climb). Indian River Trail is an easy 4 miles with a gradual climb to a waterfall. Mt. Verstovia Trail is difficult, its 2.5 miles consisting of steep terrain.

If you rent a bicycle, a good ride is along Sawmill Creek Road to **Heart Lake** with a stop on the way at **Whale Park** for its waterfront views (about 10 miles in total). A longer and more strenuous ride can include **Blue Lake**. Another attraction in the area is **Fortress of the Bear**, adjacent to Sawmill Farm, where orphaned brown bear cubs can be viewed (admission is $10 for adults).

Outlying Ports

Sitka is steeped in Russian history but visitors to outlying ports will find themselves soaking in something quite different – the region's natural hotsprings. Long used by natives, then by hunters and trappers, these hotsprings were also retreats for fishermen and gold prospectors.

The **Goddard Hotsprings**, 16 miles south of Sitka on the outer coast of Baranof Island, was one of the first to be developed in the mid-1800s when a few cottages were built to house invalids from Sitka. In the 1920s a hotel was built, then became an overflow facility for Sitka's Pioneers Home. Today two cedar bathhouses stand on the hillside and collect the hot mineral waters for visitors arriving by boat.

On the other side of Baranof Island, at beautiful **Warm Spring Bay**, a waterfall spills into the head of the bay near a pier and the Baranof Wilderness Lodge. Overlooking the falls, on the tiered hillside, are outdoor rock pools where visitors can soak in the steaming hot mineral water.

On adjacent Chichagof Island, a community has formed around one of the local springs. Called **Tenakee Springs**, this former cannery town is a weekend retreat for Juneau and Sitka residents arriving by ferry. Bathing hours for men and women are posted on the bath house door but visitors soon know them by heart, however, because the bathing hours are promptly told to any strangers arriving in town (it's presumed) for a soak in the springs. There are no cars here, just a narrow lane called Tenakee Avenue which runs the length of this waterfront village and is traveled by foot, bicycle or motorbike.

Tenakee Springs

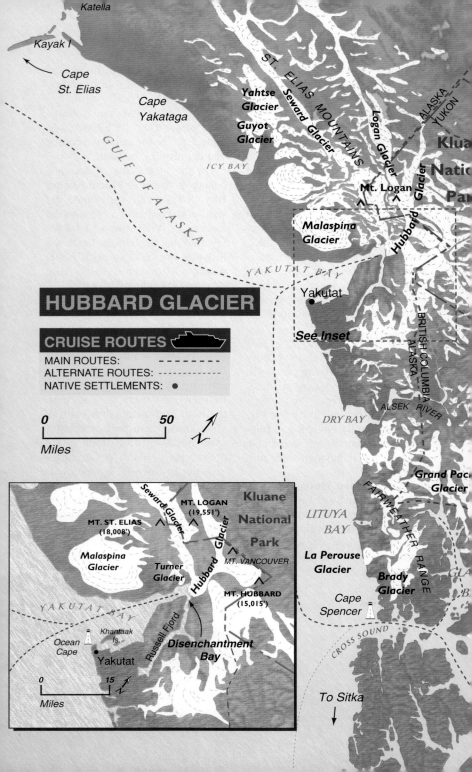

Katella

Kayak I

Cape
St. Elias

Cape
Yakataga

GULF OF ALASKA

ICY BAY

ST. ELIAS MOUNTAINS

Yahtse
Glacier

Guyot
Glacier

Seward Glacier

Logan Glacier

ALASKA
YUKON

Klua

Natio

Par

Mt. Logan

Malaspina
Glacier

Hubbard Glacier

YAKUTAT BAY

Yakutat

See Inset

BRITISH COLUMBIA
ALASKA

HUBBARD GLACIER

CRUISE ROUTES

MAIN ROUTES:
ALTERNATE ROUTES:
NATIVE SETTLEMENTS: ●

0   50

Miles

N

DRY BAY

ALSEK RIVER

Grand Pac
Glacier

FAIRWEATHER RANGE

LITUYA
BAY

La Perouse
Glacier

Brady
Glacier

GLA
B

Cape
Spencer

CROSS SOUND

To Sitka

Seward Glacier

MT. LOGAN
(19,551')

Kluane
National
Park

MT. ST. ELIAS
(18,008')

Hubbard Glacier

Malaspina
Glacier

Turner
Glacier

MT. VANCOUVER

MT. HUBBARD
(15,015')

YAKUTAT BAY

Ocean
Cape

Khantaak
Is.

Yakutat

Russell Fjord

Disenchantment
Bay

0   15

Miles

N

HUBBARD GLACIER
& Yakutat Bay

Some of the most spectacular scenery in the world is found along Alaska's Gulf Coast on the way to Yakutat Bay. Rising from the edge of the sea are some of the world's tallest coastal mountains, their slopes blanketed by North America's largest glaciers.

Few people live along this coast, where the overall landscape is one of looming mountains and sprawling glaciers. There are but three or four sheltered anchorages for mariners to pull into, and **Yakutat Bay** offers the only harbor for large ships. The bay's entrance, over 16 miles wide, is visible from great distances because it is marked by **Mount Saint Elias**, which is 18,008 feet tall and growing. Yes, growing. A piece of the earth's crust – called a terrane – is sandwiched here between two tectonic plates. This terrane (called the Yakutat Block) broke away from the edge of the Continental Plate about 25 million years ago and, riding on the Pacific Plate, was pushed 330 miles northwest along a fault until it reached the top of the Gulf of Alaska.

About 100,000 years ago, the Pacific Plate began shoving the Yakutat Block (360 miles long and 120 miles wide) against the Continental Plate at a rate of about two-and-a-half inches per year. Something must budge as the dense oceanic plate pushes underneath the more buoyant continental plate and, in this case, part of a mountain range is being forced upward. At a growth rate of two-and-a-half inches per year, it will take Mount Saint Elias quite a while to surpass 20,320-foot Mount McKinley as the tallest mountain in North America. Saint Elias also faces competition from 19,850-foot Mount Logan, only 25 miles away and also rising. All this bumping and grinding of terranes and plates is invisible to the human eye until an earthquake gives the area a good jolt, which happened at **Yakutat**

A commercial fishboat trolls for salmon near the entrance to Yakutat Bay.

in September 1899. Living in this remote village on the shores of Yakutat Bay were the original native Tlingits, a few missionaries and some mining prospectors.

The tremors and shocks began on September 3 and lasted four weeks. No lives were lost, even though at least one of the quakes was of the same magnitude as the 1906 San Francisco quake. The small community of Yakutat was at first alarmed and then terrified when, on September 10, the strongest of these quakes sent people rushing from their creaking and groaning homes, while the trees outside swayed like stalks of grass. An eyewitness report by a civil engineer camped at the time in Yakutat was published in the *San Francisco Examiner*. He described native villagers pleading with the

missionary to hold church services to pacify their god, who was obviously "angry at the earth and shaking it." They were horrified when the mission church "rocked until the church bell rang," perceiving this as an omen. When the earthquake ceased, three great waves (tsunamis) rolled in from the ocean and filled Yakutat Bay with whirlpools. Lowlands were flooded as the water level rose 15 feet. The eyewitness engineer reported that "the earthquake was undoubtedly a magnificent sight, but hardly one a fellow would hunt up for the sake of looking at it."

The U.S. Geological Survey sent a team to inspect the after-effects of the earthquake six years later, and they found that a former tidal zone of beach and barnacled rocks had been raised as much as 47 feet above the high-tide line. This uplifting was felt most dramatically by a group of prospectors camped beside Russell Fjord at the head of Yakutat Bay, not far from **Hubbard Glacier**. When the September 10 quake hit, the men ran from their tents. The glacial moraine under their feet was undulating and Hubbard Glacier was surging forward. As if that weren't enough, a lake behind the beach spilled from its bed and swept across their abandoned camp. Tons of rock came pouring down as the men fled along the beach. Four days later they made it to Yakutat where they found the

A cruise ship pulls within a quarter mile of Hubbard Glacier's massive snout.

residents camped in tents on Shivering Hill, as it was promptly named following the earthquake.

The **Harriman Expedition** had visited Yakutat just 11 weeks prior to the September earthquakes. The scientific party on board the steamer *George W. Elder*, chartered by their host Edward H. Harriman, would have had much to observe and record had they been exploring the shoreline of Yakutat Bay a few months later. As it was, the narrow inlet of **Disenchantment Bay** (at the head of Yakutat Bay) was thick with ice floes when the *Elder* arrived at its entrance and waited for the ice to disperse before proceeding. Meanwhile, some Tlingits paddled alongside in canoes filled with furs and skins for sale. Their welcome was similar to that given another scientific expedition a hundred years earlier, when the Spanish explorer **Alejandro Malaspina** visited Yakutat to investigate a rumor that a northwest passage lay at this latitude

It was the summer of 1791 when Malaspina headed north from Acapulco, setting a course that took his two ships directly to Yakutat Bay. When he saw the bay's wide opening at the latitude substantiated by the Academy of Sciences in Paris as being the location of the 'Strait of Anian' (a mythical northwest passage), Malaspina figured he was onto something. The Tlingits living at Yakutat had already dealt with Russian, French and British ships, and they anticipated a brisk trade with this new batch of white men. The Spaniards, however, seemed preoccupied with setting up a base camp and preparing two launches to explore the Strait of Anian. Others were busy collecting specimens and sketching the scenery.

Eventually the **Tlingits** engaged the Spaniards in barter. However, by the time the men in the two launches returned with disappointing reports of a huge glacier blocking their way, the mood on the waiting ships had also soured. The Spanish were not getting along with the Tlingits and tensions reached a climax when a pair of trousers went missing. A chief was detained and trading was halted

A morning arrival at Yakutat Bay where Mount Saint Elias looms above the entrance.

until the trousers were returned. The expedition's artist captured the reconciliation scene on canvas – natives approaching in a canoe, one with his arms outstretched in a gesture of friendship, another holding up the stolen trousers. Disappointed but convinced that the 'Strait of Anian' theory was false, Malaspina left. The name he gave the ice-filled inlet at the head of Yakutat Bay reflects his dashed hopes – **Disenchantment Bay**.

By the time the Harriman Expedition pulled into Yakutat Bay, the wall of ice that had stopped the Spaniards dead in their tracks was now retreating up the inlet. The *Elder* was able to pick its way through the ice floes and be the first ship to enter Disenchantment Bay. On board was a Yakutat Tlingit named James who had impressed Harriman with his detailed knowledge of the area and was invited to join the elite party of scientists as a consultant to the ship's pilot.

Harriman's scientific party included John Muir, John Burroughs and **Dr. William H. Dall** (Paleontologist of the U.S. Geological Survey). Dall had made several trips to Alaska and his keen observance and recording of what he saw resulted in several animal species receiving his name, such as the Dall porpoise and Dall sheep. **Grove Karl Gilbert** was the expedition's glaciologist. He made careful empirical studies of each glacier they visited, drawing dozens of maps and taking plenty of his own photographs in addition to those taken by the expedition's two official photographers, one being **Edward S. Curtis**. Gilbert studied each glacier's topography and the eroded fjords, valleys and rutted plains left behind by receding glaciers. Gilbert's work was a major contribution to the emerging science of glaciology which today measures the thickness of ice with radar, uses aerial photography to monitor a glacier's movements, and employs satellite technology to determine the exact height of a mountain.

Hubbard Glacier at the head of Disenchantment Bay is the longest tidewater glacier in North America. This massive river of ice originates in the St. Elias Mountains of Kluane National Park in Canada's Yukon, and

The sheer cliffs of Hubbard's terminus are typical of an actively calving glacier.

flows for 76 miles before reaching its terminus – an ice-cliff face that is six miles wide. At one time, perhaps as recently as 600 years ago, the glacier completely covered Yakutat Bay. When the Harriman expedition examined the glacier in 1899, it had just finished retreating and was starting to readvance.

Hubbard received widespread attention in the summer of 1986 and was dubbed the 'Galloping Glacier' when it advanced hundreds of feet within a few weeks. The glacier's snout over-ran a small island and dammed the entrance to **Russell Fjord**, trapping seals inside what became a huge lake. Its water level rose 83 feet and threatened to overflow, the run-off potentially pouring into the Situk River where salmon would be washed away in a flood of debris. Then, on October 8, the dam ruptured and 3,500,000 cubic feet of water per second was dumped into Disenchantment Bay. Shrimp lying on the bottom of this deep fjord were lifted by the turbulent water and thrown onto shore. Scientists speculate

(Above) A ship's boat is launched to retrieve a chunk of Hubbard's calved ice. (Below) A chef transforms this piece of glacial ice into a sculpture for the dining room.

Hubbard Glacier is the longest tidewater glacier in North America.

that an equivalent discharge of water last took place near the end of the Great Ice Age, when Lake Missoula emptied into the Columbia River.

Surging glaciers are still not completely understood but it's surmised that faulty plumbing is the culprit. A healthy, slow-moving glacier slides on its base while its top layer flows steadily forward, transferring ice from its source (where snow accumulates) to its snout (where the ice melts). When a glacier isn't flowing smoothly, its upper end becomes clogged with accumulated snow and ice. Then, in a year of high runoff due to heavy rain or spring thaw, the glacier's motion is suddenly eased and the glacier is pushed forward as its top-heavy mass of ice surges down the slope.

Hubbard Glacier was a major media attraction in the summer of 1986 when the fishermen of Yakutat found themselves chauffeuring reporters and camera crews to the head of the bay. In summer of 2002, Hubbard again advanced across the entrance to Russell Fjord, causing its water level to rise as mountain streams and glacier melt flowed into the blocked fjord. Again the ice and moraine dam burst before the rising water spilled over a low pass at the far end of the fjord.

Yakutat is an important port for Alaska's fishing fleet, the only one with dock facilities between Juneau and Cordova (in Prince William Sound). Most of Yakutat's 700 residents run fishboats or work in fish processing plants, and many will tell you that Yakutat is the most beautiful port in Alaska. The town overlooks Monti Bay, on the southeast shores of Yakutat Bay, with Khantaak Island lying opposite and acting as a breakwater to the swells which roll into

Yakutat Bay off the Gulf of Alaska. Beautiful beaches ring much of the area's shoreline, and stretching across the northern horizon is a breathtaking vista of mountains and glaciers, including **Malaspina Glacier**. It is the largest piedmont (foot-of-the-mountain) glacier in North America, measuring 45 miles from east to west and 30 miles from north to south. Its fan-like terminus is almost 60 miles in circumference and ends within three miles of the Pacific Ocean.

Malaspina Glacier is fed by more than two dozen **tributary glaciers**. As these smaller glaciers merge with the main glacier, they bring along rock and gravel eroded from valleys. These dark stripes of moraine run in parallel lines like feeder lanes joining a main highway. From the air the Malaspina Glacier looks like an abstract painting with its parallel moraine stripes twisted into swirls or folded into zigzags by surges within the glacier.

Jet planes land daily at Yakutat on regularly scheduled flights. For travelers approaching Yakutat by ship, the landscape looks so uninhabited that the sight of a jet plane coming in for a landing seems completely out of place. These planes touch down on Alaska's longest runway – built during World War II when 15,000 troops were based at Yakutat.

For most of this century, Yakutat's main industry has been the commercial catching and processing of salmon, cod, halibut and crab. The town's first cannery was built in 1904. Timber harvesting is also underway on Tongass National Forest lands between Yakutat and Dry Bay.

Dry Bay lies at the mouth of the Alsek River and is slowly being turned into a huge delta. The **Alsek River** drains 9,500 square miles of Alaska and Canada while carving its way through the Saint Elias Mountains, past glaciers and through canyons, to reach the Gulf of Alaska. Canada's **Tatshenshini River** flows into the upper Alsek. In 1993 it was declared a wilderness park by the British Columbia government after environmentalists opposed an open-pit mine planned for the summit of Windy Craggy Mountain. The Tatshenshini-Alsek watershed, considered North America's wildest river, is now completely protected. Intrepid kayakers occasionally paddle the white waters of this river but it is normally not well travelled. The natives used the Alsek – 'Raven's River' – as a trade route until a burst ice dam wiped out a riverside village. Afterwards, they restricted their settlements to the river's headwaters and its mouth at Dry Bay.

In August 1999, three hunters on a limited-entry hunt for Dall sheep stumbled upon a remarkable archeological find at the foot of a retreating glacier in **Tatshenshini-Alsek Park**. They photographed but did not touch the preserved body of an aboriginal hunter who died there, possibly caught in a fierce snowstorm as he was crossing the glacier about 600 years ago. A team of scientists has since been studying Kwaday Dan Sinchi (Long Ago

The small fishing port of Yakutat is located near the mouth of Yakutat Bay.

Person Found) – examining everything from his gopher cloak and cedar-and-spruce root hat to his stomach contents. As the glaciers continue retreating, they are expected to reveal more such artifacts and specimens that have been frozen in time.

During the Gold Rush, some prospectors tried to reach the Klondike via the Alsek River. In the spring of 1898 more than 300 men arrived at Yakutat Bay and hauled their mining outfits 50 miles across Hubbard Glacier to the Alsek River. At this point most turned back, but those who ascended the river set up their winter camp in a desolate area almost devoid of fuel. Freezing and sickness took its toll, with only a handful surviving the ordeal. That spring the survivors reached Dalton Post on the Tatshenshini River. Had they taken a different route from the coast, they would have reached Dalton Trail after a few days of travel.

Some prospectors tried to cross the massive **Malaspina Glacier**

to reach the Yukon. Those who made it were in bad shape – both mentally and physically. When the *George W. Elder* stopped at Yakutat, members of the Harriman Expedition met groups of bedraggled and penniless miners who were hoping to catch the next steamer home. A few were panning for gold in the creeks around Yakutat.

Specks of gold lie in the black sand beaches of **Cape Yakataga** – about 70 miles west of Yakutat Bay. To this day, the residents of Cape Yakataga work their claims by hauling sand and running it through sluice boxes. These modern-day prospectors are mainly summer residents, with about a dozen people living year-round at this remote cape. They grow small gardens in summer, make preserves from wild berries, can or smoke fish and wild game, and collect firewood for their stoves. Stands of spruce and hemlock grow right to the beach, and alder, willow and cottonwood flourish along the river banks. Leisure time is spent beachcombing to see what the gulf has thrown onto the exposed shores of the cape. On clear nights the northern lights can often be seen. In spring and fall thousands of migrating birds – swans, geese, cranes and ducks – stop here briefly.

Cape Yakataga is backed by mountains and flanked on either side by massive icefields – Malaspina to the east, Bering to the west. Lying at the base of Bering Glacier is Cape Suckling. Offshore, jutting into the gulf like a sore thumb, is **Kayak Island**. In July of 1741 a Russian ship under the command of the Danish captain Vitus Bering anchored in the lee of Kayak Island. The ship remained there for only a few hours, just long enough for naturalist Georg Steller to go ashore to sketch and name a few plants and animals, such as the Steller's jay. He was thus the first European to step on Alaskan soil.

Kayak Island rises from the water like a wedge of rock, and **Cape Saint Elias** – one of the most feared capes on this coast – is located at the south end of Kayak Island, where it is connected by a low, narrow strip of land to Pinnacle Rock. Fishermen give this stark cape a wide berth, for strong winds funnel off its sheer cliffs and turbulent currents create erratic waves. This is one of the most dramatic capes on the entire Alaskan coastline and well worth the effort to spot during your cruise. The seas south of Cape Saint Elias were considered perilous until a manned light station was installed in 1916 and later automated by the U.S. Coast Guard in 1974. Today the only inhabitants of Kayak Island are brown bears and foxes.

In waters north of Cape Saint Elias, in **Katalla Bay**, the famous steamship *S.S. Portland* was shipwrecked in November 1910 but its relic wasn't discovered until 2002 by an Alaskan environmentalist exploring this remote shoreline. Nearly buried in silt at the mouth of the Katalla River, and visible only at a very low tide, all that remains of the ship that triggered the Klondike Gold Rush when it pulled into Seattle in 1897 loaded with gold nuggets, are remnants of its wooden hull.

Cape Saint Elias is a feared cape and a famous landmark.

Fairweather Range

PRINCE WILLIAM SOUND
WHITTIER & VALDEZ

Prince William Sound is the crowning glory of coastal Alaska. Situated at the top of the Gulf of Alaska, its mainland shores are surrounded by a lofty barrier of mountains and snow, and are indented with dozens of glacier-carved fjords that wend their watery way inland. These fjords contain Alaska's greatest concentration of tidewater glaciers – 20 of them active.

Glaciers are not the only feature found here in abundance. The numerous forested islands are habitat for Sitka blacktail deer, black and brown bears, wolves, red fox, river otters, mink and other fur-bearing animals. Marine mammals thrive in waters rich with salmon, halibut, red snapper, crab, clams and shrimp. Each summer, thousands of sea otters, Dall porpoises and harbor seals frequent the Sound, along with killer whales and more than 100 humpback whales. Several thousand bald eagles inhabit the islands of Prince William Sound, and about half a million marine birds take up residence at the 88 seabird colonies.

Human habitation of Prince William Sound has always been sparse compared to the animal life the area supports. About 3,000 Pacific Eskimos inhabited the area when the first European

PRINCE WILLIAM SOUND AT A GLANCE
Whittier: page 299
Valdez: page 300

Human habitation is sparse on the glacier-clad shores of Prince William Sound.

(Above) A seabird colony at Porpoise Rocks near Hinchinbrook Entrance. (Below) Bryn Mawr Glacier, College Fjord.

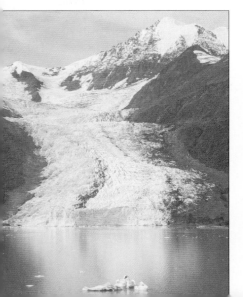

seafarers arrived, with Britain's Captain Cook naming Prince William Sound in 1778. When Spanish explorers surveyed part of the Sound in 1790, they left behind such place names as Valdez and Cordova. In 1791 Russia's Alexander Baranof visited Prince William Sound and departed with a new wife – the daughter of a local chief.

A century later salmon canneries dotted the Sound and fish processing was a going concern, with Scottish and Norwegian experts brought in to teach the locals how to cure and pack herring. A salmon cannery was in operation at **Cordova** when the Harriman Expedition stopped for a visit in the summer of 1899. American railway magnate Edward H. Harriman had chartered the steamship *George W. Elder* for his family's vacation and he invited an impressive collection of scientists to join him in exploring Alaska's coastline. This elite expedition put their time to good use in Prince William Sound. Not only did they name **College Fjord** and its numerous glaciers for the various colleges and universities with which the scientists were affiliated, they also discovered a newly formed fjord. While viewing Barry Glacier, they noticed a narrow passage unexpectedly leading past the glacier's snout – which had retreated since it was last surveyed to now reveal an unknown inlet. Harriman was a risk taker and he saw this open sliver of water as a window of opportunity. "We shall discover a new Northwest Passage!" he declared. His captain was opposed to taking the ship

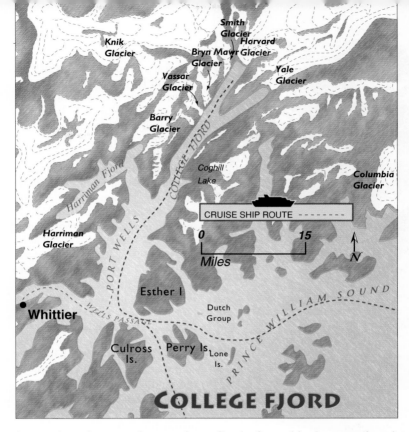

into uncharted waters where a sub-merged rock might pierce a hole in the *Elder's* hull, but Harriman took full responsibility and ordered that they proceed. Harriman's gamble resulted in their discovery of **Harriman Fjord**.

Today, fishing is the mainstay for most residents of Prince William Sound. In addition to the annual herring and salmon runs are abundant harvests of crab, clams and shrimp. The clam industry suffered a setback when the **1964 Good Friday earthquake** raised clam beds 10 feet above the water. The town of **Valdez**, sitting on silt, was shaken so violently that the entire town swayed as if riding ocean waves.

Cracks formed in the ground, and these began opening and closing, spurting water in the process. Then huge blocks of land slid out to sea, and waterfront buildings and docks collapsed. The final blow came from the tsunamis. Four of these giant, earthquake-generated waves swept ashore, devastating what was left of Valdez.

The town of **Whittier**, on the west side of Prince William Sound, was closer to the quake's epicenter but, unlike Valdez, it was built on bedrock and the ground didn't collapse. The port was, however, hit by a huge har-bor wave. A native village on Chenega Island was destroyed in the Good Friday earthquake by a tsunami, and was rebuilt at **Sawmill Bay** on Evans Island, on a former saltery site. **Valdez** was also rebuilt at a new location, about four miles from the original townsite.

In the early 1970s, Prince William Sound experienced three bad fishing years in a row, due to poor pink salmon runs. To counteract the cyclical nature of salmon fishing, an aquaculture corporation was formed and fish hatcheries were built in the western part of the sound. The one at Sawmill Bay, near the native village of Chenega, is one of the largest of its kind in the world in terms of fry released. Salmon runs became so predictable that by the late '80s local fishermen said that catching pink salmon in the sound was more like ocean ranching than fishing.

Meanwhile, a new concern had arisen for fishermen – the presence of oil tankers in their pristine fishing grounds. When oil was discovered beneath the tundra of Alaska's far north, **Valdez** was chosen as the southern terminus for an 800-mile-long pipeline. Enormous storage tanks were built at Valdez, along with a maze of feeder lines and valves, tanker berths and giant incinerators.

Starting in 1977, crude oil was regularly loaded into tankers and shipped south to refineries. The men and women who fished in local waters were largely opposed to these massive ships traversing the intricate waterways of their fishing grounds. However, measures were taken to ensure their safe movement and for years the

(Top) A cruise ship lingers near the snout of a tidewater glacier in College Fjord. (Above) An on-board naturalist provides glacier commentary.

transport of oil through the Sound ran smoothly, with no major accidents occurring. Escort tugs and harbor pilots safely saw these tankers (the length of three football fields) through the narrow entrance of the Port of Valdez, past Middle Rock (dubbed the 'can opener') and into open waters. Then, in 1986, things began to change. Budget cutbacks resulted in decreased Coast Guard staff at Valdez, and their radar system was downgraded. Tanker crews, with a proven track record of safety, were no longer required to have a pilot on board past Rocky Point.

Complacency is a mariner's worst enemy and this lesson was learned the hard way in the early hours of March 24, 1989, when the *Exxon Valdez* ran onto **Bligh Reef** and spilled 11 million gallons of crude oil into the pristine waters of Prince William Sound. Currents quickly spread the oil in a southwest direction for 1,200 miles towards the Kenai Fjords, Kodiak Island and the southern tip of the Alaska Peninsula. Reporters and photographers from around the world converged on Valdez and local residents turned their spare bedrooms into hotel rooms to meet the demand for accommodations. Others arriving at Valdez came to help, and thousands of workers were employed by Exxon to clean the oiled beaches – either by hand or with power hoses. An Alaska state ferry became a floating dormitory for workers.

Fishing fleets were hired to install, clean and repair booms used to corral the spilled oil. As the slick rode the prevailing currents toward the southwestern entrance of Prince William Sound, boats rushed to Sawmill Bay to protect its hatchery with booms. While Alaskans scrambled to keep the spreading oil off their shores, waterbirds died by the thousands – many so coated in oil they were unidentifiable. Hardest hit of the mammals were the sea otters.

Unlike other marine mammals, **sea otters** retain their body heat not with blubber but with an insulating fur coat. If this thick fur becomes coated with crude oil, it quickly loses its ability to trap warm air next to the skin and the animal dies of hypothermia. Many

Oil tankers are a regular sight in Prince William Sound.

of these oil-coated creatures climbed out of the frigid water in an attempt to stay warm. Others inhaled toxic fumes or ingested oil as they groomed their fur.

Exxon spent millions of dollars rescuing the area's wildlife, and extraordinary efforts were made to save the afflicted sea otters. Rushed to emergency headquarters, they were stabilized and sedated before enduring repeated washings with a soap solution. Local swimming pools became holding pens for the cleaned otters while they groomed themselves (which restores natural oils) and regained their strength before being returned to the wild. Some were flown to city aquariums for treatment.

The majority of Prince William Sound's shoreline was untouched by the oil spill, and attempts were made to clean the islands and beaches that were in the slick's path. However, residual oil tends to remain in streambeds where it is dispersed over time into waterways by tidal actions.

Oil tankers in Prince William Sound are now subject to stringent safety measures, including tug escorts and travel restrictions in weather too severe to contain a potential spill.

(Above) Snug Harbor on Knight Island was heavily oiled from the 1989 spill and its streams were monitored for lingering after-effects. (Below) A cruise ship plies the scenic waters of Prince William Sound.

One of the Sound's most impressive natural sights also played a major role in the 1989 oil spill. **Columbia Glacier**, largest in Prince William Sound, is one of the most studied tidewater glaciers in the world. Aerial photography has documented its rapid retreat, which began in the early 1980s when the glacier's snout receded from its moraine (an underwater shoal created by the glacier's leading edge). As the glacier moved into deeper water, this triggered an increase in calving speed.

Once this instability was initiated, the glacier began a major retreat that is expected to continue until the glacier's terminus reaches the shoreline at the head of Columbia Bay by about 2030. The glacier's icebergs pose a hazard when they drift into shipping lanes outside the nearby port of Valdez. This was the case when the ill-fated *Exxon Valdez* altered course to avoid some large ice floes and ran onto Bligh Reef.

Cruise ships usually keep their distance from Columbia Bay which is often congested with floating ice (mélange), bobbing seals and numerous seabirds attracted to the fish that feed here on plankton.

Whittier

Whittier, its port and rail facilities constructed during World War II by the U.S. Army, used to be connected only by a railway tunnel to the rest of Alaska. The tall concrete apartment buildings that comprise the townsite were built to house army personnel and their families, and the 14-story Begich Towers is now home to most of Whittier's year-round population of 300. A highway connection through the 2.5-mile-long tunnel was completed in 2000, providing easy access to Anchorage, which is 65 miles away.

Traffic in the toll tunnel is one-way and strictly controlled, with vehicles waiting at either end of the tunnel until directed through. Railcars travel through the tunnel on tracks that are straddled by the wheels of cars and buses. Whittier is an embarkation and disembarkation port for one-way cruises between Vancouver and Anchorage, and passengers connecting with their ship in Whittier have the option of transferring to or from Anchorage via motorcoach or railcar. The train station is opposite the cruise terminal.

The port of Whittier

Valdez

Valdez (population 9,600) is the most northerly ice-free port in the Western Hemisphere and is connected to the rest of mainland Alaska by the Richardson Highway, which leads north to Fairbanks. Nestled at the base of the Chugach Mountains, Valdez has been called Alaska's Little Switzerland because of its scenic alpine setting. Attractions include a tour of the Alyeska Pipeline Terminal, the local museum, and a visit to the retreating Valdez Glacier, located about four miles above the pre-1964 townsite.

Shore excursions include a motorcoach ride along the Richardson Highway (which runs parallel with the pipeline) to **Worthington Glacier**, which is accessible on foot and featured in guided hiking tours. Salmon fishing is also offered, as is sea kayaking, a boat cruise through iceberg-studded waters to **Columbia Glacier** and whitewater rafting in Keystone Canyon.

Mount Wrangell, the tallest active volcano in Alaska, looms in the distance. Termed a shield volcano because of its broad dome, Mount Wrangell rises more than 14,000 feet and the ice-filled caldera at its summit is nearly 12 square miles. Scientists believe Mount Wrangell's rounded profile

A mountain tunnel provides rail and road access to Whittier.

Shore Excursions

ANCHORAGE/ WHITTIER

Passengers transferring between Anchorage and Whittier by motorcoach have the option of booking a shore excursion that takes in the sights in between these two centers. Stops along the way include Portage Glacier (see pg 313-314), Alaska Wildlife Conservation Center (see pg 313-314) and Alyeska Resort (see pg 312). Excursions based in Whittier include kayaking past the pristine shorelines of Prince William Sound or boarding a sightseeing vessel for a cruise to Blackstone Glacier at the head of a scenic fjord.

is due partly to subglacial eruptions in which the lava flows laterally beneath the ice. Its last major eruption was between 2,000 and 10,000 years ago, although it has had several minor eruptions in the last hundred years.

Mount Wrangell is part of **Wrangell-St. Elias National Park and Preserve** – a vast wilderness of glacier-clad peaks bordered to the east by the Saint Elias Mountains of Kluane National Park Reserve in Canada's Yukon Territory. The historic copper mining towns of McCarthy and Kennicott are located in Wrangell-St. Elias.

The Chugach Mountains stretch across the horizon at Valdez (above) and along the Copper River Valley (below).

The Richardson Highway eventually converges with the **Copper River**, which traces the park's western boundary. Park headquarters are at Copper Center (pop. 400), which is also the location of the Copper River Princess Wilderness Lodge where guests enjoy breathtaking views of Mount Drum, a peak rising to the west of Mount Wrangell.

Iditarod Trail

To Denali
Willow

GLENN HWY.

Palmer

1

3

ANCHORAGE

POPULATION (METRO):   300,000
ANNUAL RAINFALL: 16 inches
DISTANCE TO WHITTIER: 59 miles
DISTANCE TO SEWARD: 127 miles
DISTANCE TO TALKEETNA: 113 miles
DISTANCE TO FAIRBANKS: 362 miles

Susitna River

1

ANCHORAGE

Anchorage
Int. Airport

KNIK ARM

SEWARD HWY.

Mt. Alyeska
Resort

Girdwood

*In summer, beluga whales are
often sighted in Turnagain Arm*

TURNAGAIN ARM

Bird
Point

Turnagain
Pass

1

Whittier

Portage
Valley

COOK INLET

Summit
Lake

Kenai

Sterling

**Kenai
Princess
Lodge**

Cooper
Landing

Moose
Pass

Kenai River

Skilak L.

Russian R.

Kenai Lake

**Seward
Windsong
Lodge**

*Sargeant
Glacier*

**Exit
Glacier**

*Marathon
Mtn.*

Seward

Sterling Hwy.

Tustumena Lake

**Bear
Glacier**

*Caines
Head*

**Harding
Icefield**

**Holgate
Glacier**

*Aialik
Bay*

*Fox
Island*

Cape Resurrection

**Rugged
Island**

KENAI   PENINSULA

*Harris
Bay*

Resurrection Bay

*Three Hole
Point*

Homer

*Granite
Cape*

GULF OF ALASK

0   20
Miles

N

CRUISE ROUTES

MAIN ROUTES: – – – – – –
ALTERNATE ROUTES: · · · · · · ·

ANCHORAGE
Seward, Kenai and the Portage Valley

Anchorage calls itself 'Air Crossroads of the World' for it was once a regular stopover for Asia-bound aircraft. The Anchorage International Airport is today one of the world's busiest in terms of cargo traffic, and nearby Lake Hood Air Harbor is the world's busiest floatplane base – handling hundreds of take-offs and landings on a peak summer's day. Anchorage is also Alaska's transportation hub, connected by air, rail and road to other parts of the state. The offices of oil corporations, as well as federal, state and local government agencies, are located in Anchorage.

Yet, even with a population exceeding a quarter-million, Anchorage remains tied to the wilderness surrounding it. Situated on coastal lowlands backed by the Chugach Mountains, Anchorage attracts a considerable moose population which triples in winter (to about 1,000) when these hulking plant-eaters show up looking for food. Many an Anchorage resident has awoken to find their yard's mountain ash and birch trees destroyed by a hungry moose who is now sleeping off a good meal in a comfortable spot beside the house next to a heating vent.

The famous Iditarod Trail Dog Sled Race – an 1100-mile race from Anchorage to Nome – starts in downtown Anchorage. Since the first race in 1977, trained dog teams have mushed their way each March across two mountain ranges and the pack ice of Norton Sound to reach the finish line at Nome.

Anchorage also supports a symphony orchestra and is home to an impressive museum of history and art. About the only thing lacking in Anchorage is a fishing fleet, due to its location at the head of **Cook Inlet**, where the tidal range is the second largest in

A view of downtown Anchorage.

the world – second only to Atlantic Canada's Bay of Fundy. Tidal fluxes in Turnagain Arm can surpass 33 feet, and surface waters are in constant motion – moving at speeds of 10 to 15 mph – with incoming tides often creating a tidal bore (a standing wave) in Turnagain Arm. From November to April the upper inlet is often frozen or packed with floe ice, and the water's high content of glacial silt is damaging to the saltwater pumps and shaft bearings of fishboat engines. The water's high silt content was likely a factor in Captain Cook's assuming the inlet was a river when he sailed into this uncharted and boulder-strewn body of water in 1778. Captain Vancouver retraced Cook's route in 1794 and determined that Cook's River was actually an inlet, renaming it Cook Inlet.

At one time, the ice in Cook Inlet was 3,000 feet thick. When the ice retreated up Knik and Turnagain Arms at the head of the

inlet, shallow estuaries formed as glacial silt was deposited by the retreating glaciers. Upon these shores human presence appeared in about 6000 BC when Southern Eskimos first arrived. Tanaina natives migrated into the area in about 1650 AD, followed by Russian fur traders and priests who established a mission near Knik (close to present-day Anchorage) in 1835.

Gold was discovered in 1882 at Crow Creek and prospectors began moving into the area. When President Woodrow Wilson authorized construction of the Alaska Railroad in 1914, job seekers flocked to the area and a tent city sprang up on the banks of Ship Creek. A grid pattern of streets and avenues was laid out by army engineers and a land auction was held, with 655 lots selling for an average price of $225 each. A month later, in August 1915, a poll was held to choose a name for the budding railroad town. The voters chose Alaska City but the federal government decided to keep the existing name of Anchorage.

World War II brought the next boom to Anchorage. Fort Richardson and Elmendorf Air Force Base were built in 1940, and the Alaska Highway was constructed in 1942. By the end of the war, Anchorage's population had increased fivefold to 43,000 residents.

In 1951, Anchorage opened its international airport to transpolar

The Captain Cook Monument overlooks the waterfront at Resolution Park.

air traffic between Europe and Asia. Seven years later, on June 30, 1958, the Statehood Act was passed, and Anchorage celebrated with a 50-ton bonfire. 'North to the Future' was the new state's motto, and the future looked promising for Anchorage. Then, on March 27, 1964, a massive earthquake – the largest ever recorded in North America – hit the city. Situated on glacial silt deposits, downtown Anchorage was devastated. Amid violent shaking, the ground beneath buildings slid into the sea. Sections of 3rd and 4th Avenues collapsed, dropping as much as 10 feet. In the Turnagain area (now Earthquake Park), 75 homes were destroyed, some of them sliding 2,000 feet. Despite such destruction, the city wasted no time rebuilding.

The discovery of North Slope oil in 1968 brought another boom, as oil and construction companies set up headquarters in Anchorage.

Getting Around

Anchorage's airport is four miles (a 10-minute drive) from downtown, where the selection of **hotels** includes the **Hilton** (at 3rd Avenue and E Street), its spacious lobby displaying an extensive Alaskan art collection and a mounted brown bear and polar bear. The Hilton lobby restaurant features Alaskan king crab and halibut on its menu. The **Hotel Captain Cook** (at 5th and K Street) is a luxury hotel featuring fine dining and panoramic views from its top-floor restaurant, and casual meals in its lobby cafe. The **Coast International Inn** is a mid-priced hotel conveniently located near the airport on Aviation Avenue, over-looking the shores of Lake Spenard where floatplanes regularly land and take off, and where flightseeing tours depart.

The Alaska Railroad provides summer passenger service between Anchorage and Seward.

The city's grid pattern (streets running north and south, avenues running east and west) makes downtown Anchorage an easy place to navigate on foot.

For an overview of the city, hour-long Anchorage **trolley tours** depart every half hour in front of the Log Cabin Visitor Center on 4th Avenue. The tour's 15-mile route takes in Earthquake Park, Westchester Lagoon, Lake Hood and other places of interest.

The Egan Convention Center, located behind the Visitor Center on 5th Avenue, is the hub for cruise passengers with **transfers** connecting to **Whittier** or **Seward**. These transfers can be combined with a sightseeing excursion of the Portage Valley (see box on page 300).

Regional flights are available from Anchorage to Alaska's far-flung northern communities, such as **Nome**, located on Norton Sound (an arm of the Bering Sea). Nome (pop. 3,500) is rich in

The Alaska Statehood
Monument commemorates
Alaska's 75th anniversary.

Eskimo culture and gold rush history. In winter, Nome residents can ski on the frozen Bering Sea and watch the Northern Lights dance across the sky. In summer, the sun never sets, or at least it appears not to because it dips just below the horizon. Flights are also available to the Eskimo village of **Kotzebue**, north of the Arctic Circle on the Bering Sea Coast.

Shore Excursions
ANCHORAGE

Excursions in Anchorage include a variety of flightseeing trips. One takes you over Knik Glacier and Colony Glacier, another to Denali National Park and Mt. McKinley. Fly-in fishing trips are also offered. A jet boat safari can be taken along the Knik River to the actively calving face of Knik Glacier.

A variety of excursions can be combined with transfers to Whittier (Portage Lake and Glacier boat trip) or to Seward (scenic train ride; Kenai Fjords cruise). City motorcoach tours are also offered.

Local Attractions

Visitor Information Center **1** A walking tour of downtown Anchorage usually begins at the Visitor Information Center. Housed in a rustic log cabin with a sod roof, the center is a much photographed sight, with a milepost out front showing directions and flying distances to various cities around the world. Outside the entrance stands a 5,144-pound jade boulder. (Jade, the state gem, is mined around the Arctic Circle.) Adjacent to the Visitor Center is the Old City Hall, containing dioramas of Anchorage's old city streets.

4th Avenue Theater **2** Many of Anchorage's original buildings are found on 4th Avenue, and this theater is a city landmark. Built in the art deco style, it first opened in 1947 and was completely refurbished in 1992. The theater contains floor-to-ceiling bronze murals and a ceiling decorated with twinkling lights in the shape of the Big Dipper.

Alaska Public Lands Information Center **3** Across the street, at the corner of 4th Avenue and F Street, is this his-

Anchorage's main Visitor Information Center.

toric center. A former post office, it was completed in 1939 and is included in the National Register of Historic Places. The building is now a source of park information for visitors planning trips to various regions of Alaska.

Stewart's Photo Shop **4** (one block east) is housed in the second-oldest downtown building, and its pressed tin ceiling dates from its earlier days as Oscar Anderson's Meat Market.

Continuing east along 4th to D Street, you will come across the North Pacific Arc Mural, a huge painting depicting the route of the Iditarod Trail Sled Dog Race.

Wendler Building **5** Built in 1925 by an early resident, this turreted building was moved here (from the corner of 4th and I Street) in 1984 and is on the National Register of Historic Places. The ceremonial start of the annual Iditarod Trail Sled Dog Race is held in front of this building and is commemorated with a large, bronze sculpture of a sled dog. Next door, at 446 W. 4th

ANCHORAGE

SHIP CREEK

Ship Creek

Port Access Rd.

Alaska Railroad Depot

Saturday Market

3rd Avenue

4th Avenue

5th Avenue Mall

6th Avenue

Gambell Street

Fairbanks Street

Eagle Street

Denali Street

Anchorage Memorial Park

Cordova Street

Barrow Street

A Street

B Street

C Street

D Street

E Street

F Street

G Street

H Street

I Street

K St.

L Street

Town Square

Tony Knowles Coastal Trail

1st Avenue

2nd Avenue

Christensen Dr.

3rd Avenue

4th Avenue

5th Avenue

6th Avenue

7th Avenue

8th Avenue

9th Avenue

Delaney Park

Centennial

200

0

Yards

N

7 **6**

7

5

4

1 *i*

12

3 **2**

13

8

11

9

10

14

Inset: Anchorage Downtown

Elmendorf AFB

3rd Ave.

20 **21**

22

15th Ave.

Alaska Zoo

19

15

A St.

C St.

"S" St.

Minnesota Blvd.

KNIK ARM

16

Northern Lights Blvd.

Spenard Rd.

Int. Airport Rd.

Point Woronzof

Postmark Rd.

17

18

Anchorage Int. Airport

Anchorage Downtown

Avenue, is the National Bank of Alaska where tapestries depicting Alaska's history are displayed in the lobby.

One block over, at 3rd Avenue and E Street, is the **Anchorage Market & Festival** – an open-air venue of booths selling local handicrafts and other items on Saturdays and Sundays.

Alaska Statehood Monument 6 If you continue north on E Street to 2nd Avenue, you will arrive at this monument, erected in 1990 to commemorate Anchorage's 75th birthday and the 100th anniversary of President Eisenhower's birth.

Ship Creek Overlook 7 To the west of the monument on 2nd Avenue is this overlook providing views of the Alaska Railroad Depot and Ship Creek – a popular salmon fishing stream for Anchorage residents. Directly west of the overlook along 2nd Avenue is an enclave of historic homes built around 1917 when the railroad was being developed.

Near the western end of 2nd Avenue is the start of the **Tony Knowles Coastal Trail** – eight scenic miles of paved trail which winds along the shoreline, leading to such attractions as Elderberry Park.

Port of Anchorage Viewpoint 8 One block south of the trail's starting point, at the end of Christensen Drive, is this viewpoint overlooking Knik Arm and the mouth of Ship Creek, where gold rush steamships anchored while unloading passengers and supplies.

Resolution Park 9 At 3rd and L Street is this park where the

Captain Cook Monument marks the 200th anniversary of Captain Cook's third and final voyage. Across the inlet stands Mount Susitna (Sleeping Lady), its rounded shape carved by glacial ice that once flowed across its summit and lay 3,000 feet deep in Cook Inlet. Three of Alaska's four tallest active volcanoes are also found on the western shores of Cook Inlet – Mount Spurr, Mount Redoubt and Mount Iliamna (all over 10,000 feet high). On an island within the inlet stands Mount St. Augustine (4,025 feet). When this volcano erupted in 1986, it sent ash eight miles high, disrupting air traffic in southcentral Alaska. Mount Redoubt erupted in December 1989, dusting Anchorage with ash and disrupting holiday air travel. An eruption from Mount Spurr in August 1992 sent ash eastward on

A bronze sled dog outside the Wendler Building marks the Iditarod's ceremonial start line.

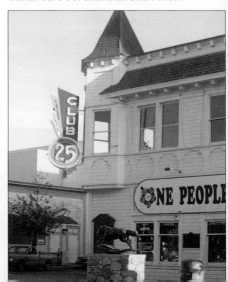

the prevailing winds to Prince William Sound and Yakutat Bay.

Elderberry Park 🔟 Accessed from the Tony Knowles Coastal Trail, this park contains the Oscar Anderson House, Anchorage's first wood-frame house built in 1915 and now a museum.

Holy Family Cathedral 🔟 Points of interest along 5th Avenue include this cathedral, transported from the town of Knik by horse and sleigh in the early 1920s.

Egan Convention Center 🔟 was named for William A. Egan, Alaska's first governor elected after statehood. Across the street is Town Square, a municipal park and popular gathering place for locals with its flower gardens, benches, outdoor amphitheater and **Alaska Center for the Performing Arts** 🔟. The Kimball Building, Anchorage's first dry goods store, stands at the northeast corner of the park. The Dena'ina Civic and Convention Center connects with the other two centers by covered walkways and skybridges.

Anchorage Museum at Rasmuson Center 🔟 The Anchorage Museum first opened in 1968 with an exhibition of borrowed Alaska paintings and a collection of objects loaned from the local historical society. The original museum has been enlarged several times since and this world-class museum at 6th Avenue and C Street now houses the **Smithsonian Arctic Studies Center** (displaying hundreds of indigenous Alaska artifacts), the **Imaginarium Discovery Center** (a hands-on science discovery center), the **Thomas Planetarium** and the **Conocophillips Gallery** (displaying contemporary Alaska Native art). The museum also contains a gift shop, restaurant and atrium cafe.

Ship Creek Salmon Viewing & Waterfowl Nesting Area 🔟 Below the Ship Creek Overlook is a viewing area where salmon can be seen swimming upstream from June through September.

Town Square is the cultural hub of Anchorage.

Westchester Lagoon Waterfowl Sanctuary 16 Further along the Tony Knowles Trail is this peaceful bird sanctuary where wild geese and ducks live year round.

Earthquake Park 17 About a mile and a half along the trail from the Westchester Lagoon is the site of Anchorage's worst destruction during the 1964 earthquake. Buildings here were leveled by landslides but, rather than rebuild in this area, Anchorage residents decided to turn it into a park with an interpretive display.

Lake Hood Air Harbor 18 Located between Earthquake Park and the International Airport is the world's largest and busiest floatplane base. A shoreside park offers visitors a view of the lake and its aerial activity. Alaska Aviation Heritage Museum on the south shore of Lake Hood contains an observation deck and displays featuring historic aircraft and pioneer aviators.

Alaska Zoo 19 Home to native and exotic wildlife, the zoo is a 15-minute drive south of downtown.

Elmendorf Air Force Base Wildlife Museum 20 Northwest of downtown Anchorage is this museum which features mounted animals.

Alaska Native Heritage Center 21 is where indigenous art and architecture can be viewed in a park-like setting. This attraction can be reached by free shuttle service from downtown.

Merrill Field 22 One mile east of downtown is this airfield named in honor of a pioneer pilot who was the first to fly a commercial flight west of Juneau and the first to attempt a night landing in Anchorage. He also discovered, in 1927, a key pass in the Alaska Range which bears his name. With half of Alaska's licensed pilots living in Anchorage, Merrill Field is a busy small-plane base.

Lake Spenard, where flightseeing tours are available, is part of the Lake Hood Air Harbor.

(Above) Alyeska Resort. (Left) Seven glaciers surround the valley town of Girdwood.

Turnagain Arm

The scenic **Seward Highway** runs between Anchorage and Seward, and in the year 2000 was designated an All-American Road – an honor given to the nation's most outstanding highways. The Alaska Railroad follows basically the same route as the Seward Highway, which starts just south of Anchorage and traces the northern shore of **Turnagain Arm**. There are several turnouts and scenic overlooks along this stretch of road, with views across Turnagain Arm to the Kenai Mountains.

Beluga whales are often sighted in Turnagain Arm, where tides can range up to 38 feet, exposing vast expanses of **mud flats** at low tide. People are warned not to venture onto these exposed mud flats which can become quicksand. More than one person has lost their life after getting stuck in the mud and drowning as the water level rose before rescue crews could save them. Beluga Point and Bird Point are good spots to view Turnagain Arm's **bore tides,** which arrive at Beluga Point about an hour after low water at Anchorage.

Tidal bores occur regularly in Turnagain Arm due to the large tidal range in Cook Inlet. When the rapidly rising tidal waters in Cook Inlet flow into the narrow, shallow, gently sloping basin of Turnagain Arm, this creates an incoming wall of water ranging from six inches to 6 feet in height, depending on the size of the tide and other factors such as wind strength and direction. Also along this stretch of the Seward Highway are several gunmounts, used to hold 105mm recoilless rifles for shooting down accumulated snow and reducing the occurrence of random avalanches, which close the highway for short periods.

At Seward Highway's junction with the Alyeska Highway is the valley town of **Girdwood**, a former mining camp and now a recreational center for skiers and hikers. The Chugach National Forest's District Office is located here, providing visitors with information on the area's natural attractions and hiking trails. At the far end of town, nestled at the base of **Mount Alyeska**, is the Alyeska Prince Hotel, a luxury resort featured in several of the cruise lines' land tours. Adjacent to the resort is an aerial tram that transports visitors above the valley floor to the 2,300-foot level of Mt. Alyeska where panoramic views can be enjoyed at a mountaintop complex and along a ridgetop hiking trail. Guided

(Right) The Ptarmigan offers boat tours to Portage Glacier.

excursions at Alyeska Resort include rainforest hikes, river rafting and a jet boat safari past waterfalls and hanging glaciers.

Portage Valley

Portage Glacier Road connects with the Seward Highway at the head of Turnagain Arm. Near this highway junction is the former townsite of **Portage** – a railroad town that was once part of a natural trade route across the Portage Valley between Cook Inlet and Prince William Sound, used by natives, Russian fur traders and gold prospectors. The land underneath Portage sank during the 1964 earthquake and, flooded by Turnagain Arm, the town was abandoned. The marshy land is now ideal habitat for waterfowl. The area's **Alaska Wildlife**

(Top, above) Begich, Boggs Visitor Center provides telescopes for visitors. (Below) A young hiker on the trail to Byron Glacier.

Conservation Center is a good place to see indigenous birds as well as large mammals, including moose, caribou and brown bear. The animals living at this center are orphaned or injured when brought here for rehabilitation.

The turnoff onto Portage Glacier Road is about three miles south of the former townsite, and this paved highway weaves across the valley floor, past campgrounds, trout ponds and salmon streams to **Begich, Boggs Visitor Center** overlooking **Portage Lake**. Named for two Congressmen whose plane disappeared in the area in 1972, the Center provides information on the Chugach National Forest and the glaciers lining Portage Valley. The retreating **Portage Glacier** flows into Portage Lake and can be viewed on hour-long boat tours. **Byron Glacier** can be accessed on foot, following a mile-long trail that traces the glacier's meltwater stream to its snout. It's possible to walk right onto the glacier's snout but be aware of the avalanche danger – a distant rumbling sound would be your cue to leave. The **Williwaw Fish Viewing Platform** is a good place to see spawning salmon from late July through early September.

Not far from the Begich, Boggs Visitor Center is **Portage Glacier Lodge**, a day lodge with a cafe and gift shop. Portage Glacier Road continues eastward, along the shores of Portage Lake to a mountain tunnel that leads to **Whittier**. Until 2000, when modification of the tunnel was completed, there was no road connection to Whittier and vehicles rode on flat railcars through the tunnel.

Kenai Peninsula

(See cruisetour information for this area on page 21).

A popular recreational area for Anchorage residents, the Kenai Peninsula has been called 'Alaska in miniature' for the diversity of its scenery, habitat and wildlife. The **Seward Highway** wraps around the head of Turnagain Arm before turning inland and ascending 1,000 feet to Turnagain Pass, then meandering southwestward past mountain lakes and creeks. The rail line diverges with the highway at the head of Turnagain Arm, paralleling the Placer River, which drains the many streams of Placer Valley. Points of interest along the Seward Highway include a scenic viewpoint overlooking Lower Summit Lake, and a stop at the **Summit Lake Lodge,** a landmark log structure with views overlooking Upper Summit Lake. There are also several hiking trailheads along the highway.

Near Quartz Creek bridge the stands of red-rust spruce trees along this stretch of highway have been ravaged by spruce bark beetles. More than a million acres of spruce forests on the Kenai Peninsula have been killed by these beetles. Their larvae, the size of rice grains, destroy the tree's ability to transport nutrients, causing it to die.

The **Sterling Highway** turn-off leads westward along the shores of the **Kenai River** where anglers will find some of the best freshwater fishing Alaska has to offer. Nestled on the banks of this beautiful river is the **Kenai Princess Wilderness Lodge**, where the setting is sublime and excursions

Kenai Princess Wilderness Lodge

include lake kayaking and river rafting, as well as nature hikes and horseback trail rides, all offering a close-up look at the area's green valleys, snowcapped mountains and turquoise lakes. Much of this area lies within the **Kenai National Wildlife Refuge**, first established as the Kenai National Moose Range in 1941 to protect the area's moose population. More than 200 species of wildlife live in this 1.92 million-acre refuge, its headquarters located in **Soldotna** (pop. 4,000), one of several rural communities in the area. Nearby **Kenai** (pop. 7,000), on the shores of Cook Inlet, is an historic homestead town containing a century-old Russian church and art galleries. **Homer** (pop. 4,700) is another enclave for local artists. This scenic fishing port is at the far end of the Sterling Highway and its famous spit extends halfway across the mouth of Kachemak

Seward is famous for its fishing.

Bay, above which rise the glaciated peaks of the Kenai Mountains.

Seward

Seward, headquarters for Kenai Fjords National Park, is the southern terminus of the Seward Highway, 127 miles from Anchorage. Located at the head of Resurrection Bay at the foot of the Kenai Mountains, Seward was established in 1903 as an ocean terminal for the planned Alaska Railroad. Named after Secretary of State William Seward (who arranged the purchase of Alaska in 1867), the town of 2,800 is today a commercial fishing and cargo port.

The waters in and around **Resurrection Bay** are prime fishing grounds, with huge salmon runs and halibut weighing over 300 pounds. The Seward Silver Salmon Derby, held each August, is Alaska's most prestigious fishing event, drawing thousands of anglers. Halibut, a seafood delicacy, is served fresh from the sea in Seward's waterfront restaurants overlooking the boat harbor.

Seward is about a mile long, so it's possible to walk its length in about 20 minutes. The waterfront bicycle trail is a pleasant route for walking from the harbor to the south end of town. **Trolley tours** leave regularly from the cruise dock on a round-trip loop past the town's points of interest.

Ship-organized excursions at Seward include tours of Resurrection Bay by sightseeing boat or by kayak; a visit to the Alaska SeaLife Center; and a coach tour to Exit Glacier. River rafting, flightseeing and dog sled-

The Alaska SeaLife Center pro-
vides a close look at Steller sea
lions and other local species.

ding on a glacier are also offered
by some cruise lines.

At the south end of town is the
Alaska SeaLife Center, a research
and educational complex operated
by the University of Alaska-
Fairbanks. Sick, injured or stranded sea mammals and birds are
brought to the Center to be cared
for by a team of veterinarians.
Those animals unable to return to
the wild will be given a permanent
home at the Center where rookeries are designed to mimic the
region's natural habitat, featuring
pools of clear sea water and seclud-
ed areas where animals can mate
and rear their young.

The Visitor Center for **Kenai**
Fjords National Park is located
on the harbor. The Park's fjords
can be viewed by sightseeing boats
which take visitors close to the
park's rugged capes, sea arches and
tidewater glaciers. The massive
Harding Icefield covers an area of
30 by 50 miles and is a remnant of
an icecap that completely covered
the Kenai Mountains at the end of
the last ice age. As recently as
1909, the Kenai Fjords were still
ice-filled bays. Fifty years later
these glaciers had staged a major
retreat, leaving in their wake fjords
which contain new islands and
cliffs freshly scoured by ice.

In addition to this dramatic glacial action, tectonic plates are colliding in the area. The Kenai
Mountains rest on the subsiding
edge of one plate and, as they are

SEWARD

POPULATION:	3,000
ANNUAL RAINFALL:	67 inches
DISTANCE TO COLLEGE FJORD	140 miles
DISTANCE TO GLACIER BAY	525 miles

Alaska Sealife Center

pulled under, glacial-carved cirques become halfmoon bays and former peaks are reduced to craggy islands. The Kenai coast is slowly slipping into the sea. All this happens very slowly of course, except when an earthquake hits.

When the 1964 Good Friday earthquake struck, the ground underneath Seward – perched on the edge of a submarine slope – lost its shear strength and became part of a massive underwater slide. The Seward shoreline dropped six feet within 30 seconds, taking with it the town's harbor and fuel docks. This was followed by a series of tsunamis that wiped out the remaining waterfront industries, including the railroad docks. Seward's death toll was 13 and a plaque in remembrance of these victims rests in the center of town near the rebuilt harbor. Film clips of this catastrophe are shown at the **Seward Museum**.

The natural forces at work along the Kenai coast are manifested in dramatic landmarks that compete

Three Hole Point is one of several dramatic landmarks in Kenai Fjords National Park.

for sightseers' attention. First there is **Aialak Cape**, a granite intrusive formed 60 million years ago, which looks like a huge boulder shoved skyward from the earth's crust. Then there is **Three Hole Point** – a towering sea arch formed by wave erosion. And of course there are the glaciers, many of which are still unnamed. Sea mammals thrive in these waters and more than 200,000 seabirds – including horned and tufted puffins – nest on the rocky islands and capes. The **Chiswell Islands** are also used by sea lions, and Barwell Island, off Cape Resurrection, is a murre colony. In Resurrection Bay, sea otters are a common sight.

Resurrection Bay, once used by Russian fur traders for ship building, was initially inhabited by a small population of Southern Eskimos. In 1918, the artist and adventurer Rockwell Kent lived with his son and a fox farmer on **Fox Island**. His book *Wilderness: A Quiet Adventure in Alaska* describes his winter experiences here. Alaska Heritage Tours offers boat tours to Fox Island and overnight stays at its lodge, which is featured in some cruise lines' land tours.

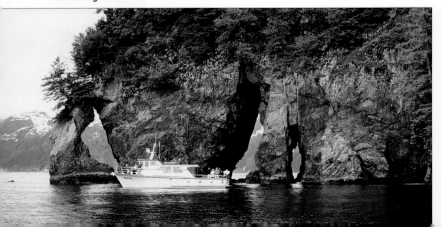

On the western shores of Resurrection Bay, six miles south of Seward, is **Caines Head State Recreation Area**. This steep headland, with its strategic view of the bay, was chosen by the U.S. Army for building a Harbor Defense System during World War II. Seward was an important wartime port, for it was Alaska's only year-round transportation center before completion of the Whittier Tunnel and Alcan Highway.

Kenai Fjords National Park also encompasses **Exit Glacier**, located northwest of Seward and reached by Exit Glacier Road (which intersects with the Seward Highway). Near this junction is the **Seward Windsong Lodge**, operated by Alaska Heritage Tours and featured in some cruise lines' land tours. At the far end of Exit Glacier Road is the entrance to the Exit Glacier fee area, which includes a ranger station with exhibits and interpretive programs. A network of hiking trails leads to the terminus of the glacier, which is retreating and actively calving large chunks of ice. It's possible to get close to the edge of the glacier while remaining on park pathways.

(Above) Exit Glacier's massive snout. (Right) Sign outside a Kenai-area hair salon. (Below) Seward Windsong Lodge.

DENALI NATIONAL PARK

& Fairbanks

Denali National Park and Preserve is symbolic of the wilderness that once dominated North America. As vast tracts of the New World's land were explored and colonized, a movement arose to preserve pockets of wilderness where the imprint of humans was barely noticeable. In Alaska, these pockets are mighty big. Of America's 95 million acres of designated wilderness areas, 57.6 million are in Alaska. By comparison, Ohio has 77 acres and some eastern states have none.

The need to preserve wilderness is deeply rooted in American thought. Thomas Jefferson, Ralph Waldo Emerson and Henry David Thoreau were the philosophical fathers of environmentalism, a movement that gained momentum in the late 19th century, with John Muir and President Theodore Roosevelt among its early proponents.

In 1916, the National Park Service was established, and the following year Mount McKinley National Park was created, largely through the efforts of naturalist and conservationist Charles Sheldon who first visited the Denali region in the summer of 1906. As chairman of the Boone and Crockett Club of New York, Sheldon led a 10-year campaign to preserve the Denali wilderness and finally, in 1917, Congress approved a bill to establish a national park. Although Sheldon wanted the name of Denali for the new park, it was called the Mount McKinley National Park from 1917 until 1980. In that year the boundary of the park was tripled and its name changed to Denali National Park and Preserve.

Mount McKinley, highest peak in North America, is the centerpiece of Denali National Park.

Denali is a native word meaning 'high one' and it refers to **Mount McKinley**, named after President McKinley. Its twin peaks stand in isolation, often shrouded in clouds that collect around the tallest mountain in North America. The north summit is 19,470 feet high and the south peak rises to 20,320 feet. Denali National Park and Preserve is huge and, at six million acres, is larger than Massachusetts.

Mount McKinley is part of the six-hundred-mile long **Alaska Range** and its massive size is likely due to its location in a bend of the Denali fault system, where one crustal block has shoved against another. McKinley is an impressive sight and a challenging climb for mountaineers, who first reached the North Peak in 1910 and the South Peak in 1913. Summer weather on Mount McKinley is cool, wet and windy.

The park contains habitat for 37 species of mammals – caribou, grizzly bear, moose, wolf and Dall sheep among others – and 155 species of birds, including golden and bald eagles. These animals live in the taiga (white and black spruce intermingled with aspen, birch and poplar) and tundra (willow, dwarf birch, sedges and grasses), alongside the lakes, rivers and alpine glaciers of the park. A 90-mile road traverses the park, providing visitors with breathtaking sights of Wonder Lake, Savage River Canyon and Muldrow Glacier, which descends 16,000 feet from the upper slopes of Mount McKinley.

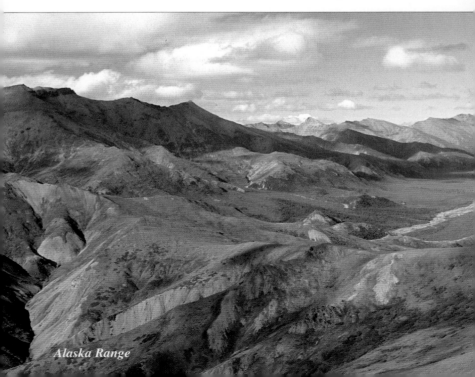

Alaska Range

Getting to Denali

The entrance to Denali National Park is located 240 miles north of Anchorage (120 miles south of Fairbanks) and can be reached by road, rail and air. From Anchorage, the rail line and Glenn Highway (#1) trace the shores of Knik Arm, where the **Matanuska Valley** lies at its head. The growing season in this farming valley is only four months but the long daylight hours produce giant vegetables – turnips over seven pounds and 70-pound cabbages. **Palmer** is the valley's trading center and its turn-off marks the junction of the Glenn Highway (#1) and George Parks Highway (#3), the latter running between Anchorage and Fairbanks. About seven miles past this junction along Highway #3 is the town of **Wasilla**, an Anchorage bedroom community with about 6,000 residents. It is also the headquarters of the Iditarod Trail Sled Dog Race. About 25 miles past Wasilla is the town of **Willow**, where mushers competing in the Iditarod line up for the race's restart. The day before (the first Saturday in March) the ceremonial start takes place in downtown Anchorage.

Talkeetna, located about 20 miles south of Denali State Park, is a major stop along the Alaska Railroad. Here passengers often disembark to visit one of several lodges in the area where the views of Mount McKinley are superb. Two excellent choices are the Princess Mt. McKinley Wilderness Lodge and the Talkeetna Alaskan Lodge.

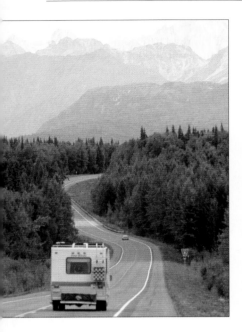

(Above) George Parks Highway.
(Below) Talkeetna is an interest-ing stop on the road to Denali.

Shuttles are available from these lodges to Talkeetna (pop. 800) where the town's pioneer past is well preserved in its original log cabins and a one-room school-house now housing the local museum. Talkeetna is a base for mountaineering expeditions to Mount McKinley, and flightsee-ing excursions depart regularly from its small airstrip. River raft-ing and dog sledding demonstra-tions are also offered.

The Talkeetna Forest Ranger Station, located two blocks west of the town's museum, is the place to obtain information on **Denali State Park**'s trails and natural attractions. Denali State Park (established in 1970 and expanded in 1976) shares its western boundary with the much larger Denali National Park and Preserve. The Parks Highway runs though Denali State Park and offers superb vantage points for viewing the Alaska Range. The roadside viewing area at **Milepost 134.8** is probably the best place to pause in your journey and gaze at snow-crowned McKinley and other peaks of the Alaska Range.

Denali National Park is the highlight of land tours available to cruise passengers embarking or disembarking in Seward or Whittier. The main staging area for visitors is just north of the park entrance where a number of lodges and services are situated. Regular bus shuttles take lodge visitors into the park where a visitor center is located near the entrance. Free shuttle buses serve the entrance area, which encompasses the Railroad Depot, Park Headquarters and several miles of trails.

South Denali Viewpoint (at Mile 134.8) provides superb views of the Alaska Range.

If you arrive at Denali with an organized cruisetour, your choice of **excursions** will include flight-seeing expeditions, river rafting and back-country ATV or jeep safaris. One of the best ways to explore Denali is on a guided tour deep into the Park. A bus will pick you up at the lodge and take you into the park, stopping at several spots where you can wander awhile and observe this beautiful landscape. The buses move along the park road at a leisurely pace, pausing at the various viewpoints along the way.

There are many species of **wildlife** you will be able to see from roadside vantage points. Caribou and moose often feed within a few miles of the road and occasionally a brown (grizzly) bear might be spotted along a ridge top or valley floor. The park is also home to wolves, but during summer months they generally hunt individually and at night, so a sighting is rare. The park also supports a variety of birds, some of which have migrated great distances, including the arctic tern (from Antarctica) and jaegers which have arrived from southern oceans. More common are grouse, jays and ptarmigan (a small goose-like bird). Some birds of prey, such as golden eagles, can also be seen riding the updrafts along ridgetops in search of food.

For visitors on an eight-hour tour, the **Eielson Visitor Center** is the most common turnaround point, providing spectacular views of Mount McKinley and

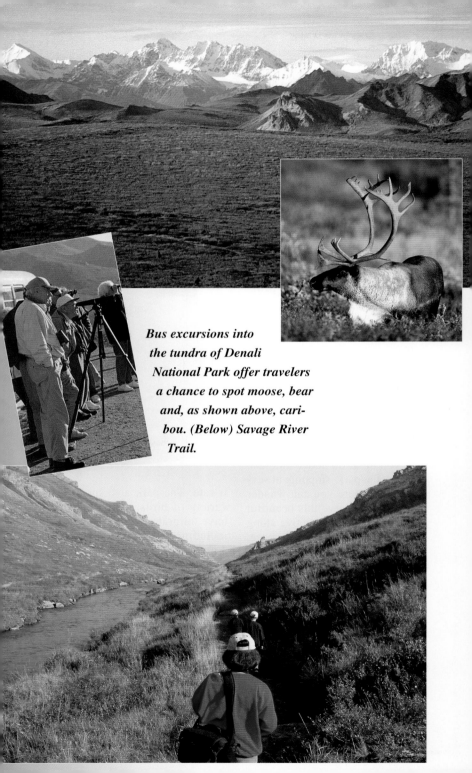

Bus excursions into the tundra of Denali National Park offer travelers a chance to spot moose, bear and, as shown above, caribou. (Below) Savage River Trail.

the surrounding tundra. Longer, 11-hour excursions extend to **Wonder Lake**. Although there are restrooms and drinking water available at the park centers, there is no food service. So, in addition to warm clothing, you should be sure to pack a lunch if it is not being provided on the excursion.

If you arrive at Denali by rental car, you can drive as far as the Savage River parking lot at Mile 15. Private vehicles are restricted beyond this point and one of the park's shuttle buses must be taken to travel further into the park. These buses depart regularly from the visitor center and seats are in heavy demand, so an advance reservation by phone or through the lodge where you are staying is recommended. If you are considering overnight camping in the backcountry of the park, permits must be obtained in person at the visitor center.

HIKING

Several good trails lie within the park's unrestricted entrance area and are easily accessible by private vehicle or by shuttle bus from the visitor center.

Horseshoe Lake Trail is a 1.5-mile roundtrip hike through taiga forest and entails a 200-foot descent to an oxbow lake. This lake, an abandoned meander of the Nenana River, was part of the river's main channel until the accumulation of silt and the building of dams by beavers caused the river to carve a new course.

The **Savage River Trail** follows the floor of a V-shaped canyon once filled with glacial meltwater. The trail runs along both sides of the narrow river which is spanned by a footbridge at the far end. It is three miles roundtrip (accessed from the parking lot) and is an easy one-hour hike along flat terrain.

(See page 85 for more tips on hiking in Alaska.)

STRANDED IN THE WILD

An abandoned bus on the north-western outskirts of Denali National Park has become a focus of interest ever since Jon Krakauer wrote his bestselling book *Into the Wild* (made into a motion picture). It tells the true story of a young man named Chris McCandless who died in this bus in the summer of 1992. The honors graduate of Emory University in Atlanta hiked about thirty miles east from the Parks Highway before setting up camp in spring. When he tried to retrace his steps a few months later, a river swollen by spring melt blocked his way. So he returned to the derelict bus and was subsisting on wild plants when he became sick from eating toxic seeds. By Alaskan standards, McCandless was a stone's throw from civilization and had several options for survival, but he was ill-prepared for what proved to be his final test. At the age of 24, he starved to death on his quest to find life's meaning in the wilderness.

Denali's Sled Dogs

Denali's most popular interpretive program – one that began in 1939 – is the sled-dog demonstration held three times a day throughout the summer at the park's kennels (reached by shuttle bus from the Visitor Center). These working dogs have played an important role ever since rangers began patrolling the park in 1921 to discourage the poaching of wildlife. When the size of Denali National Park was tripled in 1980, the original two-million-acre park was designated a wilderness area, which restricts the use of motorized equipment and mechanized transport within its boundaries. Thus, rangers would carry out their winter patrols by sled-dog team – a traditional mode of transport that has proven to be more reliable than snow machines. Trained sled dogs can sense a snow-obscured trail beneath their paws and find a patrol cabin during a wind-driven whiteout. They don't run out of gas or have mechanical parts that freeze up. Food, water and booties to protect their feet are all that's needed. Their thick fur keeps them warm when camping along the trail, and a sled dog is born to run. Those at Denali are bred not for looks but for performance, with long legs and tough feet for breaking a trail through deep snow. A friendly temperament is also required for greeting the thousands of park visitors who come to meet them each summer.

Alaskan huskies make superb sled dogs.

Fairbanks

Situated on a flat river plain, Fairbanks is a sprawling city – the second largest in Alaska with a borough population of 100,000. Named for the Indiana Senator Charles W. Fairbanks (who became vice-president to Theodore Roosevelt), the town was founded during the gold rush. Its strategic position on the banks of the Chena River made Fairbanks a major trading center for miners.

During World War II, the U.S. military built airfields and roads around Fairbanks, and this construction boom produced jobs for the local civilians. Fairbanks also benefited from the Cold War era when renewed defense spending expanded the area's existing bases, and radar systems and missile sites were installed. Today its airforce base serves as the site of a joint American-Canadian-Russian training program for coordinating search and rescue operations in the Arctic.

Sternwheel tour boats take Fairbanks visitors to sites along the Chena River.

In 1967, the Chena River overflowed and flooded Fairbanks. With the help of federal aid, local businesses were rebuilt and homes restored. A year later oil was discovered near Prudhoe Bay, and Fairbanks was, again, in a strategic location for the proposed pipeline. When construction began in 1974, the population surged but at the pipeline's completion in 1978, the city plummeted into a recession with widespread unemployment.

The hot and cold nature of Fairbanks' economic past is also reflected in its climate. Just 90 miles south of the Arctic Circle, winter days are short and bitterly cold. In contrast to the dark chill of winter are the long, hot, sunny days of summer with daylight in June and July lasting about 21 hours. The aurora borealis is regularly seen in the skies over Fairbanks.

Local Attractions

With its local sites fairly spread out, Fairbanks is best seen by car or coach tour, although guided walking tours are offered by the Fairbanks Convention & Visitors Bureau. Popular attractions include **Alaskaland Pioneer Park**, established in 1967 to commemorate the centennial of Alaska's purchase. Admission is free to this 44-acre park encircled by its own small-scale railroad to provide transportation for visitors. Sites include: Gold Rush Town, where shops and cafes are housed in relocated pioneer cabins; Palace Theater & Saloon, which holds summer musical reviews; the sternwheeler Nenana, which is drydocked in the middle of the park; the Pioneer Museum; and Northern Inva, where native athletes demonstrate their heritage sports.

Visitors can pan for gold at Gold Dredge Number 8, which operated in the Goldstream Valley near Fairbanks from 1928 to 1959.

The **University of Alaska Museum of the North**, one of the state's top 10 visitor attractions, houses displays of Alaskan animals, plants, natural history, native culture and gold rush history. Also located on campus, is the Geophysical Institute (a center for earthquake research) and the **Large Animal Research Station** where you can view musk-ox, reindeer and caribou from raised platforms The University of Alaska Fairbanks began as an agricultural college in 1922 and grew into a major institution for higher learning in Alaska.

Local **sternwheeler cruises** include a four-hour-long, narrated cruise of the Chena and Tanana Rivers aboard an authentic sternwheel riverboat, from the decks of which you will see log cabins, fish wheels and the 'Wedding of the Rivers' where the Tanana – carrying 100,000 tons of glacier sediment – meets the mouth of the Chena. Stops along the way include a dog-sledding demonstration at the kennels of Iditarod champion Susan Butcher.

A few miles west of Fairbanks is the **Cripple Creek Resort** (also known as the Ester Gold Camp). Listed on the National Register of Historic Places, its authentic gold rush buildings include the Cripple Creek Hotel and the famous **Malemute Saloon**. Continuing southwest along the Park's Highway, travelers arrive at **Nenana** where the local railroad depot houses the official **State of Alaska Railroad Museum**. Built in 1923, it too is listed on the National Register of Historic Sites.

An hour's drive east of Fairbanks along the Chena Hot Springs Road takes you to the **Chena Hot Springs**. Rustic cabins provide accommodation and soaking facilities include two jacuzzis, a hot tub and a swimming pool. The springs here circulate through fractures in the granite to depths of two miles where the rock is hotter than the surface boiling point of water.

Circle Hot Springs, discovered by a prospector in 1893, is reached by the Steese Highway which leads in a northeast direction from Fairbanks. **Manley Hot Springs** is a 45-minute flight northwest of Fairbanks or via a detour off the **Dalton Highway**, which leads north to Prudhoe Bay. A trip along the Dalton takes you across the Yukon River, the Arctic Circle, the rugged Brooks Range, rolling foothills and a vast, tundra-covered plain. Called the Haul Road, it was a supply route for trucks serving work camps during construction of the **Trans-Alaska Pipeline**.

Construction of the pipeline was Alaska's most important economic boom since the gold rush. Built by a conglomerate of oil companies called Alyeska Pipeline Service Company, it was a major engineering feat and was designed to prevent thawing of the permafrost which covers much of Alaska's interior. Other factors in construction were the region's drastic temperature range (from 90° F to -60° F) and high earthquake activity. Last but not least were concerns that the pipeline would damage the region's fragile ecosystem and disrupt migration of caribou and other animals.

The discovery of oil in 1968 set a series of events into motion. In 1971, the Native Claims

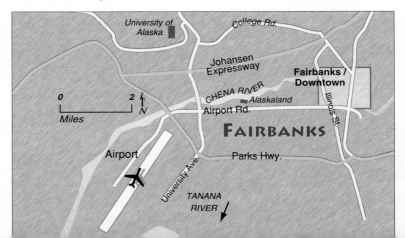

SUNSHINE

In summer, Alaska experiences protracted hours of daylight, especially north of Prince William Sound. In Fairbanks, for example, the sun rises at about 3 a.m. in late June and sets after midnight, providing nearly 22 hours of daylight. In winter, however, sunrise can be as late as 11 a.m. and sunset as early as 2:40 p.m., providing residents with less than four hours of daylight.

Settlement Act resolved the grievances of Alaska's natives who felt that neither the Alaska Purchase nor the Statehood Act had established their land rights. The 1971 Act established 13 native-owned corporations, and granted the native peoples $1 billion in revenue and 40 million acres of land.

The Alaska Pipeline and Dalton Highway wind past Galbraith Lake on the north slope of the Brooks Range.

In November 1973, Congress passed the Pipeline Authorization Act and construction of the 800-mile pipeline began. About half of its length was raised on stilts joined in a zig-zag pattern for flexibility when the pipeline expands and contracts with drastic temperature changes. The accordion-like pattern also allows the pipeline to absorb earthquake waves with minimal damage.

The oil started to flow in 1977, with friction from the pumping pressure keeping the oil at about 140° F. To absorb this heat rather than transfer it into the ground (and melt the permafrost), the stilts supporting the pipeline contain a special liquid that absorbs the oil's high temperature and releases it into the air through radiator fins. The pipe itself is protected by a layer of galvanized steel and nearly four inches of insulation. Over the years the pipeline has been shot at more than 50 times, leaving indentations but never a puncture hole until, in October 2001, someone fired at it with a .338-calibre rifle. Oil spraying from the small bullet hole was spotted by a surveillance helicopter crew about 75 miles north of Fairbanks, and four hours later a 37-year-old man was arrested. He apparently had no motive for the shooting and appeared to be intoxicated.

The pipeline is buried underground at regularly spaced intervals to allow for crossings by caribou. The caribou herds that migrate across the North Slope appear to be unaffected by the pipeline's presence, but the Western Arctic herd has been steadily declining for the past decade. The initial decline may have been triggered by a few bad winters of heavy icing and snow. Other factors include an increase in predators, such as wolves and bears. Conversely, the Porcupine herd, which often migrates across northern Yukon and Alaska, has been increasing.

The oil discovered at **Prudhoe Bay** was a long time in the making. Its source is a rich shale deposited during early Jurassic time, which was eventually covered with 6,000 feet of sandstone and other rock during the geological formation of Alaska. A chemical process transforms organic material into oil which, being lighter than water, will float through available pores and fractures in the rock above and collect in reservoirs.

Barrow (pop. 4,500) is situated 200 miles west of Prudhoe Bay and is the northernmost U.S. settlement. It lies 350 miles above the Arctic Circle and is unconnected to any other community by road. The Inupiat Eskimos who live here have traditionally hunted whales, walruses and polar bears, and are noted for their carvings in ivory and bone. Barrow's Eskimo culture, and the opportunity to see polar bears and the northern lights, draws air travelers to this remote port on the edge of the Arctic Ocean.

Mount McKinley

EXPEDITION CRUISING
Kodiak, Katmai, Aleutians and Bering Sea

Although most ships conclude a Gulf of Alaska cruise near Anchorage, at Seward or Whittier, there are still thousands of miles of spectacular coastline to explore west of Cook Inlet. Beyond is the Alaska Peninsula and such famous places as the McNeil River – where brown bears congregate each fall to feed on salmon runs – and Katmai National Park & Preserve, which contains 2.5 million acres of volcanic mountains, caldera lakes, caribou herds and the largest unhunted population of brown bears in the world. Few places are more remote than Katmai Park, except perhaps the outer islands of the Aleutian chain which stretches for 1,000 miles along the edge of a deep-sea trench separating the Gulf of Alaska from the Bering Sea.

Kodiak Island

The second largest island in the U.S. (after Hawaii), this mountainous island is covered by a dense growth of tall grass, berry bushes, alder thickets and wildflowers. Some adjacent, smaller islands contain spruce forests, but most of Kodiak Island itself is devoid of trees. It is also prime habitat for the largest carnivorous land mammal in the world – the Kodiak brown bear, which grows as large as 10 feet (when standing upright) and weighs up to 1,500 pounds. Roads here are found only in the port towns, leaving the mountainous interior the sole domain of bears and other wildlife.

The green hills above the Port of Kodiak.

Anne's Alaska Journal

Bill and I planned our sailing trip to Kodiak Island after meeting a pair of hardy Alaskan sailors named Ralph and Betty Marsh. They had just completed a five-day crossing of the Gulf of Alaska when we found ourselves docked beside them at Thomsen Harbor in Sitka. After a fascinating evening aboard their boat, we left with an armful of charts and the impression that sailing to Kodiak was a popular Alaskan pastime. Not that Ralph and Betty had in any way tried to deceive us, but their matter-of-fact approach made the trip sound like a pleasant jaunt.

Twenty months later we too were on our way to Kodiak but, as we traced the Gulf of Alaska coastline from Cape Spencer to the southern tip of the Kenai Peninsula, it gradually dawned on us that ours might very well be the only pleasure boat heading to Kodiak that summer.

Despite the obvious lack of fellow boaters, we somehow thought that once we got to Kodiak we would meet a few. However, when we pulled into St. Paul Harbor on a warm afternoon in early July, we were greeted not by other yachties but by the Kodiak fishing fleet – second largest in America.

We motored along the narrow entrance channel past canneries, fuel docks and seiners, then rounded the breakwater into a harbor containing row upon row of fishboats on which men were working or just drinking beer in the sunshine. Heaped on their decks were nets and floats in a kaleidoscope of colors. Many of them stopped working to look at us. A few called out, asking about our crossing.

There was no denying it. If our arrival could command the attention of a fishing fleet, it must be a fairly rare occurrence. This friendly reception would repeat itself time and time again over the next six weeks as we cruised the Kodiak archipelago. At one remote inlet I asked the resident fisherman if he saw many sailboats pass through this area. "Oh sure," he said. "One came through here just a few years ago."

The waters around Kodiak are also rich with animal life. Humpback whales, Dall porpoises and sea otters are frequent sights as are colorful puffins. In Kodiak's harbor, Steller sea lions are regular visitors, scavenging for fish scraps near the fishboat docks. Kodiak is a colorful fishing port – one of the largest in America – and it attracts college kids each summer in search of lucrative deckhand jobs. Many of the greenhorns, however, end up working in the canneries.

At **Larsen Bay**, site of Kodiak Island's oldest operating cannery, summer workers are housed in wooden dormitories set on pilings and joined by boardwalks to the cannery buildings. When the fish tenders pull in loaded with salmon, the assembly lines roll – regardless of the hour.

(Opposite) Larsen Bay Cannery. (Below) The author's boat makes landfall at the Kodiak archipelago.

At a couple of anchorages we were told by lodge owners on shore that we were the first sailboat ever to pull in. And everywhere we went, the fishermen were our friends. Many were outright concerned about our safety.

"How much weather can that thing take?" a crab fisherman asked us on the radio while we sat out a gale together at the southern tip of Kodiak Island. Another said, "You mean you crossed the Gulf in that little boat?" And before leaving various ports we were often told to "be careful out there."

We tried explaining that our Spencer 35 is designed for ocean crossings, but the Kodiak fishermen were more interested in our small 15hp engine. "Could it power you out of an exposed anchorage in 40-knot winds?"

After spending six weeks circumnavigating the Kodiak islands, we sailed 500 miles due east back across the Gulf Alaska to Sitka. It was a race against time for we were trying to dodge an approaching storm and made landfall just hours before it hit. From the shelter of our anchorage we listened to the wind howling in the Gulf of Alaska.

Kodiak's Baranof Museum, oldest Russian structure in Alaska.

Alaska's Russian history is closely tied to **Kodiak**, which was the colonial capital of Russian America before Alexander Baranof moved it to Sitka. Kodiak's **Baranof Museum** is the oldest Russian structure remaining in Alaska, built by the Russian-American Company in 1808 for storing fur pelts. Built of logs, it overlooks a stone wharf once used by sailing ships of the fur trade.

Behind the museum a sweep of lawn leads to the local Russian Orthodox Church – a vital presence in Kodiak since 1784 and a moderating influence on Russian fur traders who were often brutal in their treatment of natives. The Orthodox missionaries helped the natives preserve their traditions and the church has retained a faithful following among the indigenous population. Native fishermen display icons on their vessels and often ask the local priest to bless their boats before heading out.

The town of Kodiak has a history of adversity. When Mount Katmai erupted in 1912, falling ash blackened the skies for two days and residents could barely breathe. The ground shook and homes collapsed under the weight of ash that piled 18 inches thick on level surfaces and many feet deep in slides. During the 1964 earthquake, part of the town dropped two feet and seismic sea waves washed boats in the harbor onto shore. Outlying ports were also hit by tsunamis. At the native village of **Old Harbor**, residents climbed up the mountainside and watched a series of huge waves wash away their homes. The village church stood its ground against waves surging past its windows and the people of Old Harbor say it was a miracle that the church survived. It served as a refuge until outside help arrived.

In 1784 the first Russian settlement in Alaska was established just a few miles from Old Harbor at **Three Saints Bay**. An important battle took place nearby at which the invading Russians defeated the native Alutiiqs, who had inhabited Kodiak Island for some 7,000 years and whose traditions included the partaking of a *banya* (sauna). This tradition is still practised in Old Harbor, where visitors are often invited to someone's home for a steam in the family *banya*. Prominent visitors to Old Harbor include **James Michener** (while researching his book *Alaska*), singer John Denver, and David Rockefeller (who pulled into port in the summer of 1991 as the leader of a sailing expedition).

Old Harbor, Kodiak Island

Katmai National Park

Lying 25 miles across Shelikof Strait from Kodiak Island is the Alaska Peninsula. The Aleutian Range of snowcapped mountains forms the backbone of this peninsula and runs its entire length, from Cook Inlet to the Aleutian Islands. Best known of these peaks is **Mount Katmai**, around which a national park has been established. Mount Katmai erupted on June 6, 1912, and drastically altered the surrounding valleys, lakes and rivers with material spewed from its volcanic core. For a week prior to Katmai's massive eruption the surrounding area was rocked by earthquakes that were felt 130 miles away. When Katmai erupted through a vent in its base, the sound explosion was so deafening that, had it taken place in New York City, residents of Chicago would have heard it plainly. Glowing hot lava, ash and gas burst skyward from Mount Katmai, its summit collapsing as the mountain's magma chamber emptied.

It was one of the greatest volcanic eruptions in recorded history, but because of Katmai's remote location, no human lives were lost. However, plant and animal life was destroyed as molten material flowed over the surrounding terrain. For several days the skies over much of the Northern Hemisphere were darkened by a haze of ash and gas that continued spewing from Novarupta – the new cone that had formed over the vent at the base of Mount Katmai. In the end, hot ash covered an area of 40 square miles to depths of 700 feet.

Four years later, the National Geographic Society sent a scientific expedition, led by Robert Griggs, to study the aftermath of this cataclysmic event. They were awestruck at the sight of a valley completely filled with ash and thousands of smoking fumaroles, their steam still soaring 500 feet into the air. It was named the **Valley of Ten Thousand Smokes** and on September 24, 1918, President Wilson established Katmai National Monument to preserve this unique area of historical and scientific interest. In

1931 the monument was enlarged to protect its significant population of brown (grizzly) bears and other animals, such as moose and caribou. Presidents Roosevelt and Johnson each enlarged the preserve further and, in 1980, President Carter granted the area National Park status. **Brooks Camp** – located inland on Naknek Lake, about 300 air miles southwest of Anchorage – is the hub of the park with a Visitor Center and a road leading to the Valley of Ten Thousand Smokes. Adventure cruise expeditions pull into **Geographic Harbor** for a close look at the volcanic ash which lies on the park's rugged slopes and beaches. The local beachcombers here are brown bears, which are frequently seen ambling along the foreshore in search of food.

The Aleutians

Extending westward from the Alaska Peninsula, the Aleutian chain is a lonely stretch of submerged mountains, their peaks marking the edge of a deepsea subduction zone called the Aleutian Trench. The weather here is an ongoing battle between the Bering Sea's cold Arctic air and the Gulf of Alaska's warmer Pacific air. Vicious winter storms are replaced with the dense fog of summer.

Japanese troops invaded the Aleutians in June 1942, the first foreign occupation of American soil since the war of 1812. The United States had anticipated such a move and installed two secret airfields (disguised as can-

Fishboats anchor in Geographic Harbor, where brown bears wander the isolated beaches.

neries) on either side of Dutch Harbor. The Japanese, thinking the nearest American airfield was at Kodiak, were repelled in their attack on Dutch Harbor but did land on the islands of Attu and Kiska. When American pilots attempted to retake the occupied islands, violent gales and poor visibility were more of a hazard than enemy fire.

Throughout the winter of 1942-43, Japanese troops defended their positions against American air attacks. Dashiell Hammett, author of *The Maltese Falcon* and *The Thin Man*, was stationed at the Aleutians during the war and wrote about this northern battlefield in The Capture of Attu, Tales of World War II in Alaska. "Modern armies had never fought before on any field that was like the Aleutians," he wrote. "Bad weather fought against us – air reconnaissance was almost impossible."

Finally, on May 11th, 1943, 11,000 American troops landed on Attu and, after 18 days of fighting, retook the island. When

Dutch Harbor on Unalaska Island is one of few sheltered harbors in the Aleutians.

American troops landed on Kiska's shores after weeks of heavy shelling, they found the place deserted.

An earlier invasion of the Aleutians took place in the 1700s, when Russian fur traders subjugated the Aleuts as hunters of sea mammals. The islands' Russian history is evident in the onion-domed, wooden churches that still grace the native villages dotting the green slopes of these misty islands. One of the Aleuts' oldest settlements was at **Dutch Harbor**, where the Russian fur traders based their operations. Today Dutch Harbor is a major fishing port, strategically located between the Bering Sea and the North Pacific Ocean. During the king crab boom of the 1980s, hundreds of fishboats passed through Dutch Harbor on their way to the Bering Sea.

The Bering Sea

The largest Aleut population exists not on the Aleutian Islands but on the **Pribilofs,** in the Bering Sea. The ancestors of these people were brought here by Russian fur traders to harvest seals. The islands' huge fur seal colonies still bring visitors to the Pribilofs, but now they come to discreetly watch these animals from special blinds. On **St. Paul Island**, hundreds of thousands of fur seals spend the summer at various rookeries and haul-out locations. Large males – 'beachmasters' – arrive in late May and establish their territories. The females arrive in June to bear their young. Reindeer and Arctic blue fox also inhabit the tundra-covered Pribilofs, along with more than two million seabirds which arrive each summer, some migrating from as far away as Argentina. Species commonly sighted include horned and tufted puffins, rock sandpipers, red-legged kittiwakes and crested auklets.

(Below) St. Lawrence Island.
(Right) Some local islanders.

During World War II, after Japanese troops invaded the western Aleutians, the U.S. Navy evacuated the Pribilof Aleuts to Funter Bay on Admiralty Island in Southeast Alaska where they were interned for two years, living in the bunkhouses of an old cannery. After the war, reforms led to self-government for the Pribilovians.

Adventure cruises don't end at the Pribilofs, but carry on across the Bering Sea to the **Diomede Islands**, where both the Alaskan and Siberian mainlands are visible in clear weather, and to **St. Lawrence Island**, where the natives are Yu'pik-speaking Eskimos whose dialect is similar to the natives of Provideniya on the nearby Siberian coast. A few cruise expeditions visit the Russian Far East and transit the Bering Strait, proceeding far enough north to cross the Arctic Circle.

CARNIVAL CRUISE LINES:
Owned by the largest cruise corporation in the world, Carnival 7-day roundtrip Inside Passage cruises from Seattle. Carnival's 'Fun' ships attract a high number of first-time cruisers and are popular with families who enjoy the line's excellent children's facilities. Officers are Italian and service staff are international.
www.carnival.com

Carnival Legend, 2002 –
88,000 tons, 2,124 passengers

CELEBRITY CRUISES:
Founded in 1990 by the Greek line Chandris Inc., Celebrity Cruises is now owned by Royal Caribbean Cruise Lines. A premium cruise line, Celebrity is noted for its sophisticated service, gourmet cuisine and stylish ships appointed with modern art. The children's programs are excellent and family staterooms are available (but sell out quickly) on most ships. Celebrity offers 7-day roundtrip Inside Passage cruises from Vancouver and Seattle, and 7-day Gulf of Alaska cruises between Vancouver and Seward. Officers are Greek and service staff are international.
www.celebritycruises.com

Infinity, 2001 –
91,000 tons 1,950 passengers

CRYSTAL CRUISES: This luxury line operates mid-sized ships that are spacious and beautifully appointed. Crystal, which offers an all-inclusive cruise fare, is known for its tailor-made shore excursions. Alaska itineraries include 7-day cruises between Vancouver and Anchorage, and 10-day round-trip cruises from Vancouver. Officers are Scandinavian and service staff are international.
www.crystalcruises.com

Crystal Serenity, 2003
1,080 passengers, 68,000 tons

Disney Wonder, 1999 –
85,000 tons 1,750 passengers

Maasdam, 1995 –
55,000 tons 1,266 passengers
Oosterdam, 2003 – 82,300 tons,
1,916 passengers

Norwegian Sun, 2001 –
78,300 tons, 2,000 passengers

DISNEY CRUISE LINE: A premium cruise line that appeals to families, Disney offers 7-day round-trip Inside Passage cruises from Vancouver. Officers are European.
www.disneycruise.com

HOLLAND AMERICA LINE: This Seattle-based company operates a fleet of classic blue-hulled ships featuring teak promenade decks and museum-quality art and antiques displayed throughout the public areas. An ideal choice for multi-generational cruising families, Holland America's dominant presence in Alaska began with the acquisition of Westours in 1973. Today, HAL operates tour coaches, domed rail cars and the Westmark chain of hotels. This premium cruise line offers an extensive selection of Alaska itineraries. These include 7-day and 14-day roundtrip itineraries from Seattle and 7-day roundtrip cruises from Vancouver. HAL also offers one-way cruises between Seward and Vancouver. HAL's Dutch officers and service staff of Indonesians and Filipinos have built a solid reputation of well-run, immaculate ships.
www.hollandamerica.com

NORWEGIAN CRUISE LINE: NCL is a contemporary line with a casual onboard atmosphere, extensive children's facilities and unstructured dining. Also known for its excellent entertainment, notably Broadway musicals, NCL appeals to active couples and families. The line offers 7-day round-trip cruises from Seattle and 7-day one-way cruises between Vancouver and Seward (Anchorage). Officers are Norwegian and service staff are international. (www.ncl.com)

OCEANIA CRUISES: An upper-premium line of mid-sized ships, Oceania features gourmet cuisine and attentive service in a country-club casual atmosphere. The line's Alaska itineraries are varied, using the base ports of Vancouver, Seattle and San Francisco. Officers and service staff are international.
www.oceaniacruises.com

Regatta, 1998 –
30,000 tons, 684 passengers

PRINCESS CRUISES: Princess's experience in Alaska began when *Princess Italia* first steamed north in 1969. The line experienced phenomenal growth in the 1970s when the company permitted the television series *The Love Boat* to use its ships for onboard settings. This premium line offers one-way cruises between Vancouver and Whittier (Anchorage), 7-day round-trip cruises from Seattle and Vancouver, and 10-day Inside Passage cruises from San Francisco. One-way Gulf of Alaska cruises are between Vancouver and Whittier (Anchorage) The company's extensive tourist services in Alaska provide motor coaches and domed rail cars for its cruise-tour passengers, who stay at cus-tom-built Princess lodges. Officers and service staff are international.
www.princess.com

Coral Princess, 2002 –
92,000 tons, 1,975 passengers

Star Princess, 2002 –
109,000 tons, 2,600 passengers

REGENT SEVEN SEAS: This luxury line made its Alaska debut in 2000, where it currently posi-tions the 28,000-ton *Seven Seas Navigator.* This luxury ship offers mostly 7-night Gulf of Alaska cruises between Vancouver and Seward. Officers are Italian and service staff are international.
www.rssc.com

Seven Seas Navigator, 1999 –
28,550 tons, 490 passengers

Radiance of the Seas, 2001 –
90,000 tons, 2,500 passengers

Silver Shadow, 2000 –
28,258 tons, 322 passengers

ROYAL CARIBBEAN INTERNATIONAL: In 1995 RCI brought the largest ship of its time to Alaska with the arrival of the 70,000-ton *Legend of the Seas*. Power lines strung across Seymour Narrow (a major pass of the Inside Passage) had to be raised 20 feet to accommodate this ship. Larger ships have arrived on the scene since, but RCI still maintains a big presence in Alaska with 7-day roundtrip cruises from Seattle and 7-day one-way cruises between Vancouver and Seward (Anchorage). RCI's modern megaships feature impressive public areas such as a multi-deck atrium with glass elevators and the company's hallmark rock-climbing wall. Family suites, a large playroom and teen center make these ships ideal for passengers with children. Officers are Scandinavian and service staff are international. (www.royalcaribbean.com)

SILVERSEA: This six-star luxury line features oceanview suites and European styling on its all-inclusive ships. The line offers 7-day itineraries between Vancouver and Seward (Anchorage). Officers are Italian and service staff are European. (www.silversea.com)

Adventure Cruises

Small-ship adventure cruises have long been popular in Alaska, beginning in the 1970s when Chuck West – a pioneer of leisure travel in Alaska – founded Cruise West. This family-owned company no longer operates expedition cruises in Alaska, but several other small-ship lines offer this type of cruise. Passengers are taken off the beaten path in vessels that can navigate narrow channels, provide close proximity to the shore and anchor in remote coves where further exploring is done in Zodiacs or sea kayaks for close-up views of tidewater glaciers and marine life. Shore excursions focus on wildlife viewing, beach combing and forest hikes. The atmosphere on board is casual, with an emphasis on learning about the area (naturalists often give evening talks). The following lines offer adventure cruises in Alaska.

ALASKAN DREAM CRUISES: This newly founded line is owned by Allen Marine Tours, a long-time tour-boat operator owned by an Alaskan family with cruises based out of Sitka. Itineraries range from 8 to 13 nights on Inside Passage cruises. (www. alaskandreamcruises.com)

Admiralty Dream –

97 tons, 58 passengers

LINDBLAD EXPEDITIONS: This company was founded in 1979 by Sven Lindblad, son of Swedish-born Lars Lindblad who pioneered adventure expeditions in the 1950s and became known by many as the father of eco-tourism. Lindblad Expeditions partners with National Geographic to offer a wide selection of Alaska/Inside Passage itineraries. (www. expeditions.com)

PONANT: This French company offers expedition cruising to Alaska on board the luxury mega-yacht *L'Austral*, from ports that include Juneau, Vancouver and Seattle. (en.ponant.com)

UN-CRUISE ADVENTURES: Formerly American Safari Cruises, this upscale all-inclusive line is headquartered in Seattle and offers yacht-style adventure on seven- to 21-night Inside Passage and Glacier Bay cruises. (www.un-cruise.com)

Safari Explorer, 1998

36 passengers

INDEX

PHOTO CREDITS

Alaska Heritage Tours, 22, 319
Alaska State Tourism,
        Angell, Robert, 74b,
        Hyde, John, 75, 204
Alaska Stock, 234a
Alaska Trophy Fishing, 26, 65, 247
Canadian Hydrographic Service,
57, 160a
Capilano Suspension Bridge, 143a
Butchart Gardens, 120b
Celebrity Cruises, 79a, 80, 81, 260
Circa Art 4, 18, 24
Corbis Images, 74a, 78, 254b, 326b
Cruise West 16a
Defreitas, Michael, 5, 16b, 60, 69,
85, 94b, 182, 183b, 187, 188a&b,
189b, 192, 193b, 207, 210b, 211a,
231, 270, 271, 273, 275, 277b,
298b, 301b, 322/323, 324a, 329,
332, 335, 341, 342(inset)
Fairmont Hotels, 129, 145a, 149
Ferrier, Jim, 117, 191, 213, 219,
220A, 275c
Fraser River Port Authority, 152
Harvey, Al, Vancouver Aquarium, 70
Heinl, Russ, 123, 160b
Holland America, 11, 19a, 36, 252,
330
Hyde, John, Alaska Stock, 6, 64
Judd, R. H., Archives, 44, 266
Kodiak Historical Society, 61
Library of Congress, 48, 209, 215,
230, 233, 234 (inset)
Nakano, Alan, illustrations, 62, 86,
photos, 196. 197b, 202, 256/257
P&O Cruise Line, 34
Prince Rupert Port Authority, 177,
178
Princess Cruises, 33, 41b, 239b,
296a
Rocky Mountaineer Railtours, 146
Royal Caribbean Int'l , 35, 98
Schafer, Kevin, 78 Corbis Images
Seattle, Port of, 100/101, 105, 109,
110
Seattle Tourism, 106, 108b
Sequoia Company of Restaurants,
130, 140
University of Washington, 102,
Vancouver City of, Archives, 46,

124, 125, 137, 228, 246
Vancouver Tourism, 126, 136, 141,
142
Vancouver Port Corp, 127
Whistler Resort Assn, 143b
Yukon Tourism, 21, 59, 73, 77, 80b,
241b, 242, 243, 245, 247

All other photography by Anne
Vipond.